DOWN

THE HILL

DOWN
THE HILL

My Descent into the
Double Murder in Delphi

BY SUSAN HENDRICKS

hachette
BOOKS

New York

Hachette Books
Hachette Book Group
1290 Avenue of the Americas
New York, NY 10104
HachetteBooks.com
Twitter.com/HachetteBooks
Instagram.com/HachetteBooks

First Edition: September 2023

Published by Hachette Books, an imprint of Hachette Book Group, Inc. The Hachette Books name and logo are trademarks of the Hachette Book Group.

The Hachette Speakers Bureau provides a wide range of authors for speaking events. To find out more, go to hachettespeakersbureau.com or email HachetteSpeakers@hbgusa.com.

Books by Hachette Books may be purchased in bulk for business, educational, or promotional use. For information, please contact your local bookseller or email the Hachette Book Group Special Markets Department at Special.Markets@hbgusa.com.

The publisher is not responsible for websites (or their content) that are not owned by the publisher.

Some photos are used with permission of the victims' families and/or Kevin Balfe of CrimeCon. All other photos are provided courtesy of the author.

Library of Congress Cataloging-in-Publication Data

Name: Hendricks, Susan, 1973– author.
Title: Down the hill: my descent into the double murder in Delphi / Susan Hendricks.
Description: New York City: Hachette Books, 2023. | Includes bibliographical references.
Identifiers: LCCN 2023021514 | ISBN 9780306830242 (hardcover) | ISBN 9780306830259 (trade paperback) | ISBN 9780306830266 (ebook)
Subjects: LCSH: Murder—Investigation—Indiana—Delphi. | Williams, Abigail, 2003–2017. | German, Liberty, 2002–2017.
Classification: LCC HV8079.H6 H46 2023 | DDC 363.25/95230977294—dc23/eng/20230601
LC record available at https://lccn.loc.gov/2023021514

ISBNs: 9780306830242 (hardcover); 9780306830266 (ebook)

Printed in the United States of America

LSC-C

Printing 2, 2023

To Abby and Libby and their families

Contents

Advance Praise for *Down the Hill*

"With compassion, integrity, and accuracy, journalist Susan Hendricks takes a closer look inside the tragic homicides of two young girls, Abby and Libby, in Delphi. Having formed a close relationship with the victims' loved ones over several years, Hendricks provides unprecedented insight into their families' resilience, challenges, and relief once an arrest was made. Her sharp eye for detail shines through as she explores various facets of the case using her unique connections, including my thoughts about the investigation and assessment of the suspect. *Down the Hill* is an incredibly compelling read that is hard to put down; you'll never look at this case the same way again."

—**Paul Holes**, retired cold case investigator and
New York Times best-selling author of *Unmasked*

"In *Down the Hill*, Susan Hendricks deftly navigates the complexities of the Delphi case and presents a narrative of tragedy, resilience, and hope. The book offers a deep dive into the investigation and lays bare its successes, setbacks, and detours. It stands as a model for what every book in this genre should strive to be: compelling in its truth, courageous in its narrative, and compassionate in its approach."

—**Kevin Balfe**, founder and executive producer, CrimeCon

"The Delphi Murders were tragic. The Delphi Murder investigation was complicated and nuanced. To tell this story, you have to be smart, relentless, and extremely compassionate. That's why Susan Hendricks is the right person for this job. I have worked with Susan for years; I know how she uses all her investigative journalism tools to get to the truth and, more importantly, has the heart to tell the victims' story. *Down the Hill* will make you understand what it really means when two wonderful girls are taken from their families who then have to wait years for justice."

—**Vinnie Politan**, lead anchor, Court TV

"Susan Hendricks, my friend the journalist, has a heart of gold and you feel it when she tells stories of those impacted by trauma. She has told my story numerous times, so I speak from experience. Susan is raw, honest, and professional, and [she] leads with honor and integrity in her storytelling; it is no wonder Abby and Libby's families let her into their homes to share [their story while navigating] their ongoing journey of grief and healing. *Down the Hill* is a compelling read from beginning to end from a trusted source who writes with kindness, compassion, and sensitivity. Thank you, Susan, for continuing to elevate the voices of victims and survivors."

—**Kim Goldman**, victim advocate, author, and podcast host of *Media Circus* and *Confronting: OJ Simpson*

"Prepare to be deeply moved and inspired by *Down the Hill* as Susan Hendricks fearlessly steps into the heart-wrenching world of a shattered community. With unparalleled dedication and unwavering compassion, Hendricks becomes a beacon of hope for the victims and their families. In this gripping account of one of the nation's most tragic murders, she goes beyond mere reporting, immerses herself in the fight for justice, and unmasks the truth behind a heinous act of evil. Hendricks' unwavering commitment and tireless pursuit of truth make her a true champion for justice. *Down the Hill* is a testament to the resilience of the human spirit and a reminder to never relent in the search for truth and healing."

—**Deanna (Baudi Moovan) Thompson**, TV host and podcaster, *Dont F**k with Cats* and *(Re)Solved*

"Susan Hendricks is one of the most personable, talented, humble, and selfless journalists I have ever worked with. Those qualities are what allowed her to cover this tragic double murder involving children in a way few others could. Whether evaluating law enforcement's investigation, the outpouring of concern within and outside of the community, or the heartbreak endured by these brave and courageous families, *Down the Hill* delivers. Compelling, gripping, and emotional—this is a story you just can't miss. [It is] told in a way that will both enthrall and consume you."

—**Joey Jackson**, defense attorney and CNN legal analyst

"Susan Hendricks is a storyteller with a heart which is why the families of Abby and Libby opened up to her. Susan's attention to detail is coupled with her humanity as she tells the story of two girls, their families, and the town that would never be the same."

—**Ana Garcia**, host of *True Crime Daily: The Podcast*

"I've watched my friend report, advocate, and support Abby and Libby's families with respect and dignity. The double murder in Delphi stopped being a 'story' for Susan Hendricks from the first visit with Libby's family at their home. In the South we know something incredible happens once you sit with someone at their kitchen table. From that tiny table to this book, Susan brings the families center stage in this victim-centered, family-oriented, loving story of *ohana*. Susan is no longer a reporter; she is family."

—**Sheryl "Mac" McCollum**, crime scene investigator and host of *Zone 7* podcast

"Susan Hendricks' commitment and compassion for victims and their families is unparalleled. Being immersed in one of this country's most tragic murders, Hendricks takes readers deep into the heart of a community torn and broken by the deaths of Abby and Libby. Rather than just reporting on two young lives senselessly stolen, Hendricks joins the fight for justice for Abby and Libby, and she is a true champion for finding the truth at the heart of evil."

—**Kelly McLear**, co-host of *Killing Dad: The Crystal Howell Story Podcast*

"Susan Hendricks is a veteran journalist who has always captivated audiences with her soothing delivery and compassionate relatability for every interview and story told. Hendricks garnered a trusting relationship with the families of Abby and Libby and the respect of law enforcement with her long track record of telling stories with grace and empathy. Her deep dive into the Delphi case captures not only the twists and turns of the investigation but, at the human level, shows how this tragedy rippled through the victims' loved ones and ignited the strength of the community in their shared pursuit for justice. Hendricks takes us on a truly compelling journey."

—**Melissa McCarty**, true crime correspondent

Foreword

by Kelsi German Siebert

Growing up, it was Libby and me against the world. During and after our parents' divorce, we never knew whose house we would be at when, and eventually moved in with our grandparents. Throughout all of this, Libby was my constant. We went through every high and every low together. I always thought that it was inevitable that she would be with me through everything life brought our way. That was until February 13, 2017, when life as I knew it came crashing down and turned into the kind of nightmare that, until that moment, the people in small-town Delphi had only heard about on television.

Up to that point in our lives, Libby was the one I would go to when I needed someone to talk to and confide in. I would share *everything* with her, as she did with me. I spent the first year after her death trying to learn how to move forward in life without her. What was I going to do now that my whole world felt and looked so different? At seventeen, I had no idea how to cope with a traumatic loss, or even loss in general for that matter. The one thing I did know was that Libby would want me to move forward by living my life and not letting her murderer take mine also. I knew I *had* to do this to honor her life and memory.

Even though I was well aware that this was what my sister would want for me, I couldn't stop the continual roller-coaster ride of emotions. During the year that followed, I was scared to sleep in my own room alone, I quit my job because I was so uncomfortable walking to my car by myself at night, and I stopped parking in the student parking lot at school because I knew that after swim practice there would be more people walking to the front lot than the back. The knowledge that the person who had cold-heartedly murdered two teenagers in broad daylight was still out there somewhere, living their life as if nothing had happened, took hold of me and led me to a dark place, a place I prayed I was strong enough to stay away from. It was as though I had lost myself, and the person I had normally turned to for comfort and support in these times was now gone.

I felt incredibly alone. At that point, it seemed like no one in the world understood what I was feeling. My family constantly assured me that I could talk to them, but I worried that anything I said would only add to their grief. I couldn't find a counselor who knew how to help me work through the trauma I had experienced. My friends wanted to help, but the advice they gave me felt empty; even though they meant well, I knew they couldn't possibly understand the emotions I was going through. I hit rock bottom with seemingly no way out. All I could do was hold on to my faith and pray that Christ would lead me through these fires and help me to find peace.

After over a year of fighting what seemed like a never-ending battle, my family and I were invited to CrimeCon to speak about Abby and Libby's case. Up until that point, I had stayed silent and had never given any thought to putting myself out there to help in the public efforts to solve the girls' case. Before going into the event I had only planned on sitting back at the booth and handing out fliers— which is what I ended up doing. Even so, this event ended up being a turning point for me.

At CrimeCon 2018, I met Michelle Cruz—her sister, Janelle Cruz, was murdered by the Golden State Killer—along with several of the other sister survivors. These women inspired me; they still do. I watched in awe as they shared their stories without fear and celebrated the capture of their sister's killer. On the last day of the event, I found the courage to go up to Michelle and ask for her help. She told me to put myself out there and to never stop fighting for answers. She gave me the push I needed to break out of my shell and fight for my sister through social media.

Within days of starting a Twitter account for the case, I gained thousands of followers who wanted to join my family and me in our fight for justice. Making the decision to put myself out there, I became an advocate and, in the process of doing interviews and podcasts, I made many new friends. Several of the people I met through my account had also been affected in some way by violent crimes. Some of them had also lost siblings to homicide, and we were able to talk about our experiences and understand each other's feelings. For the very first time, I felt like I had a community that understood what I was going through. My prayers had finally been answered.

In the years that followed this conference, I have witnessed the best and the worst of humanity.

Social media, I have learned, is a double-edged sword. It can be a wonderful tool, sharing necessary information quickly and efficiently with the public. But it can also be filled with some users spouting hatred and untruths, ruining innocent people's lives. It was heartbreaking to read the constant speculation of what might have happened to the girls.

Luckily, there have been so many people who have supported our cause and wanted to help. I have always been a believer that good outweighs bad, and the world has shown that to be true. The people of Carroll County poured their love over us and the investigative team like no one could have ever expected. Strangers from around the world, like Michelle Cruz, Sarah Turney, Sheryl McCollum, and Susan Hendricks—to name a few, it would take dozens of pages to name them all—have stood by our side through all the ups and downs of the investigation to see justice through to the end.

My relationship with Susan has been particularly special. One of the first times my family met Susan, I accompanied her and the HLN crew to Monon High Bridge. I had met her previously and it was obvious to us how much she cared. But on this particular visit, it was even more evident. As we walked out to the bridge, we made casual conversation. I joked that they were overdressed in their winter coats; it wasn't that cold but, because they were used to the weather back in Atlanta, they had to buy warmer clothes upon their arrival in Indiana. Susan was emotional, even more so the closer we got to the beginning of the bridge. She kept reminding me that she wanted to make sure she covered Abby and Libby's story well, making sure the world knew that they were real girls, and that I was comfortable throughout the process. Over the years of knowing her, she has never failed at this. She is constantly reminding us of how much Abby and Libby—as well as our families—have impacted her life, how this has become so much more than just another story. I don't know that she realizes that she has done the same for us. Susan is one of several people who have shown us compassion and empathy in her reporting. She truly is one of the good ones and I am forever grateful for her and the friendship we have gained with her.

I have learned so much in the years that I have spent advocating for Libby, for Abby, and for others. One day I hope I am able to share some of these experiences with the world in more depth, but, for now, here are just a few of the lessons that had the biggest impact on me: I have learned how to have faith and to always remain hopeful, even when life feels hopeless. I have learned to stand up for the voiceless because I have a voice to use. I have learned to never stop fighting for what matters. And, most of all, I have learned that I am not defined by the trauma I have lived through. And neither are you.

Moving forward looks different as we reach this next chapter in the case. I have taken time to process the arrest, awaiting answers that will eventually come, and it has been a much-needed break. I am finding new ways to be a part of this community that has had my back for so long while I've worked to find myself again. Now, as a wife and mother, I will finally be living the life Libby would want me to live. I am no longer stuck in 2017 as I had been for so long.

I may not have all the answers or know what the next step is, but what I do know is this: Life has a funny way of making sure you have exactly what you need when you need it most, especially in your darkest and most lonely days. You are not defined by what has happened to you.

The Day Everything Changed

When Kelsi woke up on the morning of Monday, February 13, 2017, it seemed to be a day just like any other—well, almost. The unusually warm winter in Delphi, Indiana, had brought in fewer snowstorms than administrators had predicted earlier in the academic year, leaving unclaimed snow days in its wake, to the joy of teachers and students alike. On this snow-free "snow day" Monday, the morning rippled with glimmering promise and endless possibilities—a free day with no classes, volleyball practice, or softball.

And yet the day would forever be etched in young Kelsi's mind for a very different reason, with every choice, every step, every hint from her senses playing repeatedly in a torturous, menacing loop. It was the last day she would ever see her sister alive.

Thinking back on that morning now, years later, Kelsi is haunted most by the sounds that she once took for granted: the merry noises of her younger sister, fourteen-year-old Libby, running down the stairs with her best friend, thirteen-year-old Abby, while her grandmother Becky was in the kitchen working; the slight whispering and girlish giggling as the two young teens gossiped at the kitchen table as Kelsi and Libby's father, Derrick, made the girls breakfast.

It seems almost cruel now, the simplicity of this former morning routine, carried out by a loving family unaware that their lives would never be the same. Her grandfather Mike had already left for work by the time the rest of the house woke up, but he didn't give it a second thought; he was comforted by the parental confidence and sense of ease that he'd get to see Libby and hear all about her day with Abby later on at dinnertime, as he had every evening before.

With the afternoon quickly approaching, Libby and Abby debated how they should spend the rest of their long weekend. There were plenty of options; they had friends they could call, to laugh the rest of the day away; they could hang out with Kelsi, if she wasn't too busy; and, of course, they knew all the local hangout spots and trails they could wander.

In the end, Libby and Abby arrived at a solution that many other teens just like them have turned to countless times: they would create an adventure for themselves.

Their lips curling with mischief and unadulterated delight, the girls built up the courage to ask Becky to drive them to the local trails. Becky responded that she couldn't take the girls right away—she was too busy working through her daily to-do list—but added that they could help her by completing some quick chores before they headed out for the afternoon. After cleaning up a bit, Libby and Abby asked Kelsi whether she wanted to go with them as they explored a popular local hiking trail nearby.

Although she was seventeen and already had a social life and responsibilities of her own, Kelsi took her role as a big sister seriously and enjoyed spending time with Libby and her friends. Feeling slightly guilty, since she had been saying "no" or "I'm busy, sorry" too often lately, Kelsi readily agreed to give the girls a ride to the trailhead, but she unfortunately couldn't join them this time—she had to work.

The girls jumped up and down gleefully. Libby grabbed her sister for a big hug, and she'd thank her from the kitchen, through the front door, and all the way to Kelsi's car. In the background of this exchange, Becky, like generations of doting grandparents before her, reminded Libby, "Take a sweatshirt!"

Libby shrugged it off, and Becky repeated, "Libby, it might get chilly. Take a sweatshirt!"

"Grandma." Libby smiled back at her lovingly. "It's *OK*."

"OK. Be safe," Becky replied with an exasperated sigh. "I love you."

"Love you too! See you later!" Libby cried with a toothy smile streaking across her rosy cheeks.

Becky shut the door behind them, chuckling to herself, already thinking about what the girls might like for dinner that night when they got back. Their family always said *I love you* in place of *goodbye*. Every single time. Just in case something happened. Of course, they never expected anything actually *would* happen; it was almost as if this precaution could shield them from misfortune.

Overjoyed by the sea of possibilities in front of them, Libby and Abby jumped into Kelsi's car—Libby in the front, Abby in the back. They rolled down the windows and turned on the radio as Kelsi drove down Delphi's main road, toward High Bridge.

"Turn it up!" Libby yelled. "This is my favorite song!"

"Heathens" by Twenty One Pilots blasted through the speakers as Libby sang along with the melody:

> *All my friends are heathens, take it slow*
> *Wait for them to ask you who you know*
> *Please don't make any sudden moves*
> *You don't know half of the abuse*

The car ride was a quick one, with barely enough time to even finish the song; after all, the start of the Monon High Bridge Trail was only about five minutes away from their home. Kelsi slowed the car down to a halt as Libby and Abby clamored to undo their seat belts and bolted out of the car.

As the two girls headed toward the trail, Kelsi reminded them to stay warm, yelled out a quick goodbye, and told her sister she loved her. Watching as they scampered down the path, she couldn't help but smile, wishing she could be as young and carefree as her younger sister when she was already bogged down with work and assignments for school. As Kelsi plays the day over in her mind, this memory cuts off abruptly somewhere around a quarter to two, when she pulled her car back out and drove away—1:49 p.m., to be exact.

Now, whenever she thinks of her sister, she'll remember watching Libby and Abby grow smaller and fainter in the rearview mirror, perfectly preserved for just a moment in time.

―――

AFTER LIBBY AND ABBY SET OFF ON THE TRAIL, MUCH OF THEIR FINAL HOURS REMAINS A MYSTERY. For those who are unfamiliar with the rough terrain of Delphi's woods, the trail might appear to be a labyrinth with a monster or some other untold danger lurking in the shadows, nestled within a thick cover of ancient trees and malevolent, mangled branches. But all Libby and Abby saw before them was the start of an exciting day. They knew the twists and turns of those trails like the freckles and scars on the backs of their hands; the forest had never posed a threat to a local before, and it seemed unlikely today would be any different. Their final conversations with each other are deeply embedded in those same woods, secret murmurings that echo wordlessly within the hollows of tall sycamore and cottonwood trees.

When the girls reached the Monon High Bridge, they stopped to take a snapshot of the massive structure, much like dozens of other locals had done before. The bridge was a common feature in pictures taken by teens who'd grown up in the area; it had even gained a reputation as a popular backdrop for high schoolers posing before senior prom. Though the slats were old and the beams weathered with age, local kids knew that crossing the bridge was easy, really: just follow a few simple steps, walk slowly, and keep your eyes on the old rail bridge below your feet so you don't fall through one of the many sizable gaps.

For a visitor approaching it for the first time, however, High Bridge would appear terrifying. Looming 63 feet above the ground and spanning 1,300 feet in length, with a creek running beneath it, the course of split boards feels weary, old, uninviting. It seems near impossible that the rusted train tracks atop the bridge could carry the load of a full train if it were commanded to do so today; the old iron beams that hold the structure true seem to tremble beneath your feet, daring you to misstep.

But again, Libby and Abby—buoyed by the boldness of youth—felt no fear, and so, at 2:07 p.m., Libby took a quick picture of her best friend boldly walking across the bridge on her

Snapchat app and posted it, as if unknowingly declaring to their whole social network that they were young and invincible.

In the moments after that image was uploaded, the girls were approached by a strange man. From the start, his demeanor was troubling, his stature stocky and almost hunched. His face was covered by an old hat, and he walked with his hands stuffed into the pockets of his worn blue jacket. Alarmed, Libby began to secretly record the man using her phone, hidden within her clothing. This layer of static shrouds the recording to this day, taunting us and whispering in the cracks of the last conversation between the soon-to-be murderer and the girls.

A little after 3:00 p.m., Libby's father, Derrick, pulled into one of the parking areas and waited for the girls to emerge from the trail. After waiting for a bit, he called Libby's cell phone at 3:11 p.m. No answer, no response. By 3:30 p.m., knowing it wasn't like Libby to ignore his texts and calls, Derrick exited his car and began searching along the trails for her and Abby, worried one or both of them might be injured. Reaching the point where the trails intersected, Derrick spotted a man in a flannel shirt and stopped him to ask whether he'd happened to see two young girls. He said he hadn't, but he mentioned that he'd seen a couple on the bridge not long ago.

Derrick continued down the trail to the creek and called his mom, Becky. He was growing increasingly concerned after not being able to find or even reach the girls via phone. On his way back up the trail, Derrick tried not to run through all the nightmare scenarios in his mind, but he still wondered aloud where the girls were and what could have happened to them. Reluctantly, Derrick started his car and backed away from the pickup spot, checking his rearview mirror in hopes that Libby and Abby would run up, waving for him to turn back—that he was making a big deal out of nothing.

Meanwhile, Tara, Libby's aunt, was with her mother, Becky, around the time Derrick had called. Both Tara and Becky started repeatedly calling and texting Libby. As four o'clock approached, Becky and Tara grew more and more anxious and decided to head over to the trail to help look for them. As Tara later recalled, there were two different paths that Abby and Libby could have taken if they'd attempted to get home on their own. "So we drove both routes that they could have taken . . . and no girls. By this time, we were really quite concerned because we had [covered] the whole trail area where they should have been."

Becky called her husband, Mike, who was at work in Lafayette, to let him know what was going on. Immediately, Mike clocked out of work early and drove to the trail to help Becky, calling Kelsi along the way. Kelsi called out of work as well and headed straight to the trail.

Now sick with worry, the family members volleyed theories back and forth: Had the girls decided to go somewhere else? Were they at some other friend's house? Had something happened to them while on the trail? Could one of them have possibly fallen off the bridge? Delphi was a simple, uneventful town; *nothing* happened there. It was unfathomable that something—or someone—more sinister was to blame.

A little after five o'clock that evening, Mike contacted the police. As he remembered it, within ten to fifteen minutes of his call, the entire town of Delphi was lit up with flashlights. Abby and Libby were now officially reported missing, and their loved ones' worries continued to escalate. Desperate for answers, Becky called AT&T and begged them to get someone to ping Libby's phone so that they could find the girls more easily—to no avail.

Becky had also been trying to get ahold of Anna, Abby's mom, and was just about to drive over to her work when Anna finally answered and learned that her baby girl was missing. By six o'clock, the Carroll County Sheriff's Office, the Delphi Fire Department, and the Delphi police were all involved in the investigation. Eager to add more eyes and ears to the search effort, family members reached out for aid across social media, and what seemed like the entire town of Delphi showed up to pitch in.

The trails and surrounding streets lit up with flashlights, scouring each and every corner, behind every rock and tree. The group continued looking for hours, until the sheriff finally called off the official search at ten o'clock, saying that he did not want to expose his men to the difficult terrain in the dark. The temperature had also dropped considerably, and he was worried about exposure to the elements. Even so, many stayed behind to continue to look for the girls—in vain.

By the next morning, Indiana State Police made an official statement that they were on the lookout for two young girls in Delphi, a small town north of Lafayette, Indiana. Word spread fast. The fire station became a gathering point for volunteers. Between the families' first call to police and the first local search, Abby and Libby's disappearance had caught the attention of several news outlets. Their disappearance was beginning to capture much more attention than Kelsi and her family could have possibly anticipated.

That morning, helicopters, state troopers, the FBI, and even a K-9 unit ranged across the area in which Libby and Abby had last been seen. Exhausted after a sleepless night, the girls' families still held out hope that the teens would be found alive—maybe battered and injured, but at least alive. By now, hundreds of people—perhaps more—were on the hunt for the girls.

As one hour bled into the next, the search efforts bubbled with more energy than ever before: they were one step closer to the girls. Kelsi was so confident that Abby and Libby would be found that she even packed a backpack with granola bars, water, and blankets, thinking the girls would be hungry when she saw them again.

That cautious optimism was quickly shattered when one of the members of the search crew first discovered a shoe. Kelsi had just crossed the bridge with a small group after spending more than thirty minutes looking underneath it. The man who made that discovery used his phone to look across the creek and cried out that he'd spotted two bodies.

Kelsi's heart sank deep into the depths of her stomach, but she tried to stay hopeful. She mulled over the man's use of the word *bodies*, convinced that "he would have called out that he found 'the girls' if he had come across them." But as the minutes dragged on, she felt a pang in her gut: a part of her knew, even if Abby and Libby had been found, they weren't coming home that night.

Kelsi started to feel weak, with concerns for both the girls and their other family members, like her grandpa, who was looking nearby and had suffered heart problems in the past. She then quickly caught the eye of another volunteer, a woman who worked at the middle school and had lost her own brother in high school. Kelsi fell into her arms. The woman tried to comfort her, but she also convinced Kelsi that they didn't know what they would find and it was best to turn back.

But as more and more firefighters arrived at the tragic scene, followed by a member of the coroner's office, it became quite apparent that their search was coming to a tragic end.

At two o'clock on the afternoon of Tuesday, February 14, officials announced that the bodies of two young girls had been discovered along the trails where Libby and Abby had been reported missing. Twenty-four hours later, the bodies were identified as fourteen-year-old Liberty German and thirteen-year-old Abigail Williams. They said the matter was now being investigated as a crime and they suspected foul play.

For the public, the news was shocking and disturbing, but for the girls' families, the crushing weight of the announcement felt suffocating, utterly inconceivable. Expressing heartfelt regret, the local police force reassured their fellow citizens, confident they'd solve the heinous crime within forty-eight hours.

———

I WAS ON SET AT THE CNN CENTER IN ATLANTA WHEN DETAILS FROM THIS DOUBLE HOMICIDE STARTED to emerge. I'll never forget the day of February 14, 2017: the first time I saw images of the girls. Not knowing the ties that I would form with the families. How close I would get. How much I would come to care for them and for their community.

I've spent more than twenty-five years covering heartbreaking and harrowing stories from the field and in a studio as a journalist—from smaller stations and local affiliates of ABC and NBC to the very headquarters of CNN and HLN. There was even a five-year span in my career, when my daughter was very young, that I spent about fifteen hours a day inside the CNN Center in Atlanta—by design. I *wanted* to be there. I anchored an afternoon show on HLN until 4:00 p.m., then I'd go home at 5:00 for forty-five minutes, and then I'd drive back to CNN for Anderson Cooper's 8:00 show, *AC 360*. I was on the B block of the 8:00 hour, then again at 11:00 p.m., usually in the D block, which meant I was there until midnight. Looking back on that time now, I'm so grateful for my parents, who came to help me during that period. But I also realize that the intensity of those five years was a real crash course in compartmentalization.

I'm often asked whether it ever gets easier, reporting on the darkest depths of humanity, and I wish I could tell you it does, but I'd be lying. No matter how many crimes you cover, no matter how many people you interview, no matter how many gruesome details you hear about, it *never* gets easier. You just get better at pretending that it does.

Here's what makes it possible:

Moving fast: You are *forced* to move on. Once your mic turns off, once you hear that "all clear" from a producer, or a director, or a photographer, you're already on to the next story or assignment.

Story count: There is no shortage of horror to cover—and it's your job as a journalist to get the story out there, so you gather up the facts, interview those involved, and move on. Never linger.

No follow-up: Often, each story that a reporter is assigned to is for that day only. There is no continued communication about the case, which allows you to create a protective shield, a safe barrier, that protects you from truly feeling anything. The accompanying emotions of sadness, anxiety, helplessness, and fear—those aren't really a concern, as long as you don't get too close.

The ability to suppress your feelings is at risk if you really connect to the who, what, when, and where of the story. It can happen if the town reminds you of where you grew up, or if the particulars of the crime itself trigger uncanny memories and sensations that maybe you can't even place. Or if the victim or victims remind you of former classmates, friends, your own children, or even yourself.

Whatever it is, you have to be vigilant about maintaining your boundaries, because all it takes is a single snip—one story that cuts a little too close to the bone—and suddenly, all your tightly wound threads start to unravel. And for me, that's what happened in Delphi.

Everyone hoped that this case would be solved immediately, wrapped up quickly with a bow. But it didn't happen that way. And so all of the tactics that I normally used to protect myself from the pain no longer worked, no matter how hard I tried.

For Libby and Abby, February 13, 2017, would come to represent the end of their story. But for their loved ones and law enforcement, February 13 came to represent just the beginning.

2

On the Set

"Sir, it's Susan Hendricks. Can you hear me?" I asked, waiting for confirmation.

"Yes, I can," Ron Logan replied.

"Great. We're in a commercial break right now, but we'll be up in a few minutes."

I'd found out I'd be interviewing the guest only a few minutes before the live newscast. The producers told me they'd booked Ron Logan, the man who owned the property where Abby's and Libby's bodies had been discovered, as a guest this hour, and I'd be talking to him in the B block. Filled with anticipation of what he might say, I glanced over just in time to see the floor director say, "Stand by in two, one . . ." before pointing right to the camera.

"Welcome back. The search for a killer continues after the bodies of two young girls were found in Delphi, Indiana, near the

Monon High Bridge. They were dropped off at the trails on February 13; their bodies were discovered the next day. With me now is Ron Logan, who owns the property where the bodies were discovered."

Ron Logan described the scene to me as chilling, as if the region had been marked by their deaths. He mentioned that his son often spent time on those same trails. Logan said he was still in shock, that he "just can't believe something like this happened on my property in my backyard."

I thanked him and threw to a commercial break. If there's one thing I've learned when it comes to live TV interviews, it's that you have to wrap up an interview in whatever time you're allotted. Some producers are more patient than others, but in general, you *have* to hit the time. *On* time. The commercials are paid for specially for that block, and not hitting that mark, that exact time, is considered unacceptable.

So, I learned to get the interview, get the sound bite, and get *out*. *Fast*. It took some practice, but it became an almost robotic response over the years. And I was good at it; it's what I fixated on, above just about everything else. It's not that I didn't care about the story itself—I just didn't allow myself to focus on it. I didn't want to feel. *Anything*.

———

BACK IN DELPHI, AS THE SCENE ERUPTED AROUND THE DISCOVERY OF BODIES, POLICE ON-SITE quickly blocked off the area in Ron Logan's backyard. They were hoping to keep volunteer searchers and curious onlookers away and the chatter and noise to a minimum, but once the media caught wind, there was a frenzy. Within hours, news teams across the country who had been following the search launched breaking updates about bodies being discovered around the region where Abby and Libby had gone missing just the day before. It was a heartbreaking yet incredibly gripping story that had everyone involved scrambling to get more information from police on the scene.

Amid the bustling chaos, Kelsi and her family had to be escorted from the riverbank and back to the fire station, where they were taken upstairs, away from the crowd of people, to talk to police directly and hear the news first. Later that afternoon, Carroll County sheriff Tobe Leazenby, Delphi police chief Steve Mullin, and Indiana State Police PIO Sergeant Kim Riley stepped into a room brimming with reporters and news crews waiting for the first press conference in which police would discuss the events that had unfolded beneath the Monon High Bridge.

Sergeant Riley was the first to speak. "We have found two bodies in Deer Creek, about a mile east of town. We are investigating this as a crime scene. We suspect foul play."

It was revealed that, yes, bodies had been found, but no positive IDs had been made, and at this point, the police were unwilling to say that they were in fact the bodies of Abby and Libby.

But Becky knew. "One of my friends, her husband was in one of the search parties that found them. They said they were found, and I asked if they were OK, and they wouldn't answer me. I ran up to some of the firemen and said, 'I need you to take me to Libby. They found her,' and they kept saying no. I knew before it was announced [that] they were not alive."[1]

Kelsi knew too. She could feel grief and sorrow scraping at the insides of her stomach, rendering her hollow. The anger came later. What was happening? Why was her little sister gone and taken from her? She couldn't bring herself to ID her sister's body;

none of her family was really willing to bear witness to the unthinkable tragedy that had befallen them.

At last, her grandfather Mike stepped forward to identify his granddaughter's body. In the years since, he's never spoken about what he saw that day. Later on, as I got to know him and his family better, I asked Mike how he'd managed to stay so strong.

"Susan, what keeps me going is thinking of the last few minutes of the girls' lives, what they went through."

I shivered, aching for him and his family. I kept my thoughts to myself, but I couldn't help wondering, *What did he see? How much had the girls suffered?*

As Becky remembered it, "We were so excited we didn't think to ask anything else once we heard the girls were found. We jumped in our cars, and we got to the trailhead. We ran up, and I said, 'Where are they? Libby needs me.' I remember looking over, and my sister was sitting on a cart, and she was crying. I went running over and said, 'They found them, they found them, they found them,' [but] all she could do was sit there and cry, and she kept saying, 'I'm sorry.' I [was] sitting there with her, and about that time, Mike came over, and I remember the coroner's van driving by, and that's when I knew that they found them, and they weren't alive."

A second press conference was held the next day, February 15, now forty-eight hours since the girls' disappearance and twenty-four hours since their bodies had been discovered. At last, the police publicly announced that the bodies had been officially identified as Abby and Libby. The room erupted immediately with questions about how the girls had died, what had happened to them. The police replied that they could not release the cause of death because they had ruled it as a double homicide. Abby and Libby had been brutally murdered and then discarded in the woods near the creek. No arrests had been made; there weren't any official suspects at that time.

Later that evening, the police released a grainy photo of a man, a possible witness who they hoped may be able to shed light on what had occurred between the time Libby posted that photo of Abby on Snapchat and when the girls were supposed to meet Libby's dad at the trailhead. Police pleaded with the individual to come forward and offer any insight or clues they could to help move the case further along. But, as with everything in this case, new information only led to more questions. First and foremost, where had the photo come from? Who had taken the photo of this witness, and just when or how had it been turned over to the police?

As soon as the homicide ruling was released, speculation and suspect hunting ran rampant as the national focus ransacked the streets of Delphi. Fanciful, unfounded rumors about their cause of death started circling relentlessly around the internet; at their funerals, both girls' necks had been wrapped in scarves. But investigators remained tight-lipped.

The only thing the police would reveal to the public was that the area around Deer Creek where the girls had been discovered wasn't easily accessible by any means; in fact, it was far enough off the trail path that whoever had left them there would need to have a certain level of familiarity with the area to get around safely.

In other words, the killer was one of them.

Someone in Delphi, who had lived in Delphi, who the girls possibly even knew or were at least familiar with, had been the one to take their lives. Knowing that someone in their community was likely at fault, Kelsi's family, and others just like them, felt as though the sense of safety they had long taken for granted had been ripped from their hands. It was like a sick "locked-room" mystery—a killer among them—with a villain more devious than any that Agatha Christie could muster up. Before long, half the population was at risk of becoming a suspect, and it was hard to know who to trust. Thinking back on that lingering fear, Kelsi described the days surrounding the discovery of the girls as an out-of-body experience.

"The full two weeks after they were found, we have this big blur of time where we weren't really in our bodies. We were there, but we weren't there." Kelsi remembered pulling up to her house and looking up at Libby's room to see whether her light was on. "I was in denial."[2]

On Wednesday, February 22, 2017, police held another, much larger press conference, this time at Delphi United Methodist Church.

Standing behind the podium was the multiagency team who had banded together to solve this double murder, including members of the Delphi Police Department and the Carroll County Sheriff's Office; Indiana State Police superintendent Doug Carter; and a number of investigators, including the FBI's Greg Massa.

Indiana State Police sergeant Tony Slocum was the first one to greet the media, stepping up to the mic. "If you would allow me a little bit of latitude here before we get into the meat and potatoes of the press conference to give a couple of thank-yous, I would like to do that now."

Slocum paused, then began to recite his planned statement. "We volunteer because we care." He made sure to repeat that line for emphasis. "We volunteer because we *care*."

Slocum then noted that he'd seen a message on the side of a firetruck in Delphi the day before that struck a chord within him. "I believe it's a way of life here in Delphi and the Carroll County community. Because of the way this community has wrapped their arms around this investigation and provided not just the resources for officers as they're investigating this case, but also their willingness to give us information and anything that we have asked [for], including this church today for the press conference, [which] Pastor Todd has given us." Sergeant Slocum mentioned that the reward for information relating to the murders of Abby and Libby had reached $41,000. He thanked everyone who contributed, including the FBI, who added $25,000 to the pot. Slocum then turned his attention to the person I believe they were counting on to help them solve this double murder: the so-called missing link.

"I would also like to thank, in advance, the person who's gonna call our tip line and give us that tidbit of information that's going to lead to the arrest of the *murderers* of Liberty German and Abigail Williams."

His use of the word *murderers* piqued my attention. Was he saying that there were two (or more) people involved?

Slocum closed out by thanking the media for their patience, explaining that "this investigation is too important to make any mistakes and give out the wrong information."

Agent Massa approached the podium next and implored members of the Delphi community to think back to nine days before, urging them to think about how those around them had acted after the murders of Abby and Libby. There were certain behavioral indicators that could prove to be important, such as a change in that person's appearance or comportment, or even a change in their sleep patterns. Massa also asked them to consider anyone they knew who had unexpected travel come up all of a sudden, or anyone who had been following the case and the media's involvement to a degree that was "not normal."

"Please," Massa said, addressing the cameras, "if you have that information, call that into the tip line. After this press conference, the FBI will be putting out a series of these indicators on our social media, so it will be available not only to the citizens of this community but across the state of Indiana and nationally as well. We'll also be utilizing digital billboards, and in any way that we can spread this message, we will."

Massa reassured Delphi that he wouldn't stop until the investigation ended. "To the community at large, nine days ago, the FBI stood shoulder to shoulder with you: we're not going anywhere. We will be here until this case is solved, and I am confident this case *will* be solved. Thank you."

Chief public information officer Captain Dave Bursten announced that he was going to play the voice of the man they believed murdered Abby and Libby. But how? Clearly weirded out by an encounter with a stranger in the woods not long before the girls' deaths, Libby had started recording the interaction on her phone, which had been tucked away in her pocket.

"This young lady is a hero, there's no doubt," Bursten reiterated, "to have enough presence of mind to activate that video system on her cell phone, to record what we believe is criminal behavior that's about to occur."

Libby knew something was off and, like Hansel and Gretel, left behind a digital trail of breadcrumbs for us to follow.

"Micha, play the clip, please," Bursten instructed.

The audio was fuzzy, but you could clearly hear an older man say, "Down the hill."

It was on a loop—his voice, that order, strung together four times. Bursten asked Micha to play it once more in hopes that someone in the audience might recognize the man's voice.

"If you hear this today and think, *My God, that sounds like . . .* fill in the blank, call us," Bursten told the public. "Make an anonymous tip. Tell us who you think it is. Let us investigate it. If it's not the right person, they'll just be out a little bit of time and they'll be cleared, and they can go on and they'll never know that you called, *but* you may tell us who the right person was, and you could be the person that helps us to solve this horrible crime."

Indiana State Police superintendent Doug Carter reiterated what Sergeant Slocum opened with: he believed that a tip from the right person would lead them to the monster on the bridge. Referencing the poster near the podium, Carter pleaded with those watching to take another look.

"Someone knows who this individual is." He paused, then said it again. "Is it a family member? Is it a neighbor? Is it an acquaintance? Is it an associate? Or maybe that one guy that lives over at that one place that's just . . . kinda not right. Maybe it's his jeans, maybe it's his jacket or his sweatshirt, maybe it's his shirttail, maybe it's his posture, maybe it's the right hand in his pocket. You see, even with technology, we need human intelligence. In other words, we need you. I'm not suggesting that science, that everything that we can do with science, has been done, because we are just getting started."

The superintendent spoke about our obligation to these innocent young girls.

"Abby and Libby deserve us. They deserve every single one of us, and not just the people standing up here on the stage that have given so much of their lives to not just this but to this profession, but each and every one of you. Each and every person listening, watching, or seeing this in some form, we need you. Libby and Abby need you.

"Please do not rationalize tips away, rationalize what you think that might not be important away, by thinking, *He would never do that to another human being*, or think, *What I know doesn't matter*. Let folks like the people that are standing behind me with such incredible passion and commitment and dedication to this profession make that determination.

"Tips are anonymous. Some might not want to talk about it because they don't want to get involved because they know the individual—again, he may be a family member, probably has family. No one will ever know. No one will ever know. There's not an agency on the planet better at helping us facilitate this than the FBI, and they are as entrenched in this as anybody. No one will know. As poor as this picture is, somebody knows. And if you're watching"—pause—"we'll find you."

Was Doug Carter speaking to the murderer, or was he talking to a person unaware or, worse, unwilling to see what their loved one was capable of?

Then he asked the question those living in Delphi, including Abby's and Libby's family members, were asking themselves.

"Who's next? I hate to ask you that question. I'd give my life to not have to."

Sergeant Slocum wrapped up the presser with the same sentence he had started with, emphatically stating that "we volunteer because we care." He was confident that the missing link was still out there, and he hoped this presser would "prompt people to give us information."

"We need to get the *murderer* of Liberty German and Abigail Williams into custody sooner rather than later," he said. I noticed that he'd only mentioned one possible murderer this time. Was it a simple mistake, or did investigators know more than they were letting on? How many people did they believe were involved?

After the Q&A part of the presser wrapped, it was anyone's guess.

Captain Dave Bursten then came forward to talk about the question that was on everyone's minds: the mystery of what exactly Libby had captured on her phone. Was the "man on the bridge" involved, and if so, was he the only one? Was it his voice that Libby recorded saying, "Down the hill"? Or were we listening to the voice of someone else, possibly an accomplice?

"Keep in mind, all of you are in the television business." Bursten held up his hands next to his face, palms out; he was clearly evoking the image of a box, a square TV. "What do you see out of the TV? You [only] see this." He looked pointedly out at the members of the media.

"You don't see what's over here," he said, pointing to the left. "You don't see what's over here." He was pointing to the right now. "There's lots more that we're looking at." It was obvious he was reminding everyone in the audience that we weren't seeing the full picture.

After the audio was released, many in the community—if not the nation—were expecting there to be an arrest within hours, possibly days. But days became weeks, weeks turned into months, and that call just never came. The citizens were restless, growing more and more frustrated. Delphi was a *very* small town—there were fewer than three thousand residents.[3] Surely *someone* must have recognized that person's voice. Were they too afraid to come forward? We had all heard Doug Carter say they would be protected.

Rumors circulated until five months later, on July 17, when the police released another clue: a sketch of the potential suspect. The facial composite featured a middle-aged or possibly older man, scruffy in appearance, slightly heavyset, wearing a hoodie. Tufts of hair peeked out from behind a newsboy-style hat. He had dark eyes and a large nose; a light shadow of unshaven facial hair lined his mouth. It was, supposedly, a close-up look at the man on the bridge. Unfortunately, it also resembled most of the men in Delphi, as Kelsi and many others from Delphi said later on, reinforcing the fear that the murderer could be anyone.

Hoping for that one tip to come in, the missing piece of the puzzle, Superintendent Doug Carter pleaded again, speaking to anyone who would listen. "We need you. Abby and Libby *need* you."

————

WHEN I FIRST BEGAN REPORTING ON THE DELPHI MURDERS, I KNEW SOME OF THE FACTS, LIKE everyone else: who, what, when, and where. The why, on the other hand—well, that has been and always will be more difficult to grasp or make sense of.

At the time, the media had dubbed them "the Snapchat Murders," since Libby and Abby had been posting on Snapchat in the hours leading up to their deaths. I'd read the same name off the prompter myself, during a two-hour newscast in Atlanta. It was one of twelve stories in the A block.

Just shy of two years later, on February 9, 2019, I found myself heading to Delphi to meet with the families who had gone through the unthinkable. In the twenty-four months since those first few press conferences, little information had been released, and it seemed like the police were getting nowhere fast. It still wasn't clear whether the voice that Libby had recorded belonged to the man on the bridge.[4]

Driving into Delphi from the airport was like driving into a postcard image of small-town America; you could pick out the mom-and-pop shops that had always been there, lined up side by side like little soldiers along the sparse streets. Abby and Libby's elementary school was just up the road.

Before long, we pulled up to a pale yellow ranch-style house with a dark green roof and lighter, almost sage-colored shutters; a welcoming wraparound porch; and a large star, hanging like a beacon, right over the garage door. We rang the doorbell, and Becky, Libby's grandmother, greeted us with a warm smile, inviting us in. I saw Libby memorialized in a silver frame sitting right next to a cross. Kelsi walked into the room, and I turned toward her.

"Hi. I'm Susan."

"Hi," she said and smiled back. "I'm Kelsi."

3

Arrival in Delphi

As I walked farther into Libby's family home, the ever-present existence of loss and heartache were palpable, the wounds fresh, as if no time had passed—even though it had been almost two years since Abby and Libby were murdered.

Not much headway had been made in the official investigation. Authorities had seized an enormous amount of evidence recorded on Libby's phone; they knew what the man's voice sounded like. And yet no one seemed to know who this person was. In a town this small, it was reasonably assumed that the perpetrator would be found somewhat quickly. Surely *someone* must know *something*. The tip line was open. Authorities promised to protect anyone who knew anything and was willing to share it. Thousands of calls came in, though they rarely led to any new developments.

Every few months a name would surface, someone who police were "looking into," but so far no arrests had been made. The frustration surrounding the lack of progress in the case grew with every passing day. No one felt this more than Libby's and Abby's families, who spent each day hoping the news they were waiting for would finally come. It was almost like everything else stopped until they had answers; the case was their focus, their everything.

Kelsi herself was forced to mature quickly in the public eye, as much of the national attention had shifted to her. But the worst of it came from inside her own heart. As the last person to see Abby and Libby alive, Kelsi was overwhelmed with guilt that she just couldn't get past. She blamed herself for taking her sister to the bridge that day, even though it was not and could never be her fault.

"I don't want him to win," she told me. "I'm not going to let this person kill me too."

For almost two years, Kelsi and the other members of Abby's and Libby's families had done everything they could to make it through each day without their beloved girls, while the person who had brutally ended their lives was still out there, walking free among them. Where could he be hiding in a town that small?

Delphi had a charm and peacefulness to it, but it also felt isolated from nearby towns, as though it existed in its own separate world. I was expecting Delphi to have a cinematic, picturesque small-town vibe, with homes built in close proximity to one another, lined along cul-de-sacs—but the opposite was true. The abundant rural landscape was sectioned off by fencing and farm posts, with animals milling about in the cold of the late winter. Unlike the downtown area, the most striking feature of outer Delphi was how spread out the homes were, barely in the vicinity of their own neighbors.

As small and rural as Delphi is, it's the only city in Carroll County, a county I became quite familiar with over the next few years. Carroll County was first established around the end of 1824. Like many midwestern regions, it was "discovered" by settlers venturing west—mostly originating from states like Pennsylvania, Ohio, Virginia, and Kentucky. Just two years later, several hundred settlers lived within the county, building their own cabins and constructing sawmills and gristmills to stimulate the burgeoning economy.[1] The town of Delphi itself was established a little over a decade later, in 1835, but it was officially declared a city in 1866 as brand-new canals and railroads continued to bring more and more people to the area.[2]

Over the next century and a half, the population of Carroll County continued to ebb and flow; by 2017, Carroll County had a little over 20,000 residents, with 2,885 of them living in Delphi.[3] Delphi is tiny, composed of just 2.7 square miles.[4] The population is overwhelmingly white (89.73 percent), and about 38 percent of the residents consider themselves religious, primarily Christian.[5]

Delphi was, and still is, a predominantly agrarian community; the biggest industries in Carroll County are agriculture, food processing, and manufacturing, and in Delphi, about 40 percent of the workforce is centered on manufacturing and construction.[6]

In many ways, Delphi resembles so many places across the American heartland; it has that small-town feel to it, where people know their neighbors, and no one really locks their doors and the crime rate reflects that.

I looked into the crime statistics and found out there are seventeen registered violent or sex offenders in the city—which is significantly lower than the state average. The violent crime rate is also considerably lower than the national average (16.4 percent for Delphi, 22.7 percent for the US as a whole), and from about 2003 to 2015, the murder rate was virtually nonexistent, with theft and property crimes accounting for the majority of reported crimes.[7] One of the reasons why the double homicide of two young girls had shocked the community (and the nation at large) was because it seemed absolutely unfathomable that a crime like this could even happen in Delphi. As I looked out the car window, watching the fields and animals pass before my eyes, it wasn't hard to see how someone might get that impression.

As we headed back to the center of town, the buildings got closer and closer together, and that familiar small-town feel returned, but the atmosphere felt different, almost uncanny. Everyone seemingly knew one another, yet if the killer still lived in the area, it made me wonder, how much did anyone really know?

Then again, I guess the same could be said about any one of us, in any town, in any state—do we ever truly know those we live closest to? And what do statistics really tell us about a specific crime? Can past criminal behavior necessarily predict how someone else may act in that same town the future?

⎯⎯⎯

After our initial hellos, we made our way into the kitchen, where Libby's family shared with us their favorite memories of her. Kelsi beamed with pride as she showed me photos of Libby on her phone—photos of Libby playing sports, hanging out with friends, relaxing on vacation with Becky, Mike, and Kelsi. This wasn't Libby as a snapshot on a flyer; these were candid moments of Libby's life, captured right as she *lived* them.

"Our annual trip to Florida was our favorite," Becky said while looking down at a picture of Libby and Kelsi on the beach, digging their toes in the sand while standing near the water. "We would pack up the car and drive ten hours, but we'd break it up by spending the night at the halfway point . . . Susan, she was filled with so much joy, and she would pass that along to everyone in the family. She was full of energy that contagiously spread to all who knew her."

As more and more memories resurfaced, I could feel this sullen weight of grief draping its way around the room we were nestled in. It felt like someone, or something, was smothering us in a heavy quilt. The sorrow permeated every memory, and yet it also sparked a sense of resolve, a mission, for the survivors Libby had left behind. They were determined to find the man who'd been on the bridge with the girls that day. And this mission, to pursue justice for Abby and Libby, seemingly kept the family from falling further into the depths of their own grief.

"She gave us what we needed, Susan," said Mike, resolute. "Now it's up to us to get this guy."

As we settled in, Kelsi shared stories about high school and what her life had been like the last 726 days without her sister. She talked about how an essay contest at school had helped her; through writing, she felt free enough to express her darkest days and all her conflicting feelings and thoughts. I completely understood.

Mike shut the photo album, and we made our way to the living room, a large space right by the front door. I spotted a brown leather couch in front of us, next to a side table filled with photos and memories of Libby.

"Do you mind if I sit down?" I asked. "I'm exhausted."

Mike was quick to respond, his tone lightened by a touch of humor. "Of course, go ahead and sit," he said. "We know how tiring the cold weather can be, especially if you are not used to it coming from Atlanta."

"Thanks," I said with a smile as I sat down on the couch next to Kelsi. "I'd love to see it—the essay—if you don't mind."

She nodded, ran upstairs, and grabbed her laptop. Once she'd returned, everyone else migrated toward her. Kelsi mentioned it wasn't terribly long, but Becky suggested she read it to us anyway.

"You should," I reassured her.

Kelsi agreed with a sad smile and started to read.

———

If there is one thing I've learned about life, it's that it's unpredictable, erratic, inconsistent, and totally extraordinary. One minute, everything is totally normal, and the next, it's all taken away from you. There are moments you wish you could take back and things you wish you wouldn't have done and actions you wish you wouldn't have taken.

February 13, 2017, my life changed forever.

There was no school. I woke up late to my sister and Abby watching a movie that was turned up way too loud. I walked into her bedroom and sat with them.

"We've been up all night," they said. Oddly enough, they were wide awake and ready for an adventure around 11:00 a.m. I began getting ready to go to a friend's house before work. Libby walked into the bathroom and asked, "Hey, will you come to High Bridge with us?"

Knowing I had plans, I said no and told her I would drop them off if she could get a ride home. At 1:35 p.m., we arrived at the entrance of the bridge. The girls got out of my car, and I never saw them alive again.

Everything after that moment goes in slow motion. When I allow myself to actually go over that day and the week that followed, I hardly remember where I was or who I was with at the time. I was asked to remember things that I had dismissed, interrogated by countless police officers and FBI agents, followed by strangers with cameras and news reporters in vans.

It was just like everyone sees in Hollywood movies, only this time it wasn't a movie mystery—it was real. And my sister was the victim. She was gone . . .

For weeks after the loss, I tore myself down, contemplating how I should have said yes, I should have been with her. I told myself I could have saved them. I may not have made it, but at least maybe my sister would be here and I wouldn't be hurting. Asking myself if I would have been there, could I have really helped? My sister would then be here mourning the loss of her big sister, or, worse, would my family have to suffer a double loss and have to plan two funerals? I wouldn't let the what-ifs take over my life, but as I reflect now, they did teach me four lessons that will forever cause me to look at my life in a different way.

First, life is truly unpredictable. For every action a person chooses to take, there are a couple thousand more they could have taken. Over the last year, I have had to tell myself this every day. There's absolutely no way I could have known what was going to happen to the girls that day. Though normally I would have gone with them, that afternoon I had to work, and I couldn't hang out with her because of it. It's a decision I may regret at times but one that I cannot take back and will have to live with for the rest of my life.

Second, life is extremely erratic; one minute, you could be lying on the floor in your bedroom, listening to your little sister complain about middle school antics, and the next, you may be laying a flower over her grave. Tomorrow is never promised to everyone. I believe life is more understandable when you live every day as if it will be the last one you spend here on earth.

Life is also inconsistent. Things cannot stay the same forever, whether it's moving house to house, my parents' divorce, my sister's death, or being out of the granola bars I ate for breakfast. Every day, something's always changing, but if I allow the changes to rule my life in a negative direction, I will no longer be living the life that inspires myself or others.

Lastly, life is absolutely extraordinary. I have been through more than any eighteen-year-old ever should have to experience, and from those obstacles and struggles come amazing memories and experiences that outweigh all the bad. Not all high schoolers can say they've been on national TV or even that they've been to New York City. Not everyone can say they've met a Victoria's Secret supermodel, been to both sides of the United States in a month, met every news reporter and FBI agent in the state, or had the opportunity to make thousands of great friends in just a short year.

Though all of these experiences have been because of such tragic circumstances, I am grateful for every one of them. Life has taught me a multitude of lessons over the last year, but if there is one thing I have really learned from it all, it is that life can be unpredictable, erratic, and inconsistent—but in the end, it's absolutely extraordinary.

SHE LOOKED UP FROM THE PAGE. I REACHED OUT AND PUT MY HAND ON HER ARM.

It's easy to forget how young Kelsi was when her sister was murdered. Essentially overnight, at the age of eighteen, she was thrust into the glaring spotlight, becoming an advocate for her sister and Abby while trying to process everything she was feeling: guilt, sadness, anger, and loss. Her ability to focus on hope instead of despair showed a level of emotional maturity far beyond her years. When I told her this, she was quick to point out it was still something she had to work on every single day.

Meanwhile, Mike had headed back into the kitchen and started cooking. I certainly didn't want Mike and Becky going out of their way for us and reassured them that we didn't need anything.

"No, we insist." Mike shook his head, stirring the sauce on the stove. "It's my secret sauce; you'll love it." The four of us began to gather around the table, our eyes on Mike as he spoke. "You know, this house has never felt the same."

Kelsi nodded, adding, "I always knew when she walked in the door; I could hear her laugh all the way upstairs."

"Oh, her laughter—we miss that," Becky chimed in as Mike began to fill our plates.

It seemed like I'd barely started eating when I looked down and realized I'd eaten everything on mine—it was *that* good.

Mike, Becky, and Kelsi all started to laugh.

"Didn't I tell you!" Mike grinned and offered me a second helping.

The family continued to share stories of Libby, like how she'd loved to place sticky notes in the most unlikely places.

"I pulled down the visor in my car the other day and found one," Becky said. "She is still sending us messages." Just then, Becky opened a drawer and read from another note: "Thanks for all that you do, Grandma."

I glanced over and noticed photojournalist Leonel Mendez shifting in his seat, his camera equipment tucked under the table. "I'm so sorry," he murmured.

Becky looked at Leonel with tears in her eyes and nodded, knowing this probably wasn't going to be the last time she heard that during our visit.

"I'll be right back," Kelsi said, getting up from the table. I watched her walk out of the kitchen and listened as she ran upstairs, soon returning to the table with her phone in her hand. "I have a video of Libby if you want to see it."

We all nodded eagerly.

Kelsi held up her phone and tapped the icon to replay the recording. In it, Libby is standing in the very same kitchen, wearing a light blue Superman T-shirt, about four feet away from where I'm sitting. She's near the sink, holding a small watermelon, with Kelsi behind her. There is a crack in the melon. Libby grabs both sides and pulls, and it unexpectedly breaks in two. Libby falls back a bit into Kelsi, and laughter erupts.

For a brief moment, everyone at the table laughed too, remembering how it used to be.

"She was standing right there," Becky said, looking toward the back wall, thinking about the last time she'd seen her granddaughter. "I talked to her about a sweater. I knew it was going to get cold as the day went on."

She'd known that it was going to get cold, Becky whispered as she looked at the spot where Libby had been standing. "[But] she didn't want one. I told her to take it just in case. She said, 'It's OK. I love you, Grandma,' and I said it back, and that was the last time I saw her."

I tried to bite the side of my lip again. In our line of work, it's so important to keep your composure, at least in my mind it is.

I always tell myself that I'm there to gather the facts, not mourn with the family. But sometimes you can't control it and your emotions just seep out. Tears started falling so I immediately started walking toward what looked to be a bathroom, telling the group I'd be right back. I was relieved that I made it before anyone could see that I was crying. I did everything I could not to make a sound. Then, I wiped my eyes, took a deep breath, and headed back to face the family.

Before long, I was sitting next to Kelsi in the passenger seat of her car. She'd agreed to drive me out to the bridge, to the trailhead where she'd dropped the girls off that day. It wasn't far, just a few minutes down the road. She smiled, thinking back on how happy and carefree Abby and Libby seemed that day.

"The windows were down," Kelsi told me. "Not all the way but cracked. Libby was excited to have the day off, and when she heard her favorite song, she yelled to 'turn it up!'"

Kelsi also talked about what the last two years had been like for her, how everything had changed. She described how the end of high school had brought on new challenges and how her relationships with friends became strained. She was not the same person she had been before February 13, 2017, and she never would be. How could she be? She'd lost a big piece of herself that day. "Libby would always ask me to take her to places, [and] it seemed like I was always saying no. This time I decided I had said no enough and that I could handle taking her this time. Sometimes I wish I would've been a mean sister and just said no."

"You know, it's not your fault," I reminded her as I looked over at her, hands gripping the wheel.

"I'm getting there. I'm learning that, I guess," she answered quietly.

I reached out and touched her arm, wishing with my whole heart that she wouldn't have to endure this pain forever.

Within minutes, Kelsi stopped the car, and the SUV behind us (carrying the two photographers and producer from our team) stopped too. We'd arrived at the entry point of the trail, right where Kelsi had dropped off Abby and Libby, experiencing with her a sequence of events she was reliving and would have done anything to change.

When we got out of the car and walked down the trail to the Monon High Bridge, I passed a sign with the words "Mary I. Gerard Nature Reserve" carved into wooden planks, with an arrow pointing to the right and the number of steps it will take to get there: 501. I stopped and walked closer, noticing what looked like a laminated note about the size of an index card with holes on each side and a black rope securing it on the left corner. The girls' names were written at the top, followed by a message that read, "ABBY and LIBBY We are still searching for the truth. We refuse to give up until Justice is served. In Hope and Love, The Justice Seekers (SP, DS, LSH, NEF, SN, SA, JR)." Below the note, at the base of the sign, there were three cement crosses leaning against each other, accompanied by bunches of wilted faux flowers and a statue of an angel. There was also a small toy: a minion placed on a rock. I wondered if a child had been here before me and placed it there for Abby and Libby.

I continued walking, feeling like we were getting close. That's when it appeared: The Monon High Bridge. The bridge that I had seen countless times in our news programs. I thought I had an idea of what it would look like before I got there. But I never could have imagined this. I was shocked at just how menacing it appeared. Located high above a winding creek bed, it was clearly aged, ravaged by the brutality of seasons long past. It had an unforgiving presence that made me question why *anyone* would have wanted to come here in the first place, let alone on a rare day off from school.

But then I found myself thinking back to my own childhood. There was a similar place that my sister and I used to love, tucked away behind our house. While our hidden spot didn't have an abandoned railroad bridge, the same sense of discovery and adventure, of the wild unknown, was still palpable. We were eighteen months apart and did everything together, even if it was at my mother's insistence. I was the shy one, my sister the leader. As I studied the expansive tracks of the bridge and considered its staggering height, the intensity of the scene before me provided a much more definitive image of what they saw where they were standing. This was something I *needed* to see. This scene had served as the backdrop to Abby and Libby's tragic moments and the bravery it took to record the man who'd first crossed paths with them on this bridge.

We were there for about forty minutes, enough time for me to record a "stand-up" that would go in the two-hour special that would air in a few days.

Leonel wanted to make sure that the viewer would be able to see the size of the bridge behind me. He would start with the camera focused on me and then pan out slowly as I spoke.

"Can you walk on the bridge?" he asked. "Just a few steps."

I have *always* been scared of heights, but I thought maybe a step or two wouldn't bother me. I was wrong; I couldn't do it. Not even a foot. It was terrifying. I knew what I wanted to say, but I could hardly get the words out. My lips felt numb. It was nineteen degrees.

I counted down: three, two, one. "The plan was to come here, have some fun, take some pictures, and be together on their day off." Ugh. I couldn't move my lips.

I started over: three, two, one. "The plan was to come here, have some fun, take some pictures, be together on their day off." Shit, sorry.

Three, two, one. "The plan was to come here, have some fun, take some pictures, and be together on their day off. Now, two years later, [there are] still so many questions, no true suspects, thirty-five-thousand-plus tips. The big question remains, what happened to Abby and Libby after they were dropped off and walked to this bridge."

Finally, after five takes, we had it—and not a moment too soon. We headed back to the house.

I followed Kelsi into the kitchen. I watched as Mike pulled her aside, checking in to see whether she was OK. More than ever, I could imagine just how difficult it must be to revisit that place, a place that had taken so much away from this family.

I was at the sink washing my hands when I spotted a bright red cardinal perched on a tree outside the window.

"Oh, look! A cardinal!" I said, pointing at the glass. Becky smiled as I continued, "My mom says it means someone you love is visiting you."

She pulled up an image on her phone that she had taken in December 2018: two cardinals, as crimson as could be, settling into the branches facing her kitchen window. Becky remembered how long both cardinals sat in the one tree right outside the window. "Susan, they sat there for the longest time."

Becky believed that Libby had come to visit her through those birds because that was the sort of kind soul Libby was, full of compassion and exuberance. I believed it too. It is these small moments, like rays of sunshine that peeked out from behind the clouds, that kept Becky's hope for peace, resolution, and justice alive. Libby was still there, watching over all of them.

"Susan," she told me, "I post a different picture with the words 'Today is the day' every single day, knowing one day that it will be true."

The crew and I said goodbye and thanked the family for being so welcoming. Then we got in the rental car and started to drive. I felt different but couldn't explain it. So, I sat in silence—we all did—too tired and drained to say anything.

I STEPPED OUT OF THE RENTAL CAR AND WALKED TOWARD THE HOTEL IN LAFAYETTE, WHICH WAS ONLY about twenty-five minutes from Delphi but felt like a universe away. The automatic doors opened in front of me, and a new tiled fireplace sat in the center of the lobby. I'd seen it that morning, but it looked different now. Everything did. Something had changed. The car ride with Kelsi. The bridge. I'd been there. *Who did this to those girls?* My mind went back to Libby's house. I felt like I needed to tell someone, anyone, everyone: he was still out there.

I glanced to my left and spotted the letter *R*, white and familiar, blazing across a scarlet sweatshirt worn by what looked to be a college student. Even though I'd lived in Atlanta for more than fifteen years, I still called my childhood house my home. Being from New Jersey, I knew immediately where that *R* was from.

"Hi!" I walked over to him, my heart lifting ever so slightly. "Are you from Rutgers?"

"Ah, yeah . . . I'm with the wrestling team. We're playing Purdue," he explained.

"I'm from New Brunswick. That's my hometown!"

This emblem, this *R* on his sweatshirt, was as familiar as a framed family photo. For me, it brought up countless happy memories from my childhood. Every Saturday, from as far back as I could remember, a group of friends and family would gather at our house on Jefferson Avenue to head over to cheer on the Rutgers football team. The university was just a few miles away. My dad had gone to college and law school there. His mother, my nana, had been a campus nurse. My dad's brothers, my uncle Mickey and uncle Peter, along with his friends Roger, Joe, Bart, and Wally, would arrive at our house a few hours before kickoff. My mom would dress my sister and me in red and white. I could still remember running to my dad's station wagon, jumping in, and clambering toward the back of the car.

In my memories, the stadium is thumping, pulsing, filled to the brim with fans like us. Optimism and hope reverberate through the air as the team song echoes from the stands. I look up and see my dad and uncle cupping their mouths, screaming, "Upstream, red team, upstream! Rah, rah, Rutgers, rah!" A cannon fires as the players run onto the field. A wave of red and white spreads across the stands, the roar of the crowd chanting, "Go RU!" Whether we won or lost was not important to my sister and me—we just loved being there, feeling like we were a part of the action. On the way home, we'd look out the back window, where a red *R*, peeling at the corners, greeted cars behind us, stuck in the upper left-hand corner. Meanwhile, behind the wheel, my dad proudly donned an *R* of his own, a baseball cap with a white *R* across the bill.

I focused back on the guy in the hotel lobby wearing the letter, hoping he could save me. Hoping he could bring me back to how I'd felt before.

He asked why I was in town, and I blurted out, "I'm here reporting on a murder. Two young girls were killed in the middle of the day in Delphi. Just thirteen and fourteen years old."

"I'm so sorry," he responded, not quite knowing what to say. "My coach is meeting us in the lobby if you'd like to meet him," he added.

It was then that I realized he didn't understand. I didn't want to meet the coach. I wanted my father. I wanted to go *home*.

I smiled and thanked him, waving as I passed the rest of the team. Then I grabbed my key card and walked down the hall, past the pool, to my room. Everything was in place, exactly the way I'd left it nine hours ago. My black suit jacket was draped on the chair, makeup scattered on the desk. Gloves, a scarf, and hand warmers all lay scattered across the bed. When I checked out, the room would return to its natural state—sterile, nondescript, anonymous. I couldn't stop thinking about how different this room looked from Libby's room, where I'd been less than six hours earlier.

"We left it the way Libby did," Becky explained. She pointed out the purple paint covering three of the four walls. "It's what Libby wanted. She found the perfect shade, and she insisted on doing it herself." Becky turned to me, looked down, and whispered, "She never got the chance to finish it."

———

THE NEXT TWO MONTHS PASSED WITH FEW UPDATES, UNTIL EASTER SUNDAY, WHEN I RECEIVED A message from Sergeant Kim Riley, one of the investigators from the early press conferences, whom I had first met back in Delphi. He informed me that law enforcement was calling an immediate press conference and wanted to assemble the media. "Something big" was going to be announced, and they wanted us to be there for it. I knew that if they were telling the media to gather in Delphi then I needed to go.

When Sergeant Riley sent the text, I was downstairs in my house in Atlanta, sitting next to my two-year-old son, Jack. Flush with holiday excitement, he gripped with chubby fingers a stuffed bunny while biting the ears off a chocolate one. I hugged him tight before heading up to my room to pack.

A few hours later, my plane landed, and I found myself in Delphi for the second time in two months.

4

The Bridge

Jack knew I was leaving, but it was early enough for me to sneak out of the house before he was awake. As a toddler, he had a memory comparable to that of the iconic and ever-optimistic Dory, an animated fish suffering from short-term memory loss in *Finding Nemo*. He wasn't overly fond of good-byes, and I wasn't either, but I hoped I'd be back before he had much time to miss me.

Remembering how cold it had been the last time I'd visited Delphi, I stopped to check the weather app on my phone. High in the forties, low in the thirties. I ran back upstairs and grabbed a scarf and gloves—just in case. After living in Atlanta so long, that sounded pretty chilly to me for April.

I passed my nine-year-old daughter, Emery, on the way out the door. She understood my job—well, kind of. She knew that I was going to "report on a story"—that's what I'd told her. We hugged and I told her I'd be back before she knew it. Emery just nodded and smiled; she took pride in helping to take care of her younger brother while I was gone.

After a quick flight, I hopped in another rental car and drove back to the now familiar hotel in Lafayette, a quick twenty-five-minute drive from Delphi. Yet through it all, I couldn't stop thinking about the bridge. In fact, I hadn't stopped thinking about it for months, and anyone I'd crossed paths with since then hadn't stopped hearing about it either. The structure itself had a long, complicated history.

I was shocked at how massive and decrepit it looked in person. It was built in 1891, and the more research I did, the more surprised I was that it was still standing. It is sixty-three feet high, although it looks a lot taller than that in person. I learned that for almost a century, the bridge ushered trains and travelers across the local Deer Creek, until it was abandoned by CSX Transportation, a national freight railroad company, in 1987. Decades before Abby and Libby were murdered, the bridge had gained notoriety as a majestic landmark for local photo shoots, but the actual structure itself had long been in need of repairs.[1]

Apparently, back in 2016, shortly before the girls were killed, a state-run nonprofit organization called Indiana Landmarks had included the bridge on their list of "10 Most Endangered" historic sites, "places on the brink of extinction and too important to lose."[2] The group had been attempting to take ownership of the bridge as far back as 2012, but liabilities regarding the bridge's deterioration had slowed things down considerably, until April 2017.[3]

That's when Indiana Landmarks announced that they were expecting CSX to hand over the land title by June of the same year, after which they could hand it over to Deer Creek Township. Deer Creek was planning to extend a trail to the bridge, and another nonprofit, Heartland Heritage, had agreed to lease it and maintain it as a trail bridge. But before any of that could happen, the groups still needed to assess both the environmental and structural damage, and the initial projected repairs surpassed $120,000.

So, what was the holdup, you ask? My theory is that the project was cumbersome and expensive, so no one wanted to claim responsibility for fixing it. It was only when the bridge became part of a national news story that those who were ignoring the problem finally had to pay attention and do something about it.

I visited the bridge twice in 2019, first in February and then in April, and, to put it mildly, the bridge was in dire shape, though progress would be made shortly thereafter on the financial front. In May, Indiana governor Eric Holcomb announced that "more than $1.2 million from a $90 million trail initiative . . . will go toward rehabbing the Monon High Bridge Trail, including the abandoned rail trestle over Deer Creek near Delphi," according to a local paper.[4] I was glad to hear that restoration efforts were in motion, but I wondered about the timing and whether anyone would be able to entirely separate the bridge or even the trail from the memory of the horrific tragedy that had transpired there.

Back at the hotel, I rolled my suitcase inside my room, pulled off my boots, and plopped on the bed, closed my eyes, and exhaled. Within seconds, I was thinking of the girls' final moments again.

Think of something else, I urged myself. *A beach, clouds—anything.* I was actively trying to clear my mind through some form of meditation, but no matter how hard I tried, it just wasn't working. The same questions—the ones I couldn't escape from—were again running through my mind. The quiet times like this were the worst.

Who was capable of doing this? Was it a crime of opportunity? Did someone follow Abby and Libby on the trail to the bridge? Or had he already been there, lying in wait?

And what was happening tomorrow? Did they have a suspect in custody? Sergeant Kim Riley did say it was going to be "a big day." But just what did that *mean*? They must have *something*.

I opened my eyes and looked over at the clock next to the bed. My call time was five in the morning. The presser wasn't supposed to start until ten o'clock, but I'd be reporting live on *Morning Express with Robin Meade* bright and early, talking with her about all the possibilities we *might* learn, the news we could feasibly expect to hear. If call time was at five, my wake-up time would be two in the morning. I knew I should set my alarm now and get ready for bed, but my mind was racing. I was too tired to sleep, so I laid down to rest my eyes for a bit.

Before I knew it, I had drifted off, my mind taking me back to the bridge.

Suddenly I'm there, walking alone on the trails, ahead of everyone, when the brush clears. I can feel my heart speed up as we approach it.

From the images and photographs, the Monon High Bridge seems sturdy and secure—and if you haven't been there, I'm sure it may even seem quaint or charming. But in person, the bridge is anything but. It's terrifying. And now, while I'm "resting" in a hotel room in Lafayette, my subconscious takes me back there. I approach the bridge slowly, trepidation growing with every step, before looking up to gaze on it in fascination and fear.

The massive wooden structure dominates the surrounding area, with the highest trees of the neighboring forest just scraping the lower buttresses as it stretches out across Deer Creek.

Thirteen hundred feet long, the bridge extends several hundred feet past the creek and onto private property. From where I'm standing in the dream, you can't see the other end; the rotting railway just slowly fades away, seeming to disappear into the trees.

As I walk further onto the bridge, I feel like I have gone beyond the physical world, that I've somehow left Delphi, but then I notice Kelsi next to me. She looks to the left and spots a geocaching box, tucked away behind a plank of tethered wood.

"Look—Libby must have left this for me!" she cries.

I remember I have my cell phone on me.

The dream starts feeling like déjà vu, as I recall having this exact conversation with Kelsi a few weeks before. And now I'm reliving it—every step, every word—within my subconscious.

"Can I take a picture?" I ask.

She readily agrees, carefully opening the box.

"Every day after school," she explains, "Libby and I would go to McDonald's, get a large sweet tea and french fries, and then go geocaching."

I still have that image of Kelsi in my phone, smiling as she holds the treasure: a box with a miniature doll inside. Before meeting Kelsi, I had never heard of geocaching. Kelsi described it as a type of digital treasure hunt where you can track, leave clues, and surprise someone with a hidden object. It felt like a message, a gift, sent at just the right time from Libby.

I picture my younger self walking on that bridge, free of fear, smiling and laughing with my sister nearby, on a rare day off from school, a day full of possibilities unfurling before us.

As Kelsi and I talk, I catch sight of the two photojournalists who'd accompanied us that day, their focus unwavering as they capture footage of this massive structure from different angles.

Leonel grabs one of his bags and says decisively, "We should get the drone shots first."

"Is that difficult to fly?" I ask, perplexed.

"No," he says and smiles. "Not if you know how to use it. That's key."

I hear the drone take off, swooping down and around, above and below the bridge. It ventures closer and closer to the flimsy wooden platforms, each connected to the railroad ties. Even with the buzz of the drone, I am keenly aware of just how quiet it is all around us. How secluded. It feels eerie.

But then again, could the seclusion and distant feeling be the very things that attracted the girls to this spot in the first place?

All around me, I see the memorials left for Abby and Libby by those who knew them and strangers who had come to the bridge to pay their respects. little pieces of humanity in a place that now feels devoid of warmth and joy.

Now I'm facing the bridge, my knees shaking as I attempt to step onto one of the wooden boards. I feel dizzy. Did it happen here, in the spot where I'm standing? We still don't know much about the actual murders by this point; the investigators haven't shared any of the details. But I do know *he* was here, on this bridge. I know what he sounded like, what he was wearing, where he was standing.

I can see him now, head down, hands in his pockets, about a hundred yards in front of me, coming from the other side of the bridge toward the girls. But his face is blurry, with no distinguishable features. I look out and see Abby, just like she was in that final Snapchat picture Libby took. I wave to her and call her name. She doesn't answer. I hear his voice repeating "down the hill" over and over, taunting me—interrupted only by the loud ring of my hotel room landline.

Jolted awake, I jumped up and pulled the receiver to my ear. "Hello?"

"Susan, you weren't answering your cell phone." It was Barbara, my producer. "Do you want to meet me in the lobby to grab something to eat and talk about tomorrow?"

"Sure," I said. "I just had the *weirdest* dream. It all felt so real." I sighed, trying to shake it from my mind. "I'll see you in a few." I hung up the phone and quickly threw on a jacket before heading down to the lobby.

Barbara and I walked across the hotel parking lot to Longhorn Steakhouse and sat down in a booth. The sense of déjà vu was unnerving; we had been there just two months before, same restaurant, same booth. Everything felt like it was moving in endless circles.

"I'm going to call Joseph Scott Morgan and see what he thinks," I said, looking down at my phone. I wanted to talk to someone who might know something—an expert. JSM, as he is sometimes called, had decades of experience as a certified death investigator and is a distinguished professor of forensics at Jacksonville State University. He had also been on many of our shows discussing several cases, including Delphi.

Talking to him was comforting in many ways, but we were both limited by the scant details released by the police so far. The reality was that no one really knew much outside of law enforcement, and even then we weren't sure how far along the investigation was. Our chat devolved into a series of what-ifs by the end, but he acknowledged that if the police wanted me out there in person, it must be something big.

"I think this is going to be a significant development in the investigation," he said.

I really hoped so, for the families.

"Thanks, JSM. I'll call you after the press conference." I hung up and felt hopeful. Maybe tomorrow really would be the day.

5

A Killer in the Room

On the morning of April 19, 2019, our crew parked a live truck outside the Wabash and Erie Canal Center. The camera was propped up on a tripod, to allow producers in the control room back in Atlanta to see the location of the presser in the background. Barbara and I walked toward the building, curious; the doors were locked, but we could still see inside. There were two poster-board-sized images of Abby and Libby leaning on easels at the front of the room, next to a podium in front of a gray curtain. On the left side of the podium, we spotted two empty easels, as well as chairs stacked in the middle of the room. The lights were still off. I put my IFB earpiece back in my ear and headed back to the live truck. I turned on the mic that was clipped to the back of my pants.

"Susan, you are up in two minutes. Can you hear me?"

I walked in front of the camera and nodded.

After setting up the context for the press conference that would soon unfold, Robin Meade asked what I thought we might hear that day. I wasn't sure, but I knew anticipation was running high. I mostly talked about the families and reminded everyone to tune back in at 12:00 p.m. EST for the start of the press conference.

Even though Delphi itself is pretty small, it was clear that the police expected a large crowd, and the presser was even open to the public, which isn't standard in cases like this. Media outlets, law enforcement, and anyone else in the town of Delphi who wanted to attend were encouraged to be there.

To comply with the regulations, my team and I signed in with the rest of the attendees when we walked in. To the left of the sign-in table in front of us was the entry into the room, where volunteers started to unstack and line up chairs for the press conference. To the right, I noticed a door that led to a dark and narrow U-shaped room, one whose walls were filled with maps and historic pictures.

Three women were sitting behind a long foldout table with a clipboard and pamphlets for the tour center, while two members of the Delphi Police Department stood watchfully behind the table. An older gentleman standing off to the left motioned to me.

"These are the people that answer the tip line when we get calls," he said proudly.

"Oh, that's great," I replied as I scribbled down my name. Barbara and I had met him about forty minutes earlier, when they'd first unlocked the doors. He was one of the volunteers at the canal center who was nice enough to give us a minitour, explaining the history of Delphi and everything this small town had to offer.

The highlight for many, he said, was seeing the dozens of photographs of the old railroads that had once lined the streets. It was an interesting tour, and I was moved by his clear passion for

Delphi's history, but I was still finding it hard to pay attention to our kindly self-appointed tour guide.

I was thinking only about Abby, Libby, and their families, and what we were going to hear from investigators.

Without any new information to go off, Barbara and I had started to speculate the night before. Could it be related to the Flora fires?

On November 21, 2016, a little less than four months before Abby and Libby were murdered, a deadly fire had claimed the lives of four innocent young girls: eleven-year-old Keyana Davis, nine-year-old Keyara Phillips, seven-year-old Kerriele McDonald, and five-year-old Kionnie Welch.[1] Someone had intentionally set fire to their home, a house that sat on the corner of Columbia and Division Streets in nearby Flora, a town just under ten miles away from Delphi but nestled in the same county, Carroll. Police revealed they'd discovered accelerants at the scene of the crime, but years later the crime remained unsolved; the girls' devastated mother had left the state; and what remained on the site of their former home was little more than shattered windows, scorched walls, and rubble, with "boarded-up doors and boxes of toys on the front porch."[2]

When we looked at the cases side by side, there didn't seem to be a *ton* of similarities, other than the fact that both tragedies had claimed the lives of young girls. But still, we weren't ready to rule out any connections just yet.

Back in the conference room, I spotted Detective Jerry Holeman, one of the many familiar faces of law enforcement I had gotten to know.

"Detective Holeman, hi! How are you?"

"Hi, Susan."

I began to babble nervously—maybe too much about the weather, my flight the day before, what time we'd set up this morning—eagerly avoiding what was happening just a few feet away. Out of the corner of my eye, I already noticed officers gathering at the front of the room, and another officer guarding two large boards now leaning against the empty easels. Each was covered with a sheet of cardboard—one red, one black—blocking what was underneath.

It was hard to gauge how law enforcement felt, but I knew I was just *buzzing* with nervous energy. I'd been up since two in the morning and hadn't gotten much sleep. Breakfast had been lukewarm black coffee in my hotel room, which I knew wouldn't help much. But I quickly chugged two cups anyway. With the dregs of caffeine surely dripping through my veins, I felt jittery and just wanted to keep moving, so I headed back outside to grab my bag and my notes from our live truck.

When I walked back in, a woman behind the table asked, "Did you sign in?"

"I did, about fifteen minutes ago," I reminded her with a smile.

There were a *lot* of members of the media filing in, one after the other, and I bet it was getting harder and harder to keep track of who had signed in already and who hadn't. There were some local reporters—like the one I'd met near the restroom, who was coming in from a local Indiana news station—but the case had attracted national and international attention too, and the size of the audience reflected that.

Wandering back outside, I took off the earpiece I had been wearing for the early-morning live shots, noting that the once empty area near our live truck was now full of cars. I hurried back into the building to our designated area inside. Again, I passed the woman next to the sign-in sheet.

"Did you—" she began to ask.

"Yes, I did. Thank you." I wasn't irritated; I knew she had a job to do. It was clear she had been instructed to get *everyone* in that room to sign the sheet.

I spotted Mike and Becky near the entrance and rushed over to say hello. Becky and I gave each other a quick hug.

"I'm so nervous," she admitted.

"I am too," I told her.

We held hands, waiting impatiently for the presser to begin. Becky was wearing a scarf around her head—a subtle sign of another battle she'd been fighting. Five months earlier, she had been diagnosed with an aggressive form of cancer. But at this point, there was *nothing* she felt she couldn't get through. She was also mindful of attracting any attention, since she wanted to keep everyone's focus on the girls.

"I figure if I don't beat this, I will either see Libby sooner than expected, or else I'll continue fighting to track down the killer."

Becky and Mike joined Anna, Abby's mother, as the families were led into a back room.

"I'll see you after," I reassured them as I made my way back toward the empty podium.

Our group's setup was in the very front. Two CNN photojournalists had been assigned to Delphi and driven in the night before; they weren't familiar with the story, so I filled them in as best I could. CNN has some of the best photographers in the business. Their job involves going into sometimes life-threatening situations while remaining calm and focused, always ready to get the shot. It's storytelling *as it's happening* through the lens of the camera. Oh, and they do this year-round. They spend most of their lives on the road. If news breaks, they are the first to arrive. I have the utmost respect for all photojournalists. And there were plenty of them behind me, lined up from one side of the room to the other.

I sat down on the carpet to avoid blocking anyone's shot and took a moment to breathe. Inhale. Exhale. I hadn't sat down in a while, and it felt good. I looked up and saw a large black-and-white picture of the bridge looming before me. It was shiny, glossy, like a piece of art—nothing like how it looked in my memories, or in my nightmares.

Is the bridge guy in custody? I wondered. *Is that why we're here?*

About a minute before the press conference was to begin, I spotted Indiana State Police superintendent Doug Carter and Carroll County sheriff Tobe Leazenby waiting behind that gray curtain. In the front row to my right, Detective Holeman was sitting next to a few police officers, leaning forward and rubbing his eyes. Was he crying? My stomach dropped as the superintendent and the sheriff approached the podium.

"Wasn't sure quite what to expect when I walked out, but I gotta say to the Delphi community . . ." the superintendent started as the room buzzed around him. His gray hair contrasted sharply with his dark uniform; his glasses were perched gently on his nose.

At last, the room grew silent, voices winding down as the cameras started clicking.

He repeated, a little louder, "I gotta say to the Delphi community how grateful I am . . . You inspire people, you don't even understand, you don't even understand why." The superintendent grimaced and looked down at his notes in front of him, gripping the podium tightly, shaking his head ever so slightly.

It felt like we were all holding our breath, the shutter sounds behind me fluttering louder and louder by the moment. I started to record the audio on my cell phone, which was sitting in front of me, face down on the carpet. The superintendent reached up to smooth his hair quickly in what looked like a nervous gesture, and then he took another deep breath.

"Information being released today is the result of literally thousands and thousands of hours of extraordinary investigative efforts by Delphi, Carroll County, the FBI, the Indiana State Police, and countless other agencies. This community surrounded us some twenty-six months ago, and you did everything you could to support us, but most importantly, you surrounded the family of these two little girls. Gosh, I'll never forget it."

Barbara leaned in and whispered to me, "It's over."

A few moments later, our hopes were crushed. The superintendent brushed his hand across his mouth and continued.

"After you hear what we are going to release today, I am going to ask you for your continued support, your continued understanding, your empathy, and compassion, as we move forward to find out who did this. And we will."

So they didn't know. Wait, they still didn't know? Then why were we *here*? Empathy and compassion? For whom? For the families, or for law enforcement? Maybe it was both.

"We're seeking the public's help to identify the driver of a vehicle that was parked at the old CPS/DCS welfare building in the city of Delphi that was abandoned on the east side of County Road 300 North, next to the Hoosier Heartland Highway, between the hours of noon to five on February [13], 2017. If you were parked there or know who was parked there, please contact the officers at the command post"—he sighed—"at the Delphi city building."

I grabbed my pen and paper and wrote down "car" and "DCS building." What kind of vehicle was it? What color?

"We are releasing additional portions of the audio recording from that day. Please keep in mind the person talking is one person"—he lifted up one finger to stress the point—"and is the person on the bridge with the girls. This is *not* two different people speaking. Please listen to it very, very carefully."

He took another deep breath. "We are also releasing video recovered from Libby's phone; this video has never before been previously released. The video shows a suspect walking on the bridge. When you see the video, watch the person's mannerisms as they walk. Watch the mannerisms as he walks. Do you recognize the mannerisms as being someone that you might know? Remember—he is walking on the former railroad bridge, [and] because of the deteriorative condition of the bridge, the suspect is not walking naturally, due to the spacing between the ties."

All of a sudden, it registered. A video. There was a video! Of the last person those girls saw. Surely it couldn't be much longer.

The superintendent flipped to the next page.

"During the course of this investigation, we have concluded the first sketch released will become secondary, as of today. The result of the new information and intelligence over time leads us to believe the sketch which you will see shortly is the person responsible for the murders of these two little girls."

So, wait, the first sketch they released was *not* the guy? But the secondary one today was? Were there two people?

"We also believe this person is from Delphi"—he looked up, as if to underscore that the person could be anyone, even the person sitting next to us—"currently or has previously lived here, visits Delphi on a regular basis, or works here. We believe this person is currently between the age range of eighteen and forty but might appear younger than his true age."

The superintendent looked down, pausing for several seconds and attempting to collect himself. It seemed like this investigation had really unnerved him and he was doing everything he could to keep a strong facade. Just then, his voice became chilling as he issued a warning to the girls' killer.

"Directly to the killer, *who may be in this room*, we believe you are hiding in plain sight. For more than two years, you never thought we would shift gears to a different investigative strategy, but we have. We likely have interviewed you or someone close to you. We know that this is about power to you, and you want to know what we know, and one day you will."

Everyone around me was furiously scribbling down notes, and I was trying to catch as much of it as I possibly could.

"A question to you: What will those closest to you think of when they find out that you brutally murdered two little girls? Two *children*? Only a coward would do such a thing."

Did the murderer even *care* about those closest to him? I stopped recording; I knew I'd need my phone imminently. As soon as this press conference wrapped up, I'd definitely be getting a call from our producers back in Atlanta.

"We are confident that you have told someone what you have done. Or, at the very least, they know because of how different you are since the murders." The superintendent flipped his page yet again, furrowing his brow as he read aloud from the next set of notes. He scratched his head again and took another deep breath. I could only imagine the range of thoughts and feelings circling within him.

"We try so hard to understand how a person could do something like this to two children. I recently watched a movie called *The Shack*, and there's also a book that talks so well about evil, about death, and about eternity.

"To the murderer, I believe you have just a little bit of a conscience left." He squeezed two fingers together and held them up for all to see. "And I can assure you that how you left them in those woods is not, *is not*, what they're experiencing today."

He took another pause and a deep breath before addressing the family directly; it seemed he was doing his best not to cry. "To the family, I hope that you all will give them some time, because we're going to be asking that there's no media inquiry, or no media response for at least the next two weeks, and I hope you'll understand why. The family found out about this information this morning . . . I just want the family to know that when I take my last breath on this earth, I'll be thinking of them."

He readdressed the audience in full, gesturing right to us. "There is going to be a tremendous amount of questions—I know that. I *know* that. Never in my career have I stood in front of something like this. Please be patient with us, please . . . We're just beginning. We are just *now* beginning, and I can tell you on behalf of the sheriff and the police chief, [and] so many other partners, um . . . that have stood with us over this period of time . . . that *we will not stop*."

After enunciating the last few words, Superintendent Carter, along with Sheriff Leazenby, departed the podium. Nearby, Captain Dave Bursten stepped up and immediately removed the cardboard from the easel, showing us a new, never-before-seen sketch of the suspect.

"I just unveiled the person that we believe responsible for the murder of these two little girls, so I invite the media to take a look at that now," Bursten explained, pointing straight at the portrait.

The picture resting on the easel was shocking—not so much the sketch itself but rather how greatly it differed from the sketch that preceded it. I could hear a collective involuntary gasp in the room as the new portrait was unveiled. Instead of a middle-aged man, the subject in this sketch looked like a teenager, as young as seventeen or maybe eighteen years old. He had small deep-set eyes, a small nose, and a mouth in a thin line, with short dark hair cropped close to the scalp, framing his face.

Shortly after this portrait of the suspect was revealed, we learned that the sketch itself wasn't quite as new as it seemed. In fact, this younger-looking person had been drawn on February 17, 2017, just three days after the girls' bodies were found, by an Indiana State Police sketch artist, Master Trooper Taylor Bryant. Bryant said that the sketch was "based on the description of a man by a witness who reported seeing something they felt needed to be reported" and that it was "a ballpark estimation of what the person looks like."[3] When investigators were asked why this sketch hadn't been revealed earlier, they simply informed the media that "the agency is not commenting on investigative techniques."[4]

"We're also going to show you a video not previously released that the superintendent spoke to," the captain continued, "and also the audio that's additional to what's been previously released. It's only a slight change in it. So give Sergeant Riley just a second as he gets that up and ready."

The speakers muffled with static as Sergeant Riley adjusted the volume. And then, very clearly, we heard it.

"Guys . . . [static] . . . down the hill."

Sergeant Riley played the seconds-long clip several times over until the words, the sounds, were firmly imprinted in our minds forever.

It was him—the killer. His voice. The addition of "guys" was so small, and yet it made the whole clip seem different. It seemed like a more casual word, like something a younger person might say. Did they know him? But then, "down the hill" sounded like it came from someone older, like the initial sketch, which had just been labeled the "secondary" sketch. I briefly wondered, *Were two people involved?* But Superintendent Carter had made it clear we were listening to only one voice, not two.

"Stand by for the video, please," Bursten continued, pulling the new video up on the projector screen. "There is no sound in the video."

Blurry at first, the video clearly captures the man known only as "bridge guy" walking forward, taking two steps, almost three. His head is down, his facial features indistinct, his shoulders slightly hunched. He appears to be wearing a medium brown or perhaps dark olive-colored hat, with a dark blue jacket and light-to-medium-wash blue jeans. The video plays in a loop, but it's hard to catch all the details; the picture looks grainy. Is that a flannel shirt, or maybe a hoodie, sticking out of the jacket? And there's something brown—a bag of some sort, possibly—peeking out from beneath the jacket, close to his right hip. He still seems to match the FBI's original description of height and weight: somewhere between five feet six and five feet ten and between 180 and 200 pounds.[5] Other than that, it's hard to tell how old he really is. He certainly *seems* older than a teenager, but police warned us he could be younger than he appeared at first.

"As Superintendent Carter mentioned, he's on the railway bridge. You have to take different steps to get to it," Bursten said. "This information later this afternoon will be on the state police website. For the community that's here, we have one hundred copies of the news release. If you put in that URL, you'll be able to get to that site to play it. And we also have that same release for you in the media, and the rest of the state will get that release in about fifteen minutes, so we appreciate those of you who came here. This concludes our announcement. Thank you for your time, patience, and courtesy."

With that, Bursten stepped off the podium, and Superintendent Carter walked back out to face the crowd.

"I have a correction," Carter began. "Mike Patty wanted me to let you know that his family wants to talk to the media; *we* are the ones that are asking the media to give the family time. He wanted me to make that clear."

I wasn't surprised that Mike wanted to talk. He knew the importance of getting the word out. Later on, he told me this was even more crucial to his family after this particular conference because of the new sketch.

"Susan," he told me, "it feels like we're starting over."

BEFORE I HAD TOO LONG TO RUMINATE ON THE PRESSER THAT HAD JUST TRANSPIRED, A TEXT CAME IN from executive producer Jennifer Williams.

"Susan, we would like you to do the show live from there. It starts at 2 p.m. It will be two hours."

"OK, sounds good," I replied.

I sent a quick text off to Joseph Scott Morgan, asking whether he'd be on the show. Afterward, I immediately scanned the news release I held in my hands. Close to the bottom, in the second-to-last paragraph, was a passage that gave me pause: "We have a witness. You made mistakes. We are coming for you and there's no place for a heartless coward like you to hide that gets his thrill from killing little girls."

What? That was new. The superintendent hadn't mentioned anything about a witness. My mind raced. I figured they must be planning to arrest someone soon. Was that why the room cleared out so fast? I also spotted the words above the sketch in red letters that read "NEW MURDER SUSPECT."

I had little time to think before my phone buzzed again—this time a call.

"Hey, Susan. Here is a list of your guests. Ready?"

"OK, go ahead."

"It will be attorney Casey Jordan, who is a criminologist and behavior analyst. Also, Joseph Scott Morgan, a certified death investigator and professor of forensics at Jacksonville State University."

I was relieved to hear JSM was in. "OK, who else?"

"One more guest and Bobby Chacon, former FBI special agent."

"Sounds good. Will I be able to hear you during the show?"

"Yes."

"OK. I'll talk to you soon."

I tucked my phone away and walked toward the front, surprised to see that in the short time since the conference had wrapped, the entire room—the table, the chairs, the pamphlets, the sign-in sheet, the *people*—had cleared out. Everything was gone.

Was that why signing in had been so important—because they thought he might have shown up to this conference, been "in this room"? I've heard many times that it's not uncommon for a criminal to try to reinsert themselves into an investigation, or for them to otherwise pay more attention to it than they would another case. But still, there had been a *lot* of people in this room; crimes like this didn't happen around here, and I wasn't wholly convinced that the volunteers had been able to get *everyone* to sign in. It seemed just as likely that the man could've avoided the whole thing without calling too much attention to himself.

During the live show, I continued to jot down notes on the press release, writing that looked more like scribbling. Notes only

I could read—*barely*. I glanced down at the sheet sporadically during commercial breaks.

I wrote down one line in particular that I'd come back to again and again, words uttered by Superintendent Carter earlier that afternoon, words I recorded in some mixture of anger and hope.

"You want to know what we know, *and one day you will.*"

The back of the release featured the new sketch, with the caption "This is the face of the suspect that goes with the body of the video captured on Liberty German's cell phone."

Was the public so used to seeing the first sketch that this one didn't seem to match the body? The age range printed on the flier was eighteen to forty, which, admittedly, seemed fairly large. What did it mean when investigators said the suspect may appear younger than his actual age? The age range was big enough that it covered most of the men in Delphi.

"Susan," my earpiece buzzed, interrupting my thoughts. It was a producer talking to me from the studio in Atlanta. "You are up in twenty seconds."

"Joseph Scott Morgan, I'll start with you," I said, refocusing on the camera, eager to get back in the groove. "I called you last night to ask about the significance, what you thought, and you said, 'This is going to be huge,' and . . . wow."

"Yeah, bombshell," Morgan said. "I think that this is very significant in the fact that they've narrowed this down to Delphi. And this is quintessential to the case that we've narrowed this population down, a population, you know, we're talking about a city that's maybe twenty-five hundred people, and from a forensic standpoint, from an evidence-gathering standpoint, that's very significant."

I turned my attention to criminologist Casey Jordan and asked what she thought about Doug Carter speaking directly to this killer. I paraphrased the superintendent's words: "'You are a coward, you want to know what we know, and you will soon, and what are the people around you going to think when they find out you killed two innocent girls?' Casey, it's like he knew who he was talking to."

"Susan, it was absolutely a provocation," she said, "and usually you would argue 'Don't ever call somebody a coward on live media,' but in this case, they didn't have any particular suspect in mind. They think this could provoke that person into doing one of several things, basically: screwing up, quitting a job, leaving the area, or actually coming in and confessing. The idea that they put him in there—'We think you may have talked about what you've done to someone else'—will add a level of paranoia to whoever is out there who could be responsible for this.

"This man may think, *They know, and they might get my friends and family to turn on me.* I think what they're really trying to do, whether they have a particular suspect in mind or whether this is just a Hail Mary pass based on a very generalized FBI profile, they are trying to provoke the murderer into coming forward or doing something stupid so that they can home in on him and get the evidence they need to make an arrest."

I then brought in former FBI special agent Bobby Chacon, who was convinced that law enforcement knew the type of person they were talking to.

"I think they have a very specific profile of who this person is and what they are like," Chacon said. "I think that's why he mentioned, 'You might have a conscience left'—he mentioned, 'What are the people around going to think about when they hear what you've done?' If it's a regular true psychopath, they are not gonna care, and that's not going to appeal to somebody like that. So they have a specific profile of who this person is, and their strategy is geared toward that person.

"Basically, he said, 'We know you've been operating in our community, you've been among us, and you will find no safe haven in Delphi any longer,' because he's enlisted the community in this case now. *Everyone's* looking at this sketch—every convenience store, every supermarket, every gas station. People are going to be looking around for this person. This person is not going to be safe in Delphi any longer, and I think that was the bold move that the superintendent took today."

Before I knew it, the two-hour show had flown by. I looked around the now vacant room while I was taking off my microphone and unplugging my earpiece. The protection I'd felt while the camera was rolling, the confidence I'd felt that the killer would soon be caught, was starting to fade.

"I'm a little afraid," I said, handing the mic to the photojournalist.

"Afraid?" he asked. "Susan, don't worry. I've been in Iraq under ISIS control. You will be OK."

I smiled apprehensively. He wasn't wrong; the photojournalists I've met through the years, including the two who were next to me, *have* been in some of the most compromising, dangerous situations. Without hesitation, they go right into whatever the situation may be, capturing key moments in history. And even if a killer was still on the loose, there was a difference between reporting on an unsolved homicide and reporting in the middle of an active war zone.

"Susan . . . Susan . . ."

I'd been staring at the doorway, or at least in that direction, for a while before I finally heard someone calling my name. I was completely drained, mentally and physically.

"Susan, what's the plan for tomorrow? Are you OK?"

"Oh, sorry," I said. "I am. I'm just tired. I have ten live shots starting at 6:00 a.m. Eastern. Every show on CNN wants a live report."

"OK. Get some sleep; we will see you then."

———

I DON'T REMEMBER THE DRIVE BACK TO THE HOTEL. BUT I REMEMBER MY DREAM THAT NIGHT. I heard Libby's voice as clear as day. She told me they'd been killed in a barn.

I jolted out of bed and turned on the light.

It was her, I thought at first, only to realize that, no—it was just a nightmare.

I kept the bedside lamp on for the rest of the night. I also checked the lock on my hotel room door and made sure that the backup latch was in place and secure. Then I put a pillow over my head and tried to go back to sleep. But no matter how hard I tried, I just couldn't stop running through what I'd heard at the press conference.

Had he really been in the room? Where was he now? How could this person live with himself? Was he sleeping peacefully?

I turned on the TV to tune out my racing mind.

Was Doug Carter on to him? Did they have a witness? Did this coward really have a conscience? Would he even *care* if those closest to him found out what he had done? How had he left the girls that day in the woods?

I'm not sure when or whether I fell back to sleep. At three in the morning, I shut off my alarm, which was set to go off thirty minutes later, and quickly got ready. On the way out of the room, I grabbed the police bulletin and the new wanted poster with the revised sketch of the killer.

6

Abby and Libby

The families had a lot to process in the hours, days, and weeks following that shocking press conference. A new direction, a new sketch, a new witness? It was all very confusing.

The sketch of the initial suspect, an older-looking man, was released on July 17, 2017, five months after the girls were murdered. Becky remembers being surprised at how detailed it was. "It looked like a photograph. I thought surely there is enough there for someone to identify this guy." Certainly this latest press conference had been a lot for the families to absorb.

For 644 days, both families had diligently posted, handed out, and displayed the sketch of an older guy with scruffy facial hair and a hat.

The person they thought was the guy on the bridge.

Not the one unveiled on April 22.

For a total of one year, nine months, and five days, it had been part of Becky's routine: wake up, post "Today is the day" on social media, and share the flyer. The most up-to-date flyer they had. The family members brought copies of it everywhere—to festivals, conferences, meetings. *Any* large gathering they could think of became a new opportunity to spread the word.

In Delphi, the poster was seen in storefront windows along Main Street. You could find it inside bars and restaurants too, and taped to the side of a filing cabinet inside the Carroll County Sheriff's Office. It was in doctors' offices, dentists' offices. It had even been on the hood of a race car in Tennessee during the annual 250-lap Food City Dirt Race at the Bristol Motor Speedway in 2018. It was also plastered across the back of Mike's 2016 white Dodge Ram pickup truck, though he kept extras with him too.

Like her grandfather, Kelsi kept a stack of flyers in the trunk of her car at all times, just in case. They'd been told it was him by everyone—local law enforcement, state police, even the FBI. They *believed* it was him. Ever since the police first released the image on July 17, 2017, it had become the families' mission to let the public know more about the man on the bridge. Kelsi could close her eyes and picture the flyer exactly as it was: WANTED was spelled out in bold red letters across the top. Right below, there was a still-frame image of the "man on the bridge" from the video that Libby had taken on her phone. His hands were in his pockets, his head tilted down, his facial features pixelated. Next to that was the sketch, an image that seemed to bring the pixelated picture into focus.

It wasn't the only flyer friends and family handed out, though. There were several different versions of it, but each one included photos of the girls. In some of the flyers, Abby is pictured wearing a straw hat with a large yellow flower attached to the side of the hatband, a black ribbon with white polka dots. Her blouse is white with black polka dots. Her hair is pulled to one side, and she's smiling. The image captures a fleeting moment—Abby's carefree smile and decadent hat, trapped in time—now tied to a nationwide manhunt. Her mother, Anna, could still remember the day it was taken.

"That was at my cousin's bridal shower, and their theme was the Kentucky Derby," Anna said. "She helped me make that hat; we picked it out."[1]

As the days, months, and years passed, we learned even more about the thirteen-year-old Delphi Community Middle School student.

Abby Williams had played volleyball, and was about to play softball, but she'd been artsy too; she'd loved photography, painting, and, according to her mother, "more crafts than she knew what to do with. There were bracelets, there were canvases, there were beads, chalk for a while, paint . . . origami . . . every six months, it was something different."[2] She also played the saxophone in the school band. She enjoyed the outdoors and sharing time in nature with her friends. She was kind and had a gentle smile.[3] She was also a big animal lover and would often try to convince her mother to let her bring home stray cats to give them shelter. Anna had caved in once, even though she's allergic to cats, and welcomed a cat named Bongo into their home.

I had the good fortune of meeting Bongo myself when in September 2020 I visited the house where Abby had lived with her mother and grandmother. I was walking past the well-loved swing set in the yard and up the stairs to the side screen door when Bongo jumped out in front of me, eager to lead me into the house.

He was jet black with long, fluffy fur—actually, he looked a lot like a cat I'd had as a child (creatively named Kitty). As I stepped in through the screen door, I noticed a framed collection of Abby's official volleyball portraits from 2014–2016 hanging on the wall, with Abby wearing her black-and-gold middle school volleyball uniform. It appeared to be the most recent photo from that final 2016 season; just about everything in the house around me made it feel like she had just been here or she was just about to walk in the side screen door.

Diane and I were sitting on the couch looking through her family photo album as she shared memories of her granddaughter. "Abby always loved school and loved to read."

She even had a fun wager going with her uncle.

"Abby's goal was to beat her uncle, our youngest son's, six million words read in middle school, and she was just short of that goal before her life was ended, so her classmates read in her place."

I wanted to learn as much as possible about the girls, who they were before their lives had been so senselessly stolen from them.

The families have been working closely with law enforcement, following their lead. The goal was to get the word out, which would ultimately help them find the person responsible for these crimes. Part of that included doing interviews, a lot of interviews, and sharing special moments over and over again.

One of the questions you will hear most often from reporters when covering a crime where someone has died is, "What was he or she like?" It's an open-ended question, a chance for family members and loved ones to share as much or as little as they want. I've asked it too. But I've often wondered, *Is there ever really a way to describe someone you love and what they meant to you in a sixty-second soundbite?* No. They never can. It's an impossible task.

Before I talked with her loved ones, I knew that Abby was a daughter, a sister, a cousin, a granddaughter, a friend. But the more time I spent with her family, the more I learned about who she was and how much she was loved.

Her full name: Abigail Joyce Williams.

She was born in Michigan on June 23, 2003. Her grandfather, Clif Williams, still lives there. Abby was his only grandchild. Every summer around the Fourth of July, Abby would spend two weeks there.

Abby and her grandpa shared exciting adventures, including horseback riding, going to the movies, and watching the fireworks in Grand Rapids. They also practiced softball together, and every afternoon they would watch *The Andy Griffith Show*. It was Abby's favorite. Clif still watches it every day when he gets home from work. He can feel her right there next to him, watching along just as they used to. "She's right there with me."

They were best buds. Clif later spoke to reporter Rafael Sánchez with WRTV about their close bond.[4] He never imagined Abby would be taken from the family a week after her last visit.

"To lose her wasn't even on the radar." He shook his head, still in disbelief. "You never thought of anything like that, and now to have this happen . . . yeah, I just . . . I still don't know how to live without her."

Clif is still trying to figure out how to go on without her. He misses her. Every. Single. Day. Clif was always there at the press conferences, often sitting next to his daughter. He also kept a stack of fliers with him in Michigan, handing them out to anyone and everyone he saw.

Next to Abby on the flyer is her best friend, Liberty "Libby" German. She's wearing her middle school soccer T-shirt. It is black with a gold soccer ball on the front. Her hair is parted in the middle, and she's smiling.

But even that picture is just one snapshot, a moment in time that doesn't even come close to encapsulating everything she was and everything she loved. Soccer, for example, was just one of the many sports she played that year. She also loved volleyball, softball, and swimming. What's more, she was an excellent student and was preparing to compete in the Academic Bowl in the High Ability class at Delphi Community Middle School.

Libby was just fourteen years old, six months older than Abby, and was born on December 22, 2002, in Lafayette, Indiana, to Derrick German and Carrie German Timmons.

Libby lived with her grandparents, Mike and Becky, and she never let them forget how much she loved and appreciated them. She'd leave sticky notes around their home with genuine messages, like "I love you. Thank you for all you do for me and Kelsi."

It's this spirit of kindness that Abby's grandmother Diane told me she wants people to think of most when remembering her granddaughter and Libby.

"You know, middle school can be a hard place to be—people can be cruel—but things I heard about both girls is that they were kind to everyone. They didn't fall into the cliques and the bullies. We saw that too, with our own family members."

Before their families were the focus of news reports, before the girls' names and images were printed and broadcast across most media outlets and displayed on digital billboards nationwide, Abby and Libby had been regular girls from Delphi, Indiana. They were best friends, always giggling and laughing together, like sisters, who enjoyed their lives with family and friends. They were a good match, but different—complementary opposites. Abby was quieter and more reserved, Libby more gregarious and outgoing.

Their families were different too, but the families recognized, respected, and understood these distinctions. Mike addressed that when he spoke publicly for the first time less than one month after the girls were murdered.

It was March 9, 2017, and Mike was the voice for both families that day. Sheriff Leazenby said a few words and then introduced Mike.

"I wrote down some stuff so I wouldn't forget what we'd like to communicate. My family put this together." He looked down at his notes and began to read.

"My name is Mike Patty. This is my wife, Becky. We'd both like to thank you for showing up here today. I'd like to read a statement from Abby's family.

"'Abby and Libby loved each other. Throughout this tragedy, we have honored their memory by carrying forward and respecting each other. We respect Libby's family's decision to speak publicly at this time, just as they have respected our family's decision not to speak publicly. The family of Abby Williams.'"

Mike looked up from the podium and added his own words to the statement. "I would also ask that the media respect their choice and let them reach out to you if they so desire to do so." The families had been brought together, permanently linked by an unspeakable tragedy. He flipped the page. "This horrible crime has torn a hole in our families that will never heal. It's the small things that seem to hurt the most. It's just natural to holler for them to come to dinner or in the mornings to get up and get ready for school. Then expect them to come through the door after school. The silence when we don't hear their voice. Our girls were excited about the upcoming softball season. Just the day before all this happened—" Mike paused as his voice began to crack. He took a deep breath and started again.

"Just the day before all this happened, they had their equipment out, playing catch, working on their batting in the backyard, going to the ball field with Anna to hone their skills for the upcoming season, but they will never get the chance to play a single inning again."

You can hear it in the space between the sentiments—the words left unsaid. It's always the silence that hurts the most. A gaping hole, an emptiness. The missing puzzle piece that each family will never get back. The things we, the public, will never see.

Mike ended the presser by addressing those reporting on it.

"Now I would like to thank the news media," he said sincerely. "I've had several conversations with many of you. Your professionalism, and respect for our families, has been honorable. We've lost our children, and nothing will bring them back. But through your persevering coverage and help with this investigation, we are confident that together we can bring justice to those responsible for this horrible crime. We appreciate your time and help. Thank you very much."

I understood the importance of the coverage, to make sure that as many flyers were distributed as possible, but I also respected that not every family could or wanted to be public faces for the worst day of their lives. It didn't mean their grief mattered any less.

As the presser was wrapping up, a reporter asked Mike a question about Libby recording the man on the bridge. "I'm glad she had the wherewithal to do that, and I certainly hope that it proves to be the vital piece that helps bring resolution to this," he replied.

He then made it clear that *both* Abby and Libby were heroes, since they stuck together. "I don't know exactly what happened out there that day, but I imagine there was probably an opportunity for one or both to separate and try to make a break in different ways, but those girls loved each other. They were good friends, and neither one of them left each other's side. Both those girls are heroes in my book."

A LITTLE OVER FOUR YEARS AFTER THE MURDERS, I WAS SITTING NEXT TO BECKY, KELSI, AND TARA onstage in Austin, Texas. A large crowd had gathered to hear their story. Some of them were familiar with what had happened to Abby and Libby; others were hearing it for the first time.

By then, I had gotten close to Kelsi and Becky; I had known them for several years. However, this was the first time I'd ever met Libby's aunt, Tara. Becky had introduced us just the day before. Tara was easy to talk to, but I could tell she was guarded. I understood; this would be the first time she'd ever spoken about Libby in public.

It had been 1,573 days since she'd last seen her niece, and every single day hurt that much worse. Libby and Tara had been extremely close; they'd had a special, unique bond. This was particularly evident on Facebook. They would send each other loving messages, jokes, and silly photos. Looking back over Libby's Facebook now, which has been turned into a digital memorial for people to post their memories and feelings, I came across a message written by Libby and posted on February 17, 2014, that made me smile: "My Aunt Tara is pretty amazing. She's the best aunt." I could feel the sincerity and love in that post. They had spent *so* much time together. Libby had been Tara's movie guru, her sidekick, her buddy.

Looking at Tara onstage beside me, I knew this conversation would be extremely difficult. Images of her fourteen-year-old niece flashed across the screen behind us and could be seen on the two small monitors in front of our chairs. It was essentially a highlight reel, a slideshow of her life. Pictures of Libby at school, at home, in her backyard, playing sports, being silly, having fun, were moving across the screen. She was smiling with her cousins, posing next to her big sister, Kelsi, on the beach next to Becky, Mike, and Tara.

That's when I asked, "Tell us if you could—what was Libby like?"

There was a pause, and I realized Tara wasn't answering because she wasn't able to. Looking at the photos all strung together like that, she was overcome with emotion. I immediately regretted the question.

Shit, I thought. *I shouldn't have asked that.*

"It's OK," I said, both to Tara and to the audience. I told Tara I knew it was her first time talking about this in front of a crowd and it must be excruciatingly difficult. Just then, I looked down at the monitor in front of me. A selfie of Libby and Tara gazed back up at me, the same image the crowd was watching on the screen behind me. For a moment, I couldn't help but imagine a slide-show of Emery, my now thirteen-year-old daughter. How would I answer such a question? What would I say? I probably wouldn't be able to say anything at all. Just like Tara.

"The reality of it . . . the reality is . . . it's heartbreaking," I told the crowd. "And that's why we're here." My voice started to crack. "It's OK to not be OK."

After another long pause, I had to pivot. The voice in my head got louder. *Why did you ask that?*

I turned to Becky. "Becky, you were telling me earlier that someone here approached you and said they thought it was solved . . . That's what keeps you going."

"That's exactly what keeps us going," Becky said. "The girls deserve this. They deserve us. Libby did everything she could to help us out. And it's now our job to keep it out there, to keep the pressure on this guy. And never let him think that he got away with this. To think we aren't searching for him. Because we *are*. And we're *not* giving up. He's messed with the wrong family."

At the end of her answer, the audience started to clap.

———

IN THE DAYS AND WEEKS AFTER THE MURDERS, ABBY'S MOM, ANNA, SAID THAT SHE'D COME TO A painful realization. "There are things you just don't have to worry about anymore: getting up for school, buses, and keeping track of when school is closed and school delays. It's just different, and we don't know how to do it, but we figure it out every day."

Both families tried to remember the moments they had shared as a way to help process the loss. Abby's grandfather Eric even told me about an extended family trip to Washington State less than a year before she died. "Our niece was getting married, and we decided to take ten days and turn it into a family vacation. It was her first flight . . . Abigail got a chance to really spend time with her cousins, so to experience that with her and her mom—that is a memory I will cherish forever."

For Becky, Tara, and Kelsi, they also used Facebook as a tool— both to communicate their grief and to communicate with Libby directly.

"Sure do miss you," Becky wrote on June 9, 2017. "Don't like this new normal. Hate that man."

A few months later, on August 9, Tara let her feelings out through her fingertips:

I can't seem to find the words to say how my heart feels. So many emotions going on at once. It has been almost 6 months since Libby and Abby were ripped away from us. Tomorrow would be Libby and Abby's first day of high school, a day that every kid looks forward to and dreads at the same time. Libby would always ask me to take her school clothes shopping because grandma has bad taste. This year we didn't have that opportunity because some monster took her from us. A bright girl with endless possibilities ahead of her and he took that from her. I pray EVERYDAY that TODAY IS THE DAY. I keep my faith in LE (law enforcement) but most of all I keep my faith in God. I love and miss you, something terrible Liberty German.

You could tell Libby was never far from their minds; the family shared memories and quotes frequently, often recalling specific memories that they wanted to hold close forever. For them, Facebook offered a support system filled with loved ones who understood how they felt.

Becky would, and still does, speak of Libby in the present tense. "Because she is always here with us. Even on vacation, we do things that we know she would love to do."

A month after the murders, in March 2017, the family went to Chicago for spring break. Why? Because it was where Libby had wanted to go—and they wanted to respect that, make her proud. On March 25, Tara posted a picture of the family out to dinner, with Kelsi holding a picture of Libby at the head of the table.

"She's always with us," Becky explained, "not physically but in spirit."

On their trip to Florida, she was there too. There's a picture of eleven members of Libby's family all together on a beach, holding up a large sheet with her portrait right on the front of it.

Through it all, the one thing keeping both families united and focused was the feeling that someone, somewhere, might someday see the picture of the suspect on one of those flyers and finally come forward to the police. So when Superintendent Doug Carter announced a new direction and a very different sketch of the suspect, the families couldn't help but feel defeated.

"It was like a gut punch. I was like, come on, you've gotta be kidding me," Becky said.

Abby's mom, Anna, was just as confused. "It was like, wait . . . we put all this faith into this first sketch for all this time, this is who we thought we were looking for, and now they've changed their minds?"[5]

It felt like all that work, all the interviews, the conferences, the thousands of flyers they printed and handed out, was for nothing.

When the police had first reached out and asked to speak with them in April, they thought that maybe—finally—they would hear news of what they had spent more than two years waiting for: an arrest. That, of course, didn't happen.

And they regrouped. They refocused and somehow found the energy—the resolve—to do it all over again.

A new flyer, a new sketch, a new suspect, but the same mission.

It felt, in many ways, like they were back to square one. Faced with the daunting task of starting all over again.

And that's exactly what both families did.

7

The Hunt for "Bridge Guy"

Immediately following the now infamous April 22 press conference, the investigation appeared to pick up steam as more than three thousand new tips came in through the tip line and email set up by law enforcement. Two weeks after he announced "a new direction," the superintendent started doing public interviews again. He was often asked the same questions over and over again by most media outlets: "Why did this sketch look so different?"; "What was the information that led to a different 'investigative strategy'?"; and the one asked most often, "Did you really think the murderer was in the room?"

"If he wasn't, he was close by," Carter said. "I'm 100 percent convinced he was watching."

But how? How did he know? How *could* he know?

Back in Atlanta, plans for an *HLN: Delphi Special Report* were already in motion.

On April 30, my HLN colleague and fellow anchor Mike Gala-nos and I hosted a live prime-time show with a panel of guests—a dream team of experts. Joseph Scott Morgan and Casey Jordan were joining me on the air once again, along with criminal defense attorney Joey Jackson and retired FBI special agent Maureen O'Connell.

We began the show by addressing the press conference—both what was said and, more importantly, what was left out. In partic-ular, law enforcement had not provided specific details about the murders, such as the manner in which the girls had been killed or the make and model of the car Superintendent Carter said they were looking for.

Maureen theorized this was intentional; by leaving that infor-mation out, police could eliminate anyone who came forward with a false confession.

"Sadly," she said, "in this country, people are lonely, and they want to be part of something."

I brought up how dramatic the unveiling of the new sketch had been, how anxious the entire room felt. According to Joey, this was also very intentional.

"The tension building, the orchestrated nature of it, the deliv-ery of it, the unveiling of the new photograph. Basically, the announcement that everything we've been looking at for the last two years is moot. Pay attention because *this* is the guy we're look-ing for.

"And that one line, 'He could be in the room,' was *meant* to send shivers down your spine. I guarantee you that law enforce-ment was there, scanning the room, looking to see if anyone not only looks like this but got up and left, or looked really nervous. It was meant to *provoke* the killer. Now, do they really expect him to be in the room? No, they had to consider that was a possibility, but *really* what they're trying to do is reignite interest in this case, with this new sketch, because *this* represents who they're looking for now. They have a new vision. And two things: they either know a lot about this person, and have a particular person in mind, and the sketch really looks like him, or they have a new witness and they're really trying to bring it all together so they can actually match DNA and the evidence they do have on hand with an actual person."

Joey added that he was "very impressed by that press conference. I was impressed by the superintendent, the manner in which he conducted it, and the emotion that he had too. But I think it's important [to remember] that when law enforcement is on a case, that they don't work in a vacuum. Law enforcement often depends on communities. What do you *know* as a community? And it is heartening, also, that after a couple of years, we know that they're not slowing down. And they're sending the message 'You know what? We're on to you. We got you. We think you're a person who's in this community. We're going to release information to everyone—and every man, woman, and child, 'if you know a person that looks like this, you know someone who looks similar like this, you know someone who walks like that,' right? Releasing the audio, the video, getting all the information together, getting community involvement, and perhaps bringing this person to justice."

Casey Jordan turned to Joey and asked, "And you don't think they're bluffing?"

"You know what—here's what I think," he responded. "I think that they're working the case very diligently, but I do think . . . you know the saying 'See something, say something'? And I think they're really depending and leaning on a community, which is close-knit, tightly knit, to come forward with anything and everything you know to help us crack this case."

I brought up the fact that it seemed as though everyone in the media was there, and Maureen agreed that it was "absolutely by design. I thought it was a brilliant strategy. And you're right"—she motioned over to Joey—"they're not giving up at all. They're ramping up. And you can tell that every one of those law enforcement officers was just desperately invested. I think the reason they took so long to release the video in part is due to the fact that when you look at the way this man walks on the bridge, that's not a natural gait. It's not a normal gait. And if you look at the topography . . . those are railroad ties, partially eroded, so you're gonna hop-step, hop-step. And not only is it over for you, but it's a horrible depiction of how a person *actually walks*. I think the value in . . . releasing that extra video that showed the way he walks is to show that in the initial photograph, he looked very heavyset. But in that video, that short video, you can see that his legs are thinner. You can see that his jacket is . . . I think he's got all of the things he needs to commit the crimes stuffed under that jacket."

After this, the forensic expert jumped in to ask the other guests what they thought had been the most valuable piece of newly released information.

"One of the things that really haunted me was the audio . . ." Joseph Scott Morgan said. "Because now we have a larger sample than we previously had . . . Now you've got 'guys,' and I know that doesn't sound like a lot, but it implies kind of a connectivity here—he's identifying these little girls, giving them a specific directive. And if you listen to him say it, it's very bold when he says it. 'Guys.' He gets their attention. 'Down the hill.'

"I was talking to Maureen just a moment ago, and I think one of the things that's really compelling here is—I wonder if the FBI has come forward and assigned a linguist. Not to get a specific identity but to regionalize that accent. Because now they've got a larger sample here, and I think that that's gonna go a long way to getting this solved."

"I think it suggests a younger suspect—I really do think," Casey said, nodding. "I think it's far more likely that somebody in their twenties would say 'guys' or . . . maybe he knows them? You never know."

Before the allotted commercial break, Mike brought up how the superintendent had specifically referenced the movie *The Shack*, and we talked about the heavy themes of faith and religion at the core of the film.

"And even though [the movie] is about forgiveness and faith, he doesn't say those words," Casey said. "He says 'evil,' 'death,' and 'eternity.' And he mentions the movie, but then he says, 'And there's a book.' . . . Now *that's* interesting. I don't think the book he's talking about is *The Shack*; I think he's talking about *the* book. The Bible. And he's really trying to appeal . . . I think this is a churchgoing person in the community who believes on the surface, has faith, but struggles deeply with his identity . . ."

Shortly after this, Mike asked the panel whether they thought we were any closer to getting an arrest. JSM, Joey, and Maureen all seemed to have full confidence that law enforcement was getting closer to an arrest, that they'd be able to solve it soon, but Casey wasn't as convinced. She agreed it seemed like they were closer, but if nothing happened in the next few weeks, she argued, "I'm gonna think this was a Hail Mary pass. I'm gonna think they had *nothing*."

After we showed a brief clip from my visit with the family, where I'd driven to the trailhead with Kelsi in her car, Mike reiterated how even though we were all talking about solving a case, this was really more about the grief of a family.

I couldn't have agreed more. "At the presser, it's about *who did this*, meaning this sketch, but at the heart of this is a town left *devastated*, the community of Delphi, missing these young girls."

"The time is up for this killer," Joey reiterated. "I think if he's watching now . . . the pressure is on. I think he's living amongst that community, and I think it's a matter of time before they crack this case."

"And I think they're working on reverse genealogy right now, forensic genealogy, to home in on this killer," said Maureen.

"Trying to get him to come forward and confess," Casey added. "It's basically saying, 'That is your best bet right now. I still think you have a little bit of a conscience. Do the right thing.'"

———

AFTER THE SHOW WRAPPED, I HEADED OUT THROUGH THE PARKING DECK TO GET TO MY CAR, SCROLLING through my emails to see whether I'd missed anything during the taping. One message in particular, with "Delphi" in the subject line, immediately caught my attention: "Susan. This is First Sergeant Holeman. Could you call me. No rush."

My initial thought was that they'd found the guy. An arrest either had *just* happened or must be happening very soon.

I'd first met Detective Jerry Holeman two months prior, almost three. It was during my first trip to Delphi; he was my second interview after Sergeant Kim Riley.

At that point, the two-year anniversary of the murders of Abby and Libby had been just days away. Considering the evidence that had been collected at that point, no one would have guessed this would still be unsolved.

"Unsolved, yes, but don't call it a cold case."

I learned quickly that there was a big difference. Law enforcement officials were still actively working on this case and were dedicated to bringing the killer to justice; at the same time, they recognized the importance of releasing only tidbits of information. Cold cases were different, since those were cases where the investigations were no longer active, mostly due to all leads being exhausted or having limited evidence.

I had first interviewed Detective Holeman in the entryway of the police station. He seemed like a nice guy, personable and funny. His hair was short, a buzz cut, a no-nonsense style, but his eyes were kind and he had a strong presence about him.

"I'm not sure I want to talk to you," he said. "I may not do this." Those were his first words to me even before hello.

"OK," I replied. "That's fine."

"Wow, you didn't press me at all. I was just kidding."

We both laughed.

OK—he reminds me of the older brother I never had.

Before long, the camera was rolling. I had a newfound confidence now that I knew he had a sense of humor. Could I possibly get him to answer some of the questions everyone was asking? Did kindness equate to being forthcoming? I doubted it, but it was worth a try.

"What was the cause of death?" I asked.

He wouldn't say.

"Where is your evidence room?"

He smirked. "Did you really think I was going to answer that?"

I guess I should've known better; after all, there was a sign right above his head that literally read "DON'T TALK IN THESE HALLS. THE MEDIA COULD BE LISTENING."

I pivoted again. "Did Libby record more on her phone?"

He finally acquiesced. "There is more, but we only released a portion of it. Protecting the integrity of the investigation is key here. We can't release everything we have because there's only certain people that know the details. If we release everything, we get into false confessions."

His response confirmed Agent O'Connell's later suspicions from the HLN special.

When I asked whether the police had any DNA collected from the crime scene, he said, "Yes, we do, but I can't say much more."

For all he wouldn't say, there was a definitive message he wanted to get across to anyone who was listening.

"Susan, if somebody knows something and they're not telling us," Holeman said, "they are just as guilty as the other person, so they need to come forward. If they are scared, we'll help protect them, and they can remain anonymous. But there's somebody out there that knows who's responsible, and we need their help."

When I asked him how he'd personally been holding up the past year, he finally let down his guard—but just a little.

"It's been hard. It's always more difficult when children are involved. But I always go back to the investigator in me. We are never giving up until we find this guy."

After meeting with Detective Holeman, I'd driven a few miles down the road to meet Carroll County sheriff Tobe Leazenby. He looked *exactly* how you'd picture a sheriff might look, donning a thick dark mustache under his nose, curving down just so around his mouth, with a tall sheriff's hat and a gentle smile of pearly whites.

"Sheriff Leazenby!" I said, reaching out to shake his hand as we walked into his office. "Hi. I'm Susan."

"Susan, hello. Nice to meet you. You can call me Tobe."

I felt immediately at ease as the photographers started setting up their equipment. The sheriff stayed squarely behind his desk, and I sat down right across from him. Taped to his tall gray filing cabinet was a picture of Abby and Libby, next to the sketch of the suspect, as well as the tip-line number and email. Right below that was a sticker of a Pittsburgh Steelers helmet.

"Are you a Steelers fan?" I asked.

His face lit right up. "Yes, a big fan."

"Oh, we work with [wide receiver] Hines Ward. Do you know who he is?"

"Do I know who he is? *Of course.*"

"Oh, sorry." I laughed. "I only knew him from winning *Dancing with the Stars.* He's a great guy."

The office was small, which made setting up a two-camera shoot almost impossible. *Almost.* Somehow, they did it. It was cramped, but it worked. During the interview, the photographers started giving each other hand signals, lest they interrupt our very important *Dancing with the Stars* question. To my right, I saw photojournalist Leonel Mendez smiling and giving us a nod, which meant we were ready to go.

"I know you've done this before, but a reminder: it's just a conversation with me—ignore the cameras," I said as I glanced down at a picture of Leazenby and his family.

"OK, Susan," I heard, followed by "You can clap now" from the photographers squished in the two corners of the room. The on-camera clap was in there for the editor so they'd know where to start the interview. And just like that—"We're rolling."

"Tobe, when you first heard the recording of that man's voice . . . because I've heard it over and over, and it's chilling for me. I can't imagine living here and hearing that. What was that like?"

Leazenby paused before answering. "I guess the investigator part of me started to kick in, and I'm thinking, *I know that voice. Who is that? Who is that?* And I'm still doing that, thinking who this person is. I've heard that voice somewhere, but to this day, I can't put a name to that voice."

"You obviously watched the video. Has that changed you?"

He paused, looking down. "It's been a while . . . but honestly"—his gaze shifted again—"when I'm sitting here, I'm replaying it in my own mind as we speak, and I'm still in that investigator mode, going, *Who is that? Who is that person?* So there is still that, and I know this is the way it is with all of our investigators on board, but there's that driver, that fire, to get to that justice."

Leazenby had visited the spot where the girls were found. Just him, all by himself. He always followed the advice of Dr. Henry Lee, a scientist known by many as the founder of forensics. Lee had famously worked on the JonBenét Ramsey case, as well as "the death of Chandra Levy, the kidnapping of Elizabeth Smart, and the reinvestigation of the Kennedy assassination."[1]

"I remember Dr. Lee saying, 'Study the crime scene. It'll tell you what happened here—it will give you answers.' So there's been times . . . I know this sounds deep, but there's something to it that, going back out there, that you kinda look around and you go, *What am I missing here? What else can we develop from what we see out here?*"

We all headed outside to get a few walking shots before saying goodbye.

"Tobe, I grabbed a card. Is that OK?" I asked before we left.

"Sure. Reach out with any questions. You may want to take down my cell number."

I jotted his number down on the back of the card before stuffing it into my wallet.

ᴀɴᴅ ɴᴏᴡ, ᴊᴜsᴛ ᴀ ꜰᴇᴡ ᴍᴏɴᴛʜs ʟᴀᴛᴇʀ, I ᴛʜᴏᴜɢʜᴛ ᴀʙᴏᴜᴛ ᴛʜᴇ Dᴇʟᴘʜɪ ɪɴᴠᴇsᴛɪɢᴀᴛᴏʀs I'ᴅ ᴍᴇᴛ ᴀs I read the email again.

"Susan. This is First Sergeant Holeman. Could you call me. No rush."

I dialed his number from my car.

"Hello?" Holeman answered on the third ring.

I told him I was just returning his call.

"Hey, Susan, I watched the special."

Oh great, I thought.

"You guys did a good job, but you mentioned the FBI a lot."

"Well, you aren't telling us much," I replied. "I mentioned law enforcement in general."

"You know, Susan," he continued, "that press conference was *our* idea. The FBI didn't think we should do it."

Do what? I wondered. What was he saying? Wasn't the plan to lure the killer to the press conference, or at least make him nervous and get him to make a mistake? And why did the FBI think it was a bad idea? I thought back to what Superintendent Doug Carter had said at the February 22, 2017, press conference: "There's not an agency on the planet better at helping us facilitate this than the FBI, and they are as entrenched in this as anybody." Did "entrenched" necessarily equate to cohesiveness? I knew Holeman wouldn't or *couldn't* answer the many questions I had.

"Well," I said at last, "I hope that you catch him soon."

"We do too."

I hung up, somehow with even more questions than I'd had before the call. Was there infighting between Indiana State Police and the FBI, at least when it came to this case? Had the press conference been such a good idea after all?

Once again, my mind went back to the early days of the investigation, when multiple law enforcement agencies had flocked to the small town to assist them in catching the killer. Skilled federal and local investigators had promised to never give up, yet it was clear they were keeping what they *did* know within the walls of the new command center. FBI special agent in charge Greg Massa had reiterated the idea that all the teams were working on the case collaboratively.

"The FBI plays an important support role in this investigation, this joint investigation," Massa had explained. "On any given day, we have twenty FBI agents that are here providing investigative help. We were committed to work[ing] around the clock, as we have been for the last nine days, and we will continue to do so until this case is solved. And I believe it will be solved."

But what were the actual rules when it came to the FBI inserting themselves or being invited into an investigation? I called my cousin Kevin Hendricks, a detective with the New Brunswick Police Department who was temporarily assigned to the FBI. He's got a big job now, but I'll always think of him as a chubby blond baby, ten years younger than me, running around our house with his two older sisters.

"Hi, Kevin."

"Hey, Susie." It's what he calls me. It's what my whole family calls me—Susie or Sue. *Never* Susan. When I first appeared on CNN, the kids I grew up with were all like, "Who is 'Susan'?" Yes, it's my given name, but it almost felt like an alias growing up because it was never used. Plus, I was shy. *Painfully* shy.

"Susie, I didn't even know you could *talk* until you were twelve," I'd heard once from Bart, son of my mom's friend Marie. I understand. He thinks of me as that young girl hiding behind her mother's leg—the same way I see Kevin.

Back on the phone with Kevin, we caught up for a bit, making small talk, but then he got right to the point. "What do you need to know?"

"How does it work?" I asked. "In general, in terms of the investigation?"

"If Abby and Libby were missing, the FBI has an automatic in. When their bodies were discovered, that dynamic [between local law enforcement and the FBI] automatically changed. They had to be invited in."

Were they? I wondered. Did they have access to all the evidence? Was it really a "joint effort," or were they merely there for a show of solidarity?

I did know that from the start, there had been a united effort by multiple law enforcement agencies to solve this horrific crime, but as the days, weeks, months, and years went by, had that dynamic changed? Exactly *how* were they conducting their investigation? And *who* had the right to know *what*? The answer to the latter was rarely agreed on.

Early on, even the girls' families took different roles among themselves when it came to helping the investigation. For Libby's family, this meant speaking to anyone and everyone who would listen; telling the girls' stories became their mission. But Abby's family was more reluctant to deal with the public and the media, something that Becky understood, since every family dealt with grief and loss differently. Still, despite their differences, both families shared a deep-rooted trust of the law enforcement agencies working on the case.

Early on in the investigation, Abby's grandparents Diane and Eric had written a kind note for investigators, thanking them for everything they had done so far: "Where are the police when you need them? They are here, in Delphi, with us. We pray for your protection, and we are forever grateful for your service.—Diane & Eric."

Mike Patty had also commended the way investigators were keeping him and his family in the loop through the whole ordeal.

"I'm relying on law enforcement and the efforts that they're putting forward. They've been kind enough to walk me through the process of how they're evaluating this. I'm kind of a process-oriented guy, so they walked me through that. I'm very impressed with the steps that they go through whenever they receive tips, and trust me—every tip, every call, is checked. There is *nothing* that is going into a bucket, even if it seems so silly. The cohesive work between the state police, the county police, the FBI, and the city police and officers from all over that are coming in is just truly impressive. I truly feel we are going to get to the bottom of this, and that is why I'm asking for help out there. Any tips we could get [would be] monumental and could really bring this case to resolution. Somebody knows something, and I hope they call in."

Mike also thought a lot about how Libby would have responded to the same call for help in someone else's case, and he urged the public to do what she would have done.

"There are too many ways to count how our lives will forever be impacted to share here today. I imagine most people listening that have raised or are raising children know how kids can be. A phrase that was jokingly attached to Libby in our family, from asking her to pick up her shoes, her school backpack, her coat, her first reply would almost always be 'I will, in a minute.' We joked with her about this all the time. I believe if she were able to speak, she would ask people . . . please give her the one minute she always asked for. To really study the picture and listen to the audio clip. Someone out there knows this person or persons. He's someone's neighbor, coworker, family member, friend, husband, or acquaintance. If and when any new information is released by law enforcement, please take another minute from your day to review all the information and help us collect the pieces of this puzzle. Both of our families are requesting everyone to please help Abby and Libby. Look for someone who has recently changed their appearance, cut their hair, shaved, or started wearing different clothes. Have they changed in some strange manner that just seems a little odd? If you think it could be but then say, 'No, he's not like that,' go with your initial instinct. Let law enforcement run that information and make that determination. However small it may seem, it is extremely vital to capture every tip we can get. Please, we *need* your help."

Despite the families' public support for the investigators, the public's patience with law enforcement started to wane. Superintendent Carter knew plenty of people were losing faith and starting to question exactly what they were doing to find the guy.

"We'll be able to one day tell you what we know and why," he assured them. "We don't want to show our hand; we don't want to show the complete picture of what we know versus what we think. We have to be very careful there. Remember it's easy to give an opinion if you don't understand the factual basis for what we've done and why. We have to protect the integrity of what we know."

He wouldn't discuss any of the physical evidence collected from the crime scene, but he was confident that the case could eventually be solved based on the evidence Libby had recorded on her phone. After all, they had a considerable amount of evidence on hand.

It wasn't often that investigators knew what the man looked like and sounded like, and that meant for Superintendent Doug Carter, this had become personal. In May 2019, one month after the new sketch was revealed, Carter told me there was not a day that went by that he didn't think of what happened to those two young girls. "Very selfishly," he admitted, "other than the family of Abby and Libby . . . there's nobody that wants to find this monster more than me.[2]

"Somebody knows whose body that is," Superintendent Carter said. "Somebody knows if you take the head off a person that you know, you'd recognize the body. That is the piece we are waiting on." It became clear to me after several press conferences and pleas to the public that law enforcement was hoping for, counting on, banking on someone from the small town of Delphi to turn this person in. But was this *all* they had? Could they be sure that someone in this close-knit community would make that call? The fear was that the man on the bridge would strike again.

"Susan, a person wouldn't do this just one time, so if they haven't before, they likely will again."[3]

———

JUST BECAUSE THE DETAILS OF THE INVESTIGATORY PROCESS WERE NOT SHARED PUBLICLY DIDN'T mean they weren't looking into potential suspects. Back in late September 2017, seven months after the murders, a name had even come up: Daniel Nations. Indiana State Police had been contacted by a sheriff in Colorado about similarities in their case against Nations, who was facing a felony charge of menacing and reckless endangerment for allegedly "threatening several hikers with a hatchet."[4]

Nations had been on the registered sex offender registry since 2007, when he was convicted of indecent exposure in a Walmart parking lot in South Carolina. He'd been arrested multiple times in the years since, and he'd even registered himself as a sex offender in Morgan County, which was just south of Indianapolis and a little over ninety miles from Delphi, on January 31, 2017. By law, he was required to check in every seven days in person, and he'd even done so on February 14, the day after Libby and Abby went missing. He'd been in jail just ten days later, from February 24 to 28, and was in and out of court, as well as on the run, in the months following the murders. Two days after the police released the initial sketch of the man they thought to be the Delphi killer, he'd skipped a court appearance and gone on the run yet again.[5]

Comparing Nations to the sketch, one could easily see why authorities would think he might be the guy: he looked an awful lot like the suspect in question. Even his wife, Katelyn Nations, couldn't entirely rule it out. "I have been with Daniel for six years now and looking at that picture . . . there is a lot of similarities," she conceded.[6]

But when it came to whether she thought he was capable of committing the murders, his wife wasn't so sure one way or another. "Honestly," Katelyn said, "I do not want to say that I can see him doing it or not."[7]

Thirty-one-year-old Daniel Nations was *never* officially declared a "person of interest" in the case; still, authorities flew to El Paso County, Colorado, to interview him. Following that interview, law enforcement remained tight-lipped.

Indiana State Police said in a press release in early October that "there has been no information developed to specifically include or exclude Daniel Nations as a suspect in the Delphi homicides."[8] A few months later, when asked about it, Superintendent Carter told the press, "We spent a little bit of time with him [Daniel Nations], and he's not a person we care a whole lot about at this time," adding that "until somebody is arrested, we're interested in almost everybody."[9]

For the families, the whole ordeal felt like a big setback.

"Susan, I thought this may be the guy," Mike Patty told me. "We got our hopes up that the guy on the bridge may finally be caught, and then [it was] a letdown."

From that moment on, Mike decided he would no longer bank on a name or a face. He needed something concrete, like a call from law enforcement telling him someone had been charged. After all, he was a levelheaded guy who wasn't supposed to get ahead of himself. He was the anchor of the family.

"It was a roller coaster of emotions I swore I would never get back on unless a person was charged with the murders," he said. "Not to mention the buzz around Nations led some people to believe that it had been solved. Susan, it really took the wind out of our sails. We spent all that time showing the sketch, asking people to help. What if they thought we no longer needed them? We did damage control for months."

As the months dragged on, I started to wonder whether all this media attention toward Nations and other possible persons of interest had actually helped draw in more tips or if the opposite was true.

I'd begun to get more familiar with local law enforcement officers and felt comfortable enough to text Sheriff Tobe Leazenby and Sergeant Kim Riley about what kind of effect the news had on the investigation. The number of tips did go up slightly when a new name or face surfaced in the media. But I was curious: Just how many of those tips led to any movement in the investigation? *That* they would not tell me. By May 2019, more than three years after the murders, the total number of tips had increased to more than forty-two thousand. But there was still no one in custody and the man on the bridge remained out there.

Then, on July 22, 2019, another name surfaced. Paul Etter.

I was in Florida with my family when I got the panicked call from a producer in the newsroom.

"Susan, there may be an arrest in the Delphi case."

"What? How do you know? What's his name?"

"Paul Etter. *Inside Edition* called; they want you in a studio to do a live shot with the anchor. Oh . . . you are off all week."

"I am, and I *would* go to a studio, but I'm not even close to a local news station."

Local news stations will frequently let an anchor from CNN, or any other network, use their studio, depending on the affiliate and its connected station. We often know and have even worked with people at various stations around the country. Many reporters work in a specific town or city for a year or two and then move on to another market. The industry tends to feel small, especially when you've been in it as long as I have.

Almost immediately after the name was leaked, the media swarmed, eager to find out more information about Etter. As it happened, fifty-five-year-old Paul Etter had once been stopped by police in Lebanon, Indiana, after cops noticed he was driving what appeared to be a stolen vehicle. He then refused to cooperate with police, lifted his gun up to his head, and drove into a nearby field. Negotiators talked with Etter for almost five hours before he shot himself.[10]

Two days prior to the incident, Etter had been accused of kidnapping and sexually assaulting a twenty-six-year-old victim, holding her captive on his family farm. Nearly twelve hours later, he drove her to a residence and released her, at which point she called the police.

The comparisons to the sketch started almost immediately online. Like Nations, Etter seemed to share an uncanny resemblance to the first sketch in terms of both his face and his build, minus the scruffy facial hair. But three months prior, law enforcement said the second sketch was the one to focus on, *not* the first one. Even though his DNA was collected in the field following his death, he was never formally linked to the murders.

As Sheriff Leazenby stressed, "He's not a priority. . . . He's being looked into and pursued, but that's like all the others that we've been looking into all along."[11]

Meanwhile, as the weeks and months turned into years, tips continued to flood in, and the reward money offered for any information about the murders that could lead to an arrest kept skyrocketing. By April 5, 2021, the reward had jumped up to $325,000, after an anonymous donor added an extra $100,000.

The following day, April 6, Mike appeared as a guest on my weekend morning show. The anonymous donation had given him a bit of hope that this might just be what it took to help move the needle. I admired his optimism, but I was less convinced: Does reward money at this level actually encourage someone with the right tip to call in, or does it cause a lot of people to throw tips, with investigators hoping the influx yields enough information to overlap in facts? The goal, of course, was to hear from that *one* person, the one who had the information they needed to find the person who did this. Would the growing reward money help lead to that tip? Everyone was hoping that it would.

Thirteen days later, on April 19, there was word of a possible "big break" in the investigation.

Forty-two-year-old James Brian Chadwell was arrested at his home in Lafayette, Indiana, for kidnapping and sexually assaulting a nine-year-old girl. She had miraculously survived and been found in his basement.[12] After his mug shot was released, almost immediately there was speculation of a possible connection to the murders of Abby and Libby. The consensus seemed to be that he looked like the second sketch of the potential suspect.

Coincidentally, he also had a large tattoo on his arm that many thought resembled Libby.

When asked about Chadwell being a possible person of interest, Sheriff Tobe Leazenby stated, "Investigators are looking into Chadwell to see if there may be a connection." The next day, *that* became the headline. Local and national news outlets ran with what they considered an update. Headlines like "A man in custody with a possible connection to the Delphi murders" screamed across TV screens and newspapers, a picture of his mug shot often displayed right next to images of Abby and Libby.

This became a big concern for the families. "Susan, we don't want anyone thinking this is solved when it's not." Would someone who was watching the program and reading the news see the mug shot next to the girls and assume that the case had been solved? The families were worried this might happen, when what they needed most was for everyone to continue to actively look for the man on the bridge. They were *counting* on the public's help.

On July 29, 2021, three months after he was asked about James Chadwell, Sheriff Leazenby made an announcement. It appeared that law enforcement was reinforcing their wall of silence. "No further comment on Mr. Chadwell or any other suspect will be afforded in the foreseeable future." Tobe, it appeared, had grown tired of the fact that with every statement he released, no matter how vague, the headlines shifted.

The same pattern kept repeating itself, over and over.

There would be some kind of new lead or a new name, a blanket comment from law enforcement about "looking into every lead," followed by a great flurry of excitement and energy, then silence. The families were aware that this was happening, and Kelsi was fielding questions and reiterating on Twitter what law enforcement had been saying all along. On May 6, Kelsi tweeted, "Yes, I've seen his name all over. No new updates. No press release. There is no suspect in custody in this case. LE is looking into a tip that was sent in that is now being made way bigger than it is. Until LE says he's a suspect, he is no more than any other name they are looking at."

But was it better not to speak at all about possible suspects?

James Brian Chadwell eventually pled guilty to the child molestation and attempted murder charges related to the nine-year-old and in turn received a sentence of ninety years in prison. Even so, he was *never* formally considered a suspect in the Delphi double homicide.[13]

I kept going back to what Mike had told me in his home many months before.

"You know, Susan, I've been down that road before. I've gotten my hopes up, and so I'm going to wait [until they] call me and say, 'Mike, we got him.'" He sighed, his eyes starting to water. "You know, at one point, I really thought we had him."

8

CrimeCon

When I first heard about CrimeCon in Libby's kitchen back in 2019, I was a bit apprehensive. Mike had asked me whether I'd ever heard of it, but I couldn't say that I had. My initial thoughts: *Is it similar to Comic-Con? Do people dress up? What is the crowd like?*

He must have noticed an odd look on my face.

"I know it sounds a little weird," Mike said, "but it really helps get the word out. We hand out flyers, T-shirts, bracelets, and talk about the girls. It's a way to ask the public for help. Would you be interested in helping us tell our story onstage?"

"Sure!" I answered without hesitation. If Mike thought it was a good idea, then I trusted his judgment. Plus, I really wanted to help him and his family in whatever way I could.

"It's in New Orleans this year," he said. "Last year was in Nashville, and the response was really good."

"The first year was Indianapolis," Kelsi added, "so it was a close drive for us."

"I'm not sure how great I am onstage," I confessed.

Kelsi turned to me and cocked her head in confusion. "What do you mean? You're on TV."

I couldn't blame her for thinking public speaking came naturally, but let me tell you—being on a set with cameras in front of you is *very different* from being onstage with hundreds, if not thousands, of people looking on. In the studio, it's usually just me and the cameras and maybe a few other people.

"Don't worry—you'll be fine," Mike said.

I smiled and nodded, desperately hoping I wouldn't do anything to let down Mike and the rest of Abby's and Libby's family members.

By the time I got back to Atlanta, executives and several producers were already starting to plan how best to set up the Delphi panel for CrimeCon. Since talking to Becky, Mike, and Kelsi in their kitchen, I'd learned what a massive production the whole conference was—not just liaising with victims' families and expert speakers but also managing a conference that drew thousands of attendees. The two-day event was set for June 7–9 at the Hilton New Orleans Riverside. Fortunately, I wouldn't be the only one from the station in attendance; Mike Galanos, my colleague and anchor of *True Crime Live*, was set to broadcast from New Orleans.

When we were still about a month out, I started to outline and organize my notes, writing down both what I wanted to ask the family and what I thought the audience might want to know. A lot had happened since the previous year's meetup in Nashville. There was a new sketch, plus we'd also heard more audio of the killer's voice, not to mention the walk recorded on Libby's phone.

I was grateful that I would be moderating such a great panel; along with Mike and Kelsi, Abby's grandmother and grandfather, Diane and Eric Erskin, had also offered to join. Sergeant Kim Riley had agreed to be on the panel as well. It would be a good mix of family anecdotes and key intel from law enforcement, so I knew I would have a lot of material available.

One person who wouldn't be joining me onstage was Becky Patty. She was fighting two battles now, having recently undergone multiple rounds of chemotherapy and radiation. She'd also lost her hair, and she was adamant that she didn't want her appearance to be the focus of the audience. Even so, it seemed like nothing could dampen Becky's spirit. I spotted her down in the audience, to my left. Her head was wrapped closely in a scarf as she smiled up at us, looking on proudly as all of the participating family members got situated.

You could say I was more than a little nervous. It wasn't just about public speaking; it was about how important this audience could be in terms of helping us to spread the word. Sergeant Kim Riley, Superintendent Doug Carter, Sheriff Tobe Leazenby, and the countless members of law enforcement kept reiterating the same line over and over: it takes only one tip. Just one tip, from one person, having heard or seen something they think might be relevant but perhaps aren't certain about. Sometimes that's all it takes to connect the dots. What if that person were in the audience? What could I possibly say to them—what could the *panel* say to them—to help convince them to come forward?

The pressure was on. There was no question of my *wanting* to moderate the panel, but I began to wonder whether I *could*. I kept thinking back to when I'd been invited to my high school to give a speech during a ceremony for distinguished alumni. The incident had not gone well, to say the least; I still remember my mouth going dry, sweat beading against my skin, feeling like I couldn't catch my breath. After I'd tried to get a few words out, the room quickly went blurry, and I ran back to my seat. As bad as it may sound, trust me—it was worse.

I swore back then I would *never* speak in public again. And now, decades later, I was about to speak on the biggest stage of my life.

———

Fast-forward to June 7, 2019.

To say the ballroom was big is an understatement—it was *massive*. And there wasn't just one; there were several ballrooms lined up, one after the other, on either side of the long hallway. I picked one and very quietly and slowly walked inside the double doors. Onstage, I saw a man with light brown hair and a confident stance interacting and engaging with the audience. He kept pointing to what appeared to be a section of a home rebuilt on stage, a fictional crime scene. "Victim #1" was painted across a white door in bloodred paint. I was pretty sure there was a mannequin lying on a bed, but it was hard to see, and I was tucked into the back corner. The man seemed like a total natural up there, walking from one side of the stage to the other. The audience was completely mesmerized. *No pressure.*

I slowly walked backward toward the door, cracked it open, and quietly slipped out. I then took a sharp right and beelined to the elevator.

"Who is in that first ballroom?" I asked the woman next to me in the elevator. She had several telltale badges around her neck—surely she'd know the answer.

"On the right or left?"

"Right."

Libby German loved riding in the car with her sister, Kelsi, behind the wheel. They were more than sisters; they were best friends.

Libby posted a photo on her Snapchat account showing Abby walking across the old railroad bridge. This was the last time anyone heard from the girls: 2:07 p.m. on February 13, 2017.

The view from the Monon High Bridge, which looms over Deer Creek in Delphi, IN.

Libby's grandparents, Mike and Becky Patty, sit down in their kitchen for their first interview with Susan.

Kelsi reads her high school essay about the devastating loss of her sister to Susan in February 2019.

Kelsi and Susan drive out to the point where Kelsi dropped Abby and Libby off, shortly before they disappeared.

Kelsi discovers something Libby left behind for her through geocaching while at the Monon High Bridge with Susan in 2019.

Abby's grandmother talks to Susan about how her family is part of a club no one wants to join.

Carroll County sheriff Tobe Leazenby speaks with Susan at length in his office upon her visit to Delphi.

Susan and Sheriff Tobe Leazenby walk outside the Carroll County Sheriff's department, which is in the same building as the Carroll County Indiana Jail.

Susan's photo of Superintendent Doug Carter at the April 2019 press conference as he is delivering a powerful message. "To the killer, who may be in this room: We believe you are hiding in plain sight."

The new sketch of a visibly younger suspect (left), compared with the original sketch (right)

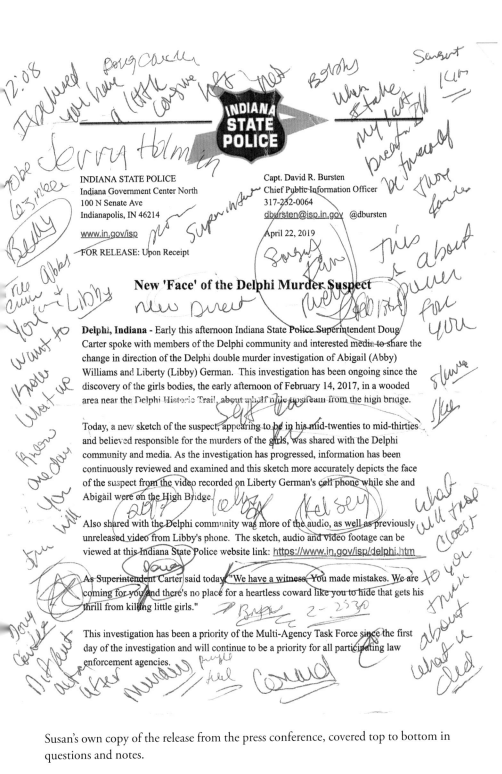

Susan's own copy of the release from the press conference, covered top to bottom in questions and notes.

Indiana State Police superintendent Doug Carter expresses his grief at the press conference in April 2019.

WANTED

Seeking Information >>   New Murder Suspect

Reward over $225,000
E-Mail:
abbyandlibbytip@cacoshrf.com
Tip Line: (844) 459-5786
Indiana State Police: (800) 382-7537
Carroll County Sheriff: (765) 564-2413

On February 13, 2017, Liberty German, age 14, and Abigail Williams, age 13, were hiking on the Delphi Historic Trail near the Monon High Bridge just east of Delphi in Carroll County, Indiana. Liberty and Abigail were reported missing to police after their parents were unable to locate them at the pick-up location. Volunteers subsequently discovered the girls' bodies in the woods east of Delphi in Carroll County, Indiana, on February 14, 2017.

The person depicted in the composite sketch is described as a White male between 5'6" and 5'10", weighing 180 to 220 pounds, with reddish-brown hair. His eye color is unknown. The suspect is believed to be between 18 and 40 years old but may appear younger.

AUDIO   VIDEO

Abigail "Abby" Williams   Liberty "Libby" German

A detailed wanted poster, featuring both the updated sketch of the subject and the infamous photo of the "man on the bridge."

Anna updated Abby's Facebook profile photo on the anniversary of her death.

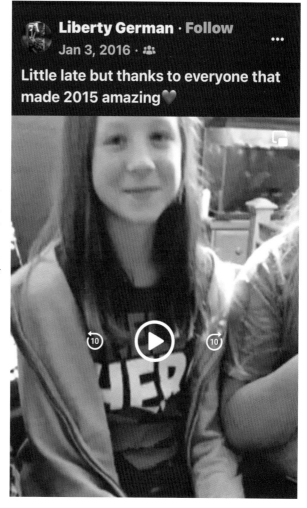

Libby was an avid social media user and frequently uploaded posts and pictures showcasing her love for her friends and family. In this roundup of 2015, she highlights her best friend, Abby (pictured), as one of the people who made her year "amazing."

Shine the brightest on the worst days ☀

Libby also posted a lot of selfies featuring positive, uplifting quotes, which she loved to share with online friends.

Susan talks on stage with Sergeant Kim Riley, Mike Patty, Kelsi German, and Diane and Eric Erskin at CrimeCon 2019 in New Orleans, Louisiana.

Paul Holes joins Libby's family for a panel at CrimeCon 2022 in Las Vegas, Nevada.

A family picture of Susan's cousin, Kathleen Keefe (far right, in blue), with her younger sisters and brother.

Dead woman is daughter of official

NEW BRUNSWICK (AP) — Police investigating the murder of a 27-year-old woman, identified as the daughter of the city's housing chief, yesterday were canvassing the neighborhood where the nude body was found under a woodpile.

Kathleen Keefe was strangled to death about two days before her body was found Thursday in the back yard of a heavy machine equipment business, said Thomas Kapsak, second assistant Middlesex County prosecutor.

Kapsak said there are no suspects and that the motive of the slaying was not known.

Kapsak would not say whether Ms. Keefe was sexually assaulted before her death or elaborate on the nature of her injuries.

He said a friend last saw Ms. Keefe Monday night in a city restaurant. Kapsak said investigators were trying to identify the person who was with Ms. Keefe in the restaurant. Detectives were also questioning people in bars and nightclubs where she might have gone after the restaurant.

Police have also talked to Ms. Keefe's two roommates, but authorities said they were not considered suspects.

Ms. Keefe was the eldest child of Richard Keefe, executive director of the city's Housing and Urban Development Authority.

Kapsak said more than 10 investigators from the New Brunswick police and the prosecutor's office have been assigned to the case.

Asked whether the slaying was being given special attention because of Keefe's position, Kapsak said that "it's getting the same treatment as any murder," adding that "when we have to fan out throughout a city, we need a lot of manpower."

Police identified the body through fingerprints on file at police headquarters, but authorities would not reveal the nature of Ms. Keefe's police record. Kapsak said he didn't believe it had anything to do with the slaying.

Ms. Keefe had worked as a waitress, but was not employed at the time of her death. Relatives said she had planned to return to college.

A local paper announces the death of Susan's cousin, Kathleen Keefe, in February 1986.

Susan and Anderson Cooper discuss current events on *AC360*. Susan delivered news headlines on the show for five years.

Susan hosts a live show with a panel of experts in which they discuss the latest developments in the case. From left to right, clockwise: Criminal defense attorney Joey Jackson, criminologist Dr. Casey Jordan, former FBI special agent and CNN law enforcement analyst Steve Moore, HLN investigative producers Barbara MacDonald and Andrew Iden, HLN contributor and attorney Jean Casarez, and retired cold case investigator Paul Holes.

RICHARD ALLEN ARRESTED FOR MURDER OF ABBY & LIBBY

HLN

Paul Holes, a retired cold case investigator and the author of *Unmasked*, offers his take on the double homicides in Delphi.

VERY SCARY PEOPLE

TONIGHT 9P ET/PT

THE CO-ED KILLER: ALMOST TOO DISTURBING TO TELL

Dr. Ann Wolbert Burgess, Boston College professor and author of *A Killer by Design*, is a pioneer in the field of criminal profiling, with key insights into potential behavioral and motivational indicators for perpetrators based on her decades of research.

Mourners still leave flowers and notes for the girls along the Monon High Bridge Trail.

"*Ohana* means family. *Family* means no one gets left behind or forgotten."
—*Lilo & Stitch*

Accompanied on either side by her loving grandparents, Kelsi German Siebert looks absolutely radiant on her wedding day.

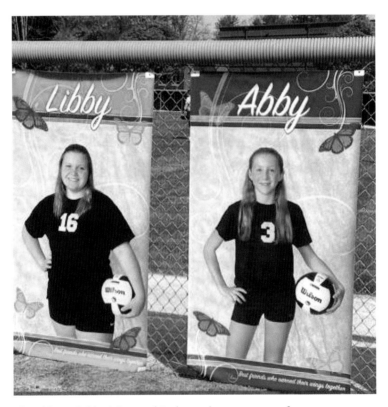

The Abby & Libby Memorial Park now hosts an array of events year-round, including sports tournaments, outdoor concerts, fundraisers, and so much more. The park features official portraits taken during Libby and Abby's final volleyball season (2016–2017), hanging proudly on the fence around the baseball diamonds.

"Oh, that's Paul Holes," she said. "He was the investigator that tracked down the Golden State Killer."

Wow. Paul Holes was a legend in the true-crime community. He'd worked at the Contra Costa County Sheriff's Office for decades, solving some of the toughest cold cases out there. After the Golden State Killer had committed a series of heinous murders, rapes, and burglaries across California in the 1970s and 1980s, it seemed that his identity might never be unveiled, until Holes and his team tracked down Joseph James DeAngelo Jr. and arrested him in April 2018.[1]

DeAngelo had terrorized those communities for *decades*. Would the search for Abby and Libby's killer take that long? Would we ever find the monster who'd done this?

Later on, ahead of entering the ballroom, I met up with my panelists in the lobby.

"Kelsi, would you mind reading this onstage?" I asked, handing her a copy of a tweet she'd written that I found particularly moving. I'd increased the font size and used the lamination paper I'd gotten at FedEx a few days before.

"Did you laminate this?" she asked, her lips curling up into a smile.

"I did," I said sheepishly. "I thought it would be easier to read."

We both let out a laugh.

"Sure, I'll read it," she said.

But in that moment, I had second thoughts. I didn't want to force it, plus I wasn't sure whether she was comfortable reading such a heartfelt personal note to her sister with hundreds of people watching. I gave her an out.

"How about this, Kelsi: I'll hold on to it. If it's too difficult, just shake your head, and I'll read it. If it's OK, put your hand out, and I'll pass it to you."

"OK," she said and nodded. "Sounds good."

I glanced again at my notes, the pictures of Abby and Libby, and the laminated tweet and headed toward the ballroom.

After passing crime scene displays and life-size cutouts of *Dateline* stars like Keith Morrison, Josh Mankiewicz, and Natalie Morales, I was relieved to spot my friends and colleagues waiting for me: criminal defense attorney Joey Jackson was there, along with fellow news anchor Mike Galanos. I have worked with them for years, and I'm not exaggerating—they are two of the nicest and funniest human beings I have ever met. We have been on set together for hours at a time; we've spent days sitting next to one another, sharing information and reporting during multiple trials and news conferences. Names from the past whirl through my head: Casey Anthony, Jodi Arias, Scott Peterson, Chris Watts—the list goes on. I've always felt so lucky to have Joey and Mike next to me on set. They're true professionals, and more importantly, they've become close friends. People I trust. It's not easy hearing and reporting, sometimes over and over again, the gruesome details of what happened to innocent victims. We share an unspoken bond.

I slowly made my way through the growing crowd, hoping to reach Galanos first.

"Hey, Tobe," he teased.

I laughed. He'd taken to calling me Tobe, as in Tobe Leazenby, the Carroll County sheriff. Mike had participated with me on most of the Delphi specials and knew that Tobe Leazenby was the sheriff and a good guy. I guess he just liked saying his name. Galanos had a real sense of humor. We'd been working together for fifteen years. I'd spent more time with him than with most of my family members. During that time, we had been through a lot. Divorce, deaths of loved ones, the excitement of new babies. And through it all, work—the CNN Center—had always been my safe space. The building, the cameras, the people—they all served as a shield. They made me feel protected. Like I belonged.

"I'm so nervous, Mike," I said. "Will you come onstage with me . . . please? I can't do it alone."

"Yes, you can," he said, "and I would, but I can't. I have to leave. You'll be *great*."

I wasn't convinced.

"Hi, Joey!" I said and waved over to my friend as a small crowd gathered around him.

Based on their excitement, you would have thought Elvis had entered the building. He definitely had fans at CrimeCon, and I understood why. Joey Jackson was the only criminal defense attorney I'd ever met with such a consistent, calm demeanor. He was also smart, considerate, and kind. Considering his line of work, that, to me, seemed close to impossible. I'd asked him several times how he did it and why he never seemed rattled or like he was in a bad mood.

"Susan, I'm grateful," he always said.

He had a wonderful wife and two sons. Maybe that was the answer. Did seeing, hearing about, and reporting on tragic events highlight not only what you could lose but what you shouldn't take for granted?

"Hey, Susan, time is ticking," Galanos said, nudging me. "Are you ready?"

OK, I was good. Familiar faces, inside jokes. I was comfortable again. There was a huge crowd now in the hallways and ballrooms—crime survivors, advocates, and fans gathered in one location, finding their way to specific panels onstage.

Mike had his own set in the hallway: two chairs and lighting, plus a backdrop and a sign that read "*True Crime Live* on Location." I sat down in one of the chairs and put my mic on. I quickly glanced at the two cameras and exhaled. This was the most comfortable I'd felt all day. This was where I was most at ease, sharing other people's stories. A way to deflect and protect my own.

Sitting next to me was Abby's grandmother Diane. Together we watched the setup piece, a quick recap of the case. Diane turned to me and said, "He's a gem," speaking of Superintendent Doug Carter.

"Stand by," I heard from a producer, and before I knew it, I was asking Diane about what it was like working with the investigators to solve this case.

"Susan, we know firsthand," Diane said. "We talk to these men and women day after day, month after month. We see pictures of our girls on their phones. They take it personally. They've spent countless hours working on the case. We have witnessed that from where we live; we have seen the manpower and hours and the time spent on the case."

Next, I wanted the viewer to know how she felt about the community that this conference encouraged.

"Diane, it's your second year at CrimeCon. What surprised you the most? I notice that people come up to you, and there is a booth honoring Abby and Libby and their life. They come up to you and share their story, in a club that they never asked to be part of—the most difficult club. What do they say to you?"

"Well, Susan, everyone has a story. And I don't know what the percentages are here at CrimeCon. But I would say it has to be very high, based on what we have witnessed. Many people are here for their own journey, to find their own peace, to make peace with a crime that's affected their own family. Whether it's their mother, their sister, their brother, their cousin, and, you know, it's awkward sometimes, when you've been a victim of this crime, to talk to someone else, but they know they can talk to us, and if they give us any inkling at all that they've been a victim of a crime, we reach right out to them."

"Because there is this kind of unspoken connection?" I asked.

"Yes," Diane continued, "an unspoken connection, that you understand when I'm looking at this person, I don't need to say, 'I am so sorry for your loss.' They already *know* that. We can say, 'We feel your pain,' because we have—we share that."

I could feel the sincerity in every syllable. What had inspired me the most about Abby's and Libby's families was their incredible, limitless capacity for empathy and compassion. I had no doubt people walked right up to them and felt comfortable enough to share their own stories, to confide about their own trauma. And despite enduring the most difficult kind of loss imaginable, these families embraced them with open arms, selflessly and wholeheartedly, eager to help ease their suffering in any way they could.

They'd done the same thing for me. Earlier that morning, I'd had a chance to sit down with Eric and Diane for a few minutes at the girls' booth. Diane had asked me whether I knew anyone who had been murdered. Instantly, I thought about Kathy.

It was 1986. I remember being in my kitchen, in the hallway, actually, near the doorway and just out of sight of my dad, who was on the phone in the kitchen. Privacy was rare back in those days, and in our house, this shared yellow phone with gray push buttons sat smack-dab in the middle of the wall in the busiest room. My sister, Lynn, and I had been playing hide-and-seek, and I'd just scrambled over to the kitchen when I heard my dad's voice break on the phone. It sounded so different from how he normally sounded; I completely forgot about the game. I then spotted my sister, who came flying around the corner, but before she could yell "You're it!" or "Found you!" I gave her the shush hand motion and then pointed to the kitchen.

We both listened closely.

"They found her body? Where? Oh no."

We heard my mom coming down the stairs.

"Eileen?" my dad called out and waited for her to walk into the room.

My sister and I were now both in the dining room, under the table. It was dark—no one could see us.

"Eileen, they found Kathy's body."

Lynn and I looked at each other. We heard more whispers before my dad started dialing another number.

"Let's go," I whispered, and we ran upstairs.

Just as we reached Lynn's room, the phone rang. We'd just received our own private line that year.

It was our friend Suzanne, who was three years older than us.

"Did you guys hear about Kathy?"

Suzanne was talking about Kathy Keefe, our cousin, whose lifeless body had just been discovered a few miles from our home. We were distant cousins, separated more by age than by location. The Keefes were a large, loving family. Suzanne's older sisters were good friends with Kathy and her siblings, so Suzanne was always telling us about how cool and fun the family was, as well as what kind of music they were listening to (mostly Stevie Nicks). Later, she would also be the one to tell us when someone had been arrested and charged with Kathy's murder.

No one in my family talked about it after that night. I'm not even sure my parents knew what we'd heard, or that we'd heard. We never asked them. That was all I understood until I stumbled on a newspaper article about her murder many years later, after I'd already started reporting on the Delphi case. Kathy had been only twenty-seven years old when she was killed. I couldn't imagine what her family had gone through. I have learned that time does not heal all wounds.

After I shared that story with Diane, she said gently, "Susan, you are part of the club."

"Well, I really never knew Kathy," I replied. "I was eleven; she was twenty-seven."

"You don't have to compare your experience or rate your pain," she said. "You saw and heard about what a senseless crime can do . . . and once you're in, you can help others heal."

I wondered whether that was part of the reason I was drawn to these families. Sometimes it can seem like the victims' families and loved ones come secondary to the crime headline, which focuses more on the person who committed the crime than the lives that person destroyed.

Before attending CrimeCon or even knowing much about it, I was concerned about what kind of approach the event might take. But, while there, I quickly discovered that CrimeCon puts the families *first*. Kevin Balfe, the conference's founder and producer, was clearly proud of the community this event was able to build.

"They're [the families] thrust into this thing involuntarily," he said. "Then they have the courage and strength and conviction to get up on a stage in front of thousands of people at our event and tell their story. It's incredible to see."

Balfe had gotten close to many of these families over the years, like Abby's and Libby's, who attended the first-ever CrimeCon. Coincidentally, the inaugural event was held in nearby Indianapolis just a few months after the girls were murdered.

"There's always been this sort of kinship that our responsibility, if you will, is to make sure that we support them however we can in keeping the case alive," Balfe explained. "And then too, just getting to know them as people, as you know. They're so phenomenal, and I cry. Every year, I see Becky, I cry, hug her. And say, 'First of all, I never want to see you again, because if you're here, that probably means we don't have a resolution, but I can't wait for the moment where you guys get to experience what the Golden State families experienced.' Susan, in that room, the standing ovation and the hugs are just insane. That's always been my hope for Delphi. I think now we're one step closer and we'll see, but that's my dream—that they get to experience that."

Balfe wasn't the only one grateful for the community at CrimeCon.

"CrimeCon is the place where my advocacy started," Kelsi said. "I don't know if I would be here today if I didn't go that first year in Indiana. That's where I created my support system."

I MADE MY WAY TO THE SIDE OF THE STAGE, SURROUNDED BY ABBY'S AND LIBBY'S FAMILIES. I FELT an immediate sense of peace. This wasn't really about me. It never was. It was about the families and telling their stories. I thought of Kathy and her family as I looked out at the crowd.

Abby's grandmother Diane was sitting to my right, next to her husband, Eric, and Sergeant Kim Riley. She told the audience she'd seen this same phenomenon earlier that morning at the table dedicated to Abby and Libby.

"Susan, it's such a raw situation when you come here," Diane said, looking my way before turning to speak directly to the crowd. "We want to hear *your* stories too—you are not alone. You are here for us, but we want to be here for you too."

Our conversation with the panel that day moved me in many ways. We talked about love and loss, grief and hope. But the thing that really stood out to me the most was the importance of building a community—a safe place where you could be truly vulnerable, share your deepest feelings, and know unequivocally that you would be supported, no matter *what* you were going through.

9

Armchair Detectives

"We *need* your help."

"We are *one* tip away."

"Only *you* can help us solve this crime."

"No matter how small or insignificant it may seem, call us. Send us an email. With your help, *we might finally be able to solve the case.*"

As time dragged on seemingly without any significant updates, law enforcement continued to call for assistance from the public in solving the murders of Libby and Abby. The Indiana State Police advised citizens to keep an eye out for suspicious behavior.

Had the habits of those around them changed before or after the crimes? Thanks to audio and visuals captured by Libby, investigators also asked the public to look for anyone who walked like the suspect, who sounded like the suspect.

As Carroll County prosecutor Nick McLeland reiterated on February 13, 2019, two years had passed, and they still needed help.

"Information is our main weapon," he said to the cameras. "This could be the missing piece that we are waiting on."

But what happens when the ask for a tip from law enforcement and family members turns into or perpetuates the public's desire to solve the crime, no matter the cost?

Can that desire lead to an online witch hunt?

The short answer is yes.

After McLeland's renewed call to action, tips started pouring in again from not just the local community but also the national true-crime community. But the desperation for closure in this case had also motivated some users online to take it one step further—by posting images of the police sketch right next to a person they thought resembled the suspect. When pictures are placed side by side, it's easy to speculate. To stare. To *assume*.

Sergeant Kim Riley made it clear this was not helping—that it in fact had the potential to cause considerable damage in its wake.

"We want to discourage this side-by-side comparison," Riley said. "It's problematic on different levels, to the individual and to the investigation."

Soon, Abby's and Libby's high school friends and classmates were being persecuted online for resembling the suspect in the sketch. The sheriff posted a message on Facebook begging the public to cease and desist.

"Please stop posting side-by-side pictures of people you think did this. You are ruining innocent people's lives." He challenged people to put themselves in the shoes of those being persecuted, to think before posting something online that could end up being quite harmful. "Before posting a side-by-side, imagine that it is *your* son, brother, or father."

———

SOMEONE WHO UNDERSTANDS WHAT CAN HAPPEN WHEN SOMEONE IS UNLAWFULLY IMPLICATED IN A crime is a woman by the name of Deanna Thompson, who was featured in the Emmy Award–winning documentary *Don't F**k with Cats*.

One of the most publicly recognized citizen detectives today, Deanna never intended to become famous. A self-proclaimed computer nerd who'd held the same job for close to thirty years, she was comfortable in her life as a data analyst for a large casino in Las Vegas. Then, in 2010, she stumbled across a sickening online video that showed a person killing cats, recording these crimes. She was determined to bring this person to justice, which eventually led her to a Facebook group and a fellow armchair detective named John Green. She said she was drawn to Green because he was "sticking to the facts." They were eventually able to track down the person responsible, a Canadian escort and porn actor named Luka Magnotta, but along the way, Deanna often wondered whether it was worth it.[1]

In February 2023, I reached out to Deanna and asked her about how she'd first gotten involved in this online investigation. She said she'd been horrified upon first seeing the video; not only was it inhumane and malicious, but it also broke "rule zero" of the internet—a set of unofficial rules that many in the online community generally accepted.

"If you google 'rules of the internet,' you'll find all the 4Chan rules, and there's like a-hundred-and-something rules," Deanna began. "Well, rule one is 'You don't talk about 4Chan,' right? That's rule one [and rule two] . . . Then rule three is 'We are anonymous.' Rule four is 'We are legion.' Rule five is 'We do not forgive, we do not forget,' and it just keeps going. [But] rule *zero* is 'Don't fuck with cats.'"

However, in the hunt to track down Magnotta, Deanna found herself investigating possible leads alongside thousands of other internet users and amateur sleuths. At its best, web sleuthing could help an active investigation, if the citizens were doing their due diligence when it came to research and open-source intelligence.

"It's using open-source intelligence tools, like software, to analyze digital forensics—that's what we do," she revealed. "Web sleuthing is just reading social media and putting the pieces of a puzzle together, things like that. So we're not drawing conclusions when we do this work. We're not drawing conclusions based on social media posts. We are taking actual evidence and coming up with a suspect and getting that over to law enforcement. We're not saying, 'Well, because he posted this on this day, he did it.' We're not doing that."

Much like an actual police investigation, there was always room for human error in web sleuthing, and this became even more problematic in large online communities that tended to become echo chambers, feeding and reinforcing false narratives.

"When you're surrounding yourself with people who only agree with you, confirmation bias can really get away from you. That's one of the reasons John Green and I work so well together. It's because we are *so* different, and we very rarely agree on anything. We're very good friends, and we both respect each other a lot, but I'll present him with a piece of evidence, and I'll be like, 'I think this because of this piece of evidence.' And he has no problem telling me, 'Deanna, that evidence is flawed, and this is why it's flawed.' Or vice versa—I will tell him the same thing. But when you get people on YouTube, who are your fans, they may respond with 'Yes, queen' and 'You're right' and 'You're always spot on.' Then you're just getting fed that *all* the evidence you're presenting is factual, when in reality, people are too afraid, until you say, 'Hey, listen, be for fucking real right now.'"

One of the primary factors in Deanna's decision to work with John in the first place was that he wasn't willing to implicate innocent people for the sake of fulfilling a narrative or feeding his own ego.

"We didn't know each other from Adam, but he and I were the only ones, out of fifteen thousand people in this group, saying, 'No, wait a minute . . . that can't be this person,' or 'Why are you posting random profiles?' So he messaged me, and he was like, 'Hey, listen, you and I seem to be the only ones really questioning things here. Let's do our own thing.' And we sort of branched off and did our own thing. If you are listening to these people who make up lies, you are just being fed garbage."

It wasn't all just egos and human error either; some content creators in particular were actively looking to profit off the public outrage.

"This is a topic I'm super passionate about," Deanna said, "because we live in an age where digital content creators are getting paid by these platforms to create content. And people *just make shit up.*"

"I know—it's true," I said. "I've seen it."

When comparing the online hunt for Luka Magnotta with the one for the Delphi killer, Deanna saw a lot of parallels, particularly in terms of the way some content creators approached the whole undertaking. It was as if the entertainment value was prioritized over the integrity of the investigation itself. Sure, posting a side-by-side picture of a Delphi resident and the police sketch might increase your video's profits and popularity, but what if it completely misled the public, damning an innocent person in the process? What if it detracted attention and resources from finding the actual person responsible for the crimes? It wasn't just that these content creators were peddling misinformation—it was that they could actively harm an ongoing criminal investigation. And it *infuriated* Deanna that these irresponsible creators often didn't seem to consider those most affected by the actual crime: the victims' loved ones.

"[The creators] don't care that the Delphi families are actively on social media. They don't care about that," Deanna said. "They care that they get three million views and $600 for that video . . .

"It's really messed up. It's *really* messed up. But I really foresee a shift happening with the true-crime space, and I think Kelsi [German] has been instrumental in that, honestly, because she is very public with her criticism of some of these people, which I respect the hell out of her for that. Not only is she dealing with this tremendous grief; now she's dealing with the public."

Fortunately, there were some people—including content creators—who genuinely wanted to help solve these cases and assisted through evidence and research. I thought of the dedicated true-crime writer and blogger Michelle McNamara, who had been relentless in her dedication to cracking unsolved cases and tracking down criminals, including the notorious Golden State Killer.[2] Unfortunately, McNamara didn't live to see the Golden State Killer prosecuted or behind bars; at the age of forty-six, she died in her sleep—nearly two and a half years before Joseph James DeAngelo Jr. was arrested. I'd recently watched a documentary on HBO called *I'll Be Gone in the Dark*, based on McNamara's book of the same name, which focused on how McNamara's meticulous and obsessive investigation brought renewed interest to the case but also slowly consumed her life.[3] In some ways, Deanna reminded me of Michelle—and I told her so.

"That is *such* a compliment. I'm not comparing myself—she was just amazing—but thank you." Deanna beamed. "So listen to me when I tell you that I am obsessed with Michelle McNamara. I'm not kidding . . . I was following her blog for a long time, and while I was investigating Luka, she was, parallelly, investigating the Golden State Killer, and I was following her the whole time. She was a huge inspiration to me, and so when she passed, I felt a personal loss."

It was a life-changing moment when Deanna heard that Michelle McNamara knew who she was, and not just that—she *respected* her.

"I have not been the same since . . . I cried, and I cried, and I cried because I so respected *her*."

"She was so in it," I said, "and for every right reason there is. But I feel like it had an effect on her, obviously, mentally. Did you feel that way during this?"

"Yes," Deanna said and nodded. "And in fact, when she died, I had to take a deep look at myself, at what I was doing, because I was going down the same path. It affected me tremendously, and that's why when I met Paul Holes [who'd worked with Michelle in the past], I was like, 'So listen, I'm not comparing myself to Michelle McNamara, but we were on the same trajectory.'" Paul got to know Michelle through her writing and eventually ended up working with her on the Golden State Killer case. "We'd go back and forth and bond over our suspects as they would get eliminated. We both really became really invested. She was case-centered. She became an investigator in this series."[4]

Deanna continued, "I was obsessed. She was obsessed. I was self-medicating. She was self-medicating. Do you know what I mean?"

I did.

"We were on the same trajectory," Deanna repeated, "and when she died, I literally had to change my life, and when the book came out, of course, I read it immediately. And of course, when the show came out, I was all in—I was all in it. I thought it was so victim-centered that it was inspiring. In fact, I met a couple of the women at CrimeCon who were victims of [DeAngelo], and they were so gracious. And I was just so impressed with that documentary, so impressed with that documentary, and the work that they did."

Hearing Deanna confess that she had to walk away from the investigation when she realized the impact it was having on her mental health reminded me of some of my own struggles.

"Deanna, I saw in the documentary that you were struggling [too], at one point," I mused, "and you said you had to kind of step away. And at times, when I would get back from Delphi, and I talked to my mom, she'd ask me, 'Can't you tell your boss that you can't report on any murders anymore?' She noticed a difference in me. But I never admitted this.

"'Mom, it's what I do,' I would always say. But I understood her concern. This story was different. I was almost *too* involved, *too* close, to the point where I was crying, randomly and often."

Deanna understood completely.

Before I left, I wanted to get her take on a quote I'd read aloud back at CrimeCon.

"These are Becky, Libby's grandmother's, words . . . 'The best revenge is none. Heal more, move on. Don't become like those who hurt you.' I think because her granddaughter was brutally murdered, she has to do what it takes to be there for her grandchildren, her family. But it wouldn't be hard to go down that dark hole . . ."

"Wow." Deanna took a deep breath. "That hit home especially from my perspective. Luka once said to me a Nietzsche quote; it's 'Battle not with monsters, lest ye become a monster, and if you gaze into the abyss, the abyss gazes also into you.' And that is exactly what Libby's grandmother is saying, right? Because if you are focused on revenge, and you're focused on getting back at somebody, you're going to become the monster you fight, right?"

"You're right," I said, blinking back tears.

"I was becoming the obsessed monster I was hunting," Deanna said. "But Libby's grandmother is absolutely right. She said it in a different way, but she's saying the exact same thing."

FROM THE START OF MY EXPERIENCE REPORTING ON DELPHI, I NOTICED HOW INVOLVED THE ONLINE community was in trying to solve the double murder. Web sleuths from across the country quickly began piecing together the facts and timeline of the crime, along with a potential suspect pool based mostly on local residents. Facebook and Reddit were especially popular, serving as open platforms for these large and diverse networks to take root and push the case in new directions.

In some ways, this was exactly what law enforcement had asked for: community involvement. However, this development quickly turned into a double-edged sword as anonymous commentators began looking for anyone and everyone to blame, even going so far as to start pointing fingers at family members.

In 2019, Kelsi felt she had to speak out to debunk the many rumors circulating around these innocent people who had been offered up to the internet as potential suspects: her own family. She agreed to an interview with a YouTuber named Gray Hughes, which was live streamed on the platform on August 19.[5] As I tuned in to the chat, I was simultaneously in awe of Kelsi and furious for her. With grace and poise far beyond her age, she defended the people she knew and loved against false statements and hurtful rumors for an hour and a half.

An hour and a half.

A then nineteen-year-old whose younger sister had been brutally murdered was now essentially forced to defend her family against the same web sleuths who proclaimed to want justice for Libby and Abby in the first place. The whole situation was absurd and hurtful.

Anna, Abby's mom, knows the accusations against the families are ludicrous, but they're painful nonetheless. "I've heard everything under the sun; it's aggravating and frustrating."

One of the rumors that continued to pop up on several platforms had to do with the timeline on February 13, 2017. "Ask me what I wore that day or what time I left the house or what time I specifically got the phone call, or who was with me, I couldn't tell you. It's not inconsistencies or changing the story any more than people said that there was a picture of Abby on the bridge wearing a sweater that I took a picture in by another bridge and that it was the same bridge, and it's not the same bridge, and it's not the same jacket, and at the end of the day it's a jacket and it had no bearing on anything. But people sure wanted to dwell." Anna, Becky, Mike, and Kelsi and their extended family were asked countless times to recall specifics of that day, over and over in the days, weeks, months, and years after Abby and Libby were murdered. "It's so in your mind of every moment of how you felt that day but don't ask me what time it was."[6]

Another sticking point on some of these sites for armchair detectives was just how much the families trusted and vocally backed local law enforcement. They were often quick to blame investigators for their inability to solve the case after several years, but the families had developed close bonds with many of these officers and felt confident that they were doing everything they possibly could.

"[The investigators] are very honest and forthcoming, super encouraging," Kelsi said. "I know they are going to get an arrest soon; they can't tell us everything, unfortunately, but to be honest, I don't really want to know everything."

After having met several of those same investigators, I could understand Kelsi's faith; it did seem like these officers were genuinely invested in solving the case. They were spending countless hours going through each and every tip that came in. Still, I sometimes wondered about the efficacy of their strategy when it came to releasing or not releasing certain information to the public, especially after enlisting the public's help to bring in those same tips and leads. The police were, and continued to be, especially tight-lipped about potential suspects, refusing to specify who *was* a person of interest and who *was not*. In the absence of definitive answers, some in the online community had apparently decided any name was fair game.

As with any modern technology, the sheer amount of information publicly available on the internet presents both a blessing and a curse. Today, just about anyone who is curious about an ongoing or even a closed investigation has the ability to access online an astounding amount of personal information, in regard to not just victims and their families but also law enforcement officers and theirs. They can also access court documents that only a few decades ago would've been virtually impossible for the public to get their hands on. There are also entire Facebook groups, subreddits, and online chat forums that focus on particular cases, providing both a dedicated hub for detailed information and an open space for questions, theories, and discussions among members.

Now, there are groups that have strict guidelines when it comes to discussing cases, especially open ones, and if you don't follow them, you are not allowed to weigh in and speak freely about them. The intentions behind a particular site or platform are usually clear from the home page. If the group is actively trying to help the investigation, the goal becomes finding the person who did this through the correct channels and then alerting law enforcement. There are others that are not nearly as rigorous, and it just seems like the users who frequent those sites simply do not care about the implications, in either the short term or the long term, of what they say and who they hurt in the process. In fact, in some cases, the more outrageous a theory sounds, the better.

When law enforcement realized the damage all this online speculation was doing, they threatened to take legal action. In July 2017, five months after the murders, Captain Dave Bursten issued a stark warning: "There has been a growing problem with 'armchair sleuthing' by people who have combed websites to find mug shots of random men who resemble the sketch; some post their dubious detective work online. A person that does that may open themselves up to some civil liability and is doing nothing to help the investigation. They will have to suffer the consequences of their own stupidity."

Despite the seriousness of his words, those who were determined to create their own online narrative did not seem the least bit deterred. And this wasn't the last time the police urged the public to stay out of the investigation—far from it. Several years after Captain Bursten's initial speech, Indiana State Police sergeant John Perrine pleaded with the public not to post falsehoods and rumors.

"When you have people who are trying to solve this case with unorthodox methods, it could not only be detrimental to innocent people, but it could harm the case as well," Perrine explained.

Nevertheless, the repeated warnings from law enforcement seemed to fall on deaf ears. The speculation, finger pointing, and blatant lies didn't slow down; in fact, the longer the case went unsolved, the more rampant these far-fetched theories and posts became.

Regardless of an individual's intentions, malicious or otherwise, there is a large margin of error when it comes to internet speculation. A remarkable characteristic of these online amateur sleuth collectives is just how quickly they can piece together a narrative that is simply not true, based on a carefully curated selection of so-called facts often devoid of any context. Within minutes, you can have a dozen people speculating about unknown details of a case. When it came to online communities dedicated to Delphi, you could scroll through the chats for hours and still not see all the different theories people had posted about why the girls had "really" gone to the bridge that day, why their murderer had been in such close proximity to them, or what the police had missed or still needed to discover in order to obtain a positive ID of the perpetrator.

When it came to the last topic, or really anything that had to do with law enforcement, some users became actively critical of officials' efforts—or, in their opinion, *lack* of effort—in bringing the murderer to justice. They were simultaneously releasing too much and not enough information. There was also a tidal wave of online criticism that flooded in after the initial sketch of the suspect was swapped out for a much younger-looking perpetrator. Libby's grandmother in particular grew weary of the callousness of some of these users, who flung wild theories and accusations without a second thought. It was like death by a thousand paper cuts.

Though I'd had years of experience as a reporter by the time the Delphi murders crossed my radar, this case ushered in my first real taste of my name being personally connected to misinformation—in other words, a blatant lie.

In February 2021, Sheriff Tobe Leazenby agreed to take questions about the case from readers of the local paper, the *Carroll County Comet*. The Q&A was then distilled into a two-part series of articles.

One reader wrote in, "You stated in last week's article that additional audio recording on Libby's cell phone would not be released, but it has been stated by the HLN interviewer, Sharon [*sic*] Hendricks, to Anna Garcia on the *True Crime Daily* podcast on YouTube that in fact, an additional two minutes of recording was shared with the family. How can you justify this?"

Leazenby gently but firmly refused to answer this, responding, "This question, being evidentiary in nature, will not be answered."

Still, the questioner persisted, trying a new route: "It was also stated by the HLN interviewer in the same program that you hosted the HLN crew to a cookout at your house when they were in the area shooting for the program. And since then, the HLN interviewer has defended your actions in public when there was criticism. Was this playing politics on your part? Were you trying to sway the perception of the investigation by doing this?"

Leazenby immediately shut this theory down, answering that these allegations were "totally false" as "this event did not occur."

After reading all this, my jaw dropped. Not only had they gotten my name wrong, but there had never *ever* been anything close to a "cookout" at Leazenby's house. I'd also never said the phone recording was two minutes long. Who was making up all these lies? And *why*?

I immediately sent a text over to Tobe, voicing my concerns and my frustration that someone had gotten everything so mixed up. He texted back right away.

"No worries regarding that improper reporting," he replied. "In fact, I chuckled because I knew the obvious truth! Plus, I haven't had or received any blowback from it. As has been the case several times, I simply brush it off and move forward."

I knew he was right, but the whole situation still irked me. The questions may not have been intentionally false, but the idea that someone was going around actively peddling misinformation was bothersome, to say the least. If they were unsure about the facts, they should've just listened to the podcast again! When in doubt, *check the source.*

As irritated as I was, I knew it was just a minuscule taste of the falsehoods the families had to deal with on a constant basis.

I also started getting criticism from web sleuths and their fans online for being "too close" to the families. One such user even went so far as to write, "Susan Hendricks seems like a very nice lady, BUT her kissing butt with the family is a real turn off for me. Sorry if I'm out of line but this has always bothered me."

At this, I couldn't help but sigh. Everyone is entitled to their own opinion, I guess.

But here's the thing: I will *never* apologize for this. When family members are interviewed, they have to relive the worst moments of their lives over and over again. To make accusatory remarks during their darkest days is unconscionable. It's unfortunate I have to reiterate the obvious, but these are *real people.* With *real feelings.*

If that means I'm "kissing butt"—well, I guess I can live with that.

10

Back to the Beginning

Superintendent Carter was in a difficult position. As much as he wanted to share information with the public about how the investigation was going, he refused to engage in any sort of speculation or discuss what his private thoughts were. He also refused to convey specific details he knew about the crime that many thought could potentially be the key to putting the perpetrator behind bars.

"We can't talk about what we think. Everybody else can. Or what they believe happened. We can't," Carter said. "There has been some criticism of me, and I'm willing to take that. I can't explain all the things that I know. He has no idea what we know, but one day he will."

Carter also stressed that he would *never* let the case go cold.

"As the tips continue to come in, we will continue to manage those tips, and when we're all done, we're going to start all over because that piece of the puzzle is in the pile someplace."

Though I understood his reasoning, as the years went on, this stance became increasingly frustrating times, and the superintendent knew and understood that. Libby's and Abby's families trusted law enforcement's efforts, but they were also free to call, ask questions, and even make suggestions to investigators. Which Kelsi often did.

Every year at CrimeCon, the families and I listened to experts discussing the latest and greatest technological advancements in the world of forensic genealogy. Becky wanted to be sure that investigators were utilizing every single tool available to help them track down the killer. She also wanted to be sure that they were reaching out to people who could help them use these tools more efficiently, like genetic genealogist and DNA investigative expert CeCe Moore and retired cold case investigator Paul Holes, who had effectively used this new technology to help identify the Golden State Killer.

"I've asked them, 'Why haven't you contacted CeCe Moore?' I know that Paul Holes and Holeman ended up exchanging cards at the first CrimeCon," Becky said. "On the outside, we don't see who they're bringing in."[1]

Becky also said that the families had wondered at times if the police should release more information to the public, like the extended clip of the video recorded on Libby's phone.

"Well, they gave us that extra word," Becky admitted, referring to the word *guys* that we heard on the audio from the most recent press conference. "I don't know their reasoning—why they don't release more. I wish there was more for the public. I have to trust that. But in the end, those officers are the ones that are going to have to make that case. They are the ones that are going to have to make sure this guy doesn't walk for any reason."

Carter knew it was difficult for the families to sustain this level of trust over a long period of time.

"There's things he wants to know that we haven't told him," Carter said, speaking about Mike. "Can you imagine? I can't. He's looking at a man that knows the answer to a question he's asking about the death of a grandchild. And I won't tell him."[2]

He also understood that he was asking *a lot* of his fellow officers, especially considering the constant criticism they were receiving from both their own community in Delphi and the online community at large. Carter said that he was willing to take the backlash but that the officers working day and night to solve this heinous crime should be off-limits.

"It's easy to be your own detective and criticize the actual ones." He sighed.

Throughout the investigation, it was apparent that law enforcement had been focusing on a few potential "persons of interest," but they refused to use that term. In fact, Sheriff Leazenby would speak only in generalities. He would always say they were "looking into" someone, never using the term *suspect* or elaborating on the extent of what "looking into" really meant.

Early on, the sheriff said they had categories of people to look into and would then narrow down that number as they combed through the evidence.

One such person they'd looked into was Ron Logan, the owner of the property where the girls' bodies had been discovered. I often thought about what he said to me during our interview when the case first broke.

"Nothing like this has ever happened in Delphi," he said, obviously shaken. "It could have been my boys."

However, unbeknownst to me and the rest of the public, at the time of this initial interview, Logan was someone investigators were actively looking into. Then again, the police were interviewing anyone who even came close to resembling that initial sketch; they'd even questioned the sheriff himself.

I'd run into Ron Logan a second time in front of his house, fourteen months after our initial conversation. My producer, Barbara, and I were walking back from the bridge on the trail when he appeared in front of us.

"They ruined my life," he said.

"Who did?"

"The police put me away, and someone stole the furniture in my house."

Ron Logan sounded very different now than he had almost two years before, after the bodies of Abby and Libby were found on his property. At that time, he'd been open and friendly. He seemed angry now, beaten down.

"I'm sorry that happened," I replied, unsure of what else to say.

I then asked Logan if he lived alone. He told me that his son had "got out of here years ago."

It was freezing that afternoon, and the temperature kept dropping. I felt my toes going numb.

"Let's go," I heard Barbara say.

We said our goodbyes to Logan and hurried to the car.

It was then I started to do some more digging into Logan's past. Back in 2017—actually, not that long after our first interview—Logan had been sentenced to almost four years in prison on illegal driving charges. Following an earlier drunk driving arrest back in 2014, his license had been suspended, and he'd been told not to drink alcoholic beverages; three years later, he pleaded guilty to violating this same probation by getting behind the wheel on the day the girls went missing *and* consuming alcohol just two weeks later. He was sentenced to four years in prison.[3]

At his sentencing, Logan was asked whether he wanted to address the court. Surprising even his own attorney, Logan turned to Carroll County superior court judge Kurtis Fouts and uttered, "Maybe in the future no one else will be murdered in my backyard," before he was led out of the room in handcuffs.[4]

A friend of his later told a local paper, "I think he was very stressed over that and upset," referring to the initial discovery of the girls.[5] Logan seemed to think he was really being persecuted for his connection to the girls, and not just violating this earlier probation. Though Logan was released after only nine months of incarceration in 2018 and was ordered to serve out the remainder of his sentence at his home in Delphi.[6]

On January 24, 2022, Ron Logan died at the age of seventy-seven, reportedly because of complications from COVID-19.[7]

Meanwhile, the investigation continued, and discussions and accusations piled up in online chat rooms. Anytime a person was arrested anywhere close to Delphi and even passingly resembled the sketch of the suspect, a whole slew of new posts would surface. Logan had managed to avoid much of this scrutiny, until a shocking revelation came out nearly four months after his death.

On May 17, 2022, a true-crime podcast called *The Murder Sheet* managed to obtain a nine-page request from the FBI for a search warrant that revealed new details about the murders.[8] Among these bombshell revelations, it was disclosed that the girls were "found dead with wounds caused by a [redacted] weapon" and that "a large amount of blood was lost by the victims at the crime scene," though the affidavit also mentioned that the girls "had no visible signs of a struggle or a fight."[9] Furthermore, "it was also discovered that the [redacted] of one of the victims was missing from the crime scene while the rest of their clothing was recovered. It also appeared the girls' bodies were moved and staged." The FBI suspected that the perpetrator may have taken a "souvenir" to "memorialize the crime scene"—possibly this missing piece of clothing; unintentionally, in its place, "unknown fibers and unidentified hairs which may later be used for comparison of similar fibers or hairs" had been left at the crime scene, both critical pieces of evidence that could eventually be used to help identify the killer.

Before releasing the document, podcast hosts Áine Cain and Kevin Greenlee said they had contacted investigators in Delphi and redacted part of the document that could later hinder the investigation. Even so, the unredacted content was more than enough to drum up a new wave of suspicion regarding Logan's possible involvement in the girls' murders.[10]

In response, Superintendent Doug Carter and the FBI quickly released statements responding to the newly leaked document, which had originally been filed back in 2017.

"I would like to remind the public that this is an active and ongoing investigation," Carter said, "and we will do everything we can to protect its integrity and to not try it in the court of public opinion. We cannot publicly convict someone based on a single document which was not released by investigators. Our profession will not allow us to speak on what we think, but to always speak about what we know. This is especially important with the heinous murders of Abby and Libby. We must continue to be mindful of their surviving family members and the entire Carroll County community who are affected by this investigation."[11]

Ignoring the superintendent's caution, self-proclaimed online detectives started firing off theory after theory, in rapid succession, claiming they *knew* Ron Logan was "bridge guy." Provocative headlines ran rampant: "Ronald Logan Was the Man on the Bridge!" "Delphi: Let's Talk About Ron Logan!" "Bridge Guy Revealed." "Ron Logan Will Prove to Be Bridge Guy."

The leaked document didn't prove that Ron was the man responsible for the crimes, but it did show that on March 6, 2017, less than a month into the investigation, law enforcement had searched Ron Logan's property "as a result of a probation violation." And though "the search was limited to the discovery of firearms and included only his main residence," what investigators had discovered was enough for the FBI to justify submitting a probable cause affidavit to the Carroll County Circuit Court— and enough for a judge to sign off on the search.

Logan had been officially identified as a person of interest. And it wasn't just because the girls had been discovered on his property, approximately fourteen hundred feet from his personal residence.

The affidavit mentioned that though Logan was seventy-seven years old, his "physical build [was] consistent with the male suspect videoed by [Liberty German] on the Monon High Bridge Trail." He also "[appeared] to be in good physical condition," and his voice was "not inconsistent with the person in the video."[12]

Logan's tendency toward violence was also mentioned throughout the document. According to the FBI, Logan owned "numerous weapons including handguns and knives that were observed . . . during the execution of the search warrant." Law enforcement had also interviewed one of Logan's ex-girlfriends, who'd met him "about seven or eight years ago." Two years prior to the murders, she had been "in a personal relationship with Logan for a couple months and would stay with him in his home on the weekends." The woman had broken up with Logan because of his physically abusive nature; "during their relationship, Logan had dragged [her] out of her car by her hair," and he'd also threatened that "he could kill her and no one would find her body." What's more, "Logan continued to stalk and harass [her] after their breakup," and "she knew that he carried a gun everywhere he went," usually in "a fanny pack . . . made out of a nicer material." It was obvious in the PCA (probable cause affidavit) that she still very much feared Logan and that she'd suspected him of being involved in the girls' murders from the start; "when she first saw the photograph of the man on the bridge, she thought the police were looking for Logan because she thought the photograph was Logan. [She] did not initially realize that the photograph was that of the suspect."[13]

Shortly thereafter, police had met with another woman, who had been Logan's "former housemate . . . from about September 2016 through December 2016" and had been in "a sexual relationship with Logan on and off for approximately three years." When she first learned of the double homicide, "her initial thought was that Logan was involved." According to her statement, "Logan had been violent with her in the past"—during one particularly brutal incident, "Logan punched her in the face knocking her down"—and she'd "even previously told her baby's father, if she ever ended up dead, Logan did it."[14]

As damning as these two accounts of Logan's exes were, his own actions and false statements of where he'd been around the time of the murders appeared to be even more incriminating. Logan's original alibi had been that he'd visited a store called Aquarium World in Lafayette at 3:00 p.m. on the day the girls went missing, and that he "was driven straight home" immediately after this errand. The affidavit noted that "these statements were found to be factually false and intentionally designed to deceive" investigators.

After giving police his alibi, Logan had apparently called his cousin and asked him to tell police that he'd picked up Logan to go to the aquarium store between 2:00 and 2:30 p.m. and returned between 5:00 and 5:30 p.m. the same day; however, a receipt found in Logan's home on March 6 indicated that he had not checked out of the store until 5:21 p.m. Given that "Logan resides approximately 22 miles from the store . . . it would take approximately 30 minutes to get to the store from Logan's home," meaning he wouldn't have arrived home until closer to 6:00 p.m.[15]

On March 7, Logan's cousin repeated the 2:00–5:00 p.m. story to police, but when he was questioned again two days later, he admitted that "he had lied when he was interviewed . . . on March 7, 2017, at Logan's request," even though his cousin "had never asked [him] to lie for him in the past." On March 12, the cousin also revealed that Logan had called him on the morning of February 14, 2017—prior to the discovery of the girls' bodies—and "asked him to provide the alibi." According to the FBI, "It is reasonable to believe that the creation of an alibi prior to the discovery of a crime indicates culpability or knowledge of the crime," which they believed might further cement Logan's guilt.[16]

The final bit of evidence in the PCA involved data that investigators had pulled from Logan's cell phone. On February 13, Logan's cell phone had been used to place a call at 2:09 p.m., and "although his exact location cannot be confirmed, the tower data shows that Logan's cell phone was in the Delphi area in the area of the Monon High Bridge Trail." Later that evening, Logan's cell phone received separate texts at 7:56 p.m. and 10:16 p.m., and at both times, the data showed that Logan's phone was "likely outside of his residence and in the proximity of where [Libby's] and [Abby]'s bodies were located."[17]

All things considered, the affidavit certainly made it seem like Logan could've been the person responsible for the crime, and that he'd been immediately considered a person of interest. However, that search had been conducted years ago, in March 2017, and in the time since, Logan hadn't been officially arrested or connected with the crime in *any* way. Surely there must be something else investigators knew—perhaps something that had come up during one of their searches or later interviews—that made them doubt whether Logan had been involved. Or were they just waiting on one final tip, one final clue that linked everything together? The affidavit also mentioned that a total of fifteen tips—from both known and anonymous sources—had come into the tip line accusing Logan of being the killer. But to me, *the* biggest clue, the most obvious one that led me to believe that Ron Logan wasn't involved, is that he was *never charged.*

Still, investigators wouldn't say if he was ruled out or not. When asked about this during a live stream on YouTube in 2020, Abby's mom explained that law enforcement didn't clear anyone. Ever. At least not officially. "Nobody including all of our family has ever been cleared of anything on the most official of capacities, but Ron has not been looked at for a considerable amount of time." She added that "he [Ron] was one of the first people they talked to us about."[18]

Although law enforcement believed that what they were doing was best for the investigation, their reluctance to disclose key details left gaps in the public's understanding of the case, leading to false accusations and unjustified assumptions. I thought back to one of the initial press conferences just weeks after the murders, when Captain Dave Bursten had urged those of us in the media to consider the limits of our own perspectives.

"Keep in mind all of you are in the television business. What do you see out of the TV, you see this . . . you don't see what's over here . . . you don't see what's over here, so there's lots more that we're looking at."

What did he mean? Was there someone or something *else* lurking nearby?

Given the inconsistencies in his account, many thought Logan had had *something* to hide. But whether that had anything to do with Libby and Abby had yet to be proven.

———

WAS IT POSSIBLE THAT THE CASE COULD BE RELATED TO OTHER CRIMES IN THE AREA, AND THAT'S WHY the police were so reluctant to release more information?

I'd been thinking a lot about this possibility when Dr. Oz invited me to be a guest on his show. I'd be reporting from Atlanta, a virtual guest on an episode that focused on the still-unsolved Delphi double homicide. The guest scheduled before me was former prosecutor Robert Ives, who'd been a chief prosecutor in Carroll County. He joined the show from Indiana.

As both a local and an expert, he offered a unique and fascinating perspective.

Ives confirmed the public theory that the killer had to have been familiar with the bridge and the trail, based on how difficult it was to get to the area. But it still wasn't clear to him whether the crime had been planned in advance.

"There is no clear motive," he said. "The crime scene is very unusual. It is all very strange."

As for whether law enforcement should keep all the information about the crime scene so close to the vest, Ives had some thoughts.

"Now, law enforcement has good reasons why they don't want to release information. I am not involved in the investigation in any way. I just . . . I hope that people who are handling the investigation will consider whether perhaps it might be time to release some more of that information, so connections to other crimes, other places, or if someone has ever spoken to the perpetrator of this crime . . . perhaps it would give them a clue that they had learned something from the perpetrator."

Ives also mentioned there had been "three or four physical characteristics at the crime scene that [law enforcement] absolutely would take pictures of."

"So just so I can connect these dots a little bit," Dr. Oz said, "if another crime scene had some of these unique characteristics that are worth photographing, could you connect that and potentially think this is the work of a serial killer?"

"I'm no expert on serial killers," Ives stated, "but I can tell you in the early days of this investigation, law enforcement—local, state, and federal—were looking for crimes in other locations that might have similar characteristics. But of course, the public doesn't know some of these similar characteristics, and even then, the characteristics they were looking for tended to be more general things than the items that I'm talking about. And I'm not certain of the exact significance of these things, but they are very unusual."

"As a former prosecutor, are you confident this will be solved?"

"*Confident* is a tough word," Ives said, "but I am hopeful."

Later on, Dr. Oz and I talked about how the crime had rocked everyone in the community, from law enforcement to the general public. During the initial search for the girls, Sheriff Leazenby had called in bloodhounds from another state to help comb the park and surrounding areas. However, after the bodies were discovered, the sheriff did something that had now become his biggest regret: he'd canceled the request for these bloodhounds, the same bloodhounds who might've been able to pick up critical clues left behind by the killer.

I also talked about Delphi—the feel of the town, the innocence that had been lost. I remembered something that Tobe had once said to me: "This used to be Mayberry. No one locked their doors, everyone could go outside, you knew your neighbor, you trusted everyone." But after officials had released two very different sketches of the possible perpetrator, just about every man in town—a town of fewer than three thousand people—had become a suspect.

Even the girls' families had become suspicious of their neighbors. According to Libby's aunt, Tara, it just wasn't the same living in Delphi anymore.

"The trust is gone," she said. "Everyone is a suspect. No matter where we are, even in different cities, if someone looks like the sketch, I can't take my eyes off them. It's horrible, but I can't help it."

The families had long insisted that they trusted law enforcement to do right by this investigation, but at times their faith wore thin. There seemed to be simultaneously so much information and yet so little. So many developments and yet so few. Where was the progress? Investigators weren't saying. The information they did release was carefully planned. The press conferences were all formulaic. First, they would thank the families for their patience and the media for their understanding, then make a plea to the person who knows the man on the bridge. Whenever any one of them was pressed on the amount of information they kept to themselves, they all answered in a similar fashion, saying either that they didn't want to "tip our hand to the person responsible for this" or run the risk of "giv[ing] out the wrong information"[19]

But were they relying *too much* on the hope that someone would come forward with that vital piece of information about the man on the bridge? It was hard to say. As the reward money continued to grow and the pleas to the public intensified, that missing puzzle piece, that "one tip," never came.

Superintendent Doug Carter would often reiterate that he understood the silence surrounding the investigation was difficult, especially for the families. And it started to show. Abby's mom, Anna, wondered why it was taking this long to find the guy on the bridge. "If he lived here, how come we don't know who he is? That's the hard part. It feels so close, and it feels so local, but if it is, *why* don't we know who he is, *why* didn't we find him?"[20]

"Susan, they owe me an arrest," Mike said to me during an interview three years after the murders. He was obviously frustrated. "Law enforcement owes me that."

No one could blame him.

II

Catfished: Kegan Kline and @anthony_shots

A fter the search affidavit for Logan's property was released, it seemed like Logan had been the primary suspect in the early days of the investigation. However, Logan wasn't the only suspicious person who police had their eyes on during this time.

Because the media had initially dubbed the murders of Libby and Abby "the Snapchat Murders," mostly because the girls had been posting pictures to the social media platform right before they went missing, there were some people, including Libby's own grandmother, who wondered whether social media was somehow responsible for their deaths. Had the girls talked with someone online who encouraged them to go out to the bridge and meet up?

At first, law enforcement had said there was no indication that this was the case, but on December 6, 2021, Indiana State Police announced a possible break in the case and asked for anyone who had interacted with @anthony_shots on Snapchat or Instagram to come forward.[1]

Libby's and Abby's families both stressed that they had no idea their daughters were communicating with this account and that they'd never met or even heard of anyone named Anthony Shots. As it turned out, *no one* had ever met Anthony Shots—because he didn't really exist.

The account was run by a now twenty-seven-year-old man and Peru, Indiana, resident named Kegan Anthony Kline, who'd created the profile using pictures he'd found online of a handsome male model with rock-hard abs and more than a handful of tattoos who portrayed himself as being extremely wealthy and owning numerous sports cars. As "Anthony," Kline successfully catfished over a dozen underage girls, first reaching out to them on Instagram and then coaxing them into communicating with him on Snapchat. Between 2016 and 2017, Kline had solicited close to one hundred pictures of these girls and around twenty sexually explicit videos. And on February 23, 2017, less than two weeks after the murders of Abby and Libby, Kline's Samsung Galaxy S5 phone had undergone a "factory reset."[2]

Two days later, on February 25, investigators issued a search warrant for the person behind @anthony_shots, including any and all electronic devices associated with the account. Kline didn't turn over his phone until February 27, and by that time, it was clear he had apparently "uninstalled and deleted several apps, including MeetMe, Snapchat and Instagram."[3]

On Monday, April 11, 2022, investigators added the social media app Yellow, currently known as Yubo. They asked for more

CATFISHED: KEGAN KLINE AND @ANTHONY_SHOTS | 153

information from anyone who communicated with the fake profile from 2016 to 2017.[4]

Kline's behavior in the days following the murders was definitely suspicious, and he appeared to be a solid lead. On the outside looking in, it seemed like a reasonable theory to explain the tragedy that had transpired; maybe Kline had presented himself as Anthony Shots assuming he'd be luring just one girl to the woods and then got nervous when two of them showed up, leading to the murders. Or perhaps Kline was working in tandem with the real killer and had used the account as a way to bring the girls right to him.

In an age where teens were becoming increasingly tied to social media and smartphones, it certainly seemed feasible. Catfishing was also on the rise, with social media platforms (including Facebook and Instagram) apparently to blame for more catfishing and romance scams than online dating profiles.[5] Data even shows that "the number of catfish scams has nearly tripled since 2016," and a Facebook audit revealed that the company detected and deactivated a staggering 1.3 billion accounts over the span of just three months.[6] The person behind the scam often targets young people—like Abby and Libby—an age group that is particularly susceptible to these schemes. According to PureSight, an organization dedicated to protecting children online, "75% of children are willing to share personal information online about themselves and their family," and roughly a third of teens have befriended people on Facebook that they haven't met in person.[7] This doesn't mean we should blame young people for disclosing this information—they are still growing into adults, after all—but we should teach them how to be mindful about what they share online and with whom they share it.

Even in cases where young people are more careful about who they talk to and when, it's not always enough to protect them.

The statistics are staggering: one in five teenagers report that they've received "unwanted sexual solicitation" online, and only a quarter of these victims have ever told their parents about these encounters.[8]

I wondered whether Abby and Libby might have gotten caught up in this digital world of fraud and falsity. The criminals that hide behind a digital facade would definitely know how to groom and target innocent victims, much like these girls.

To add more fuel to the fire, Kline wasn't the only one in his family with a criminal past; his father, Jerry Anthony Kline, had a long-standing criminal history of sexual harassment, battery, and theft, dating all the way back to 1988.[9] During his police interview, Kline fielded investigators' questions about whether his father might have had access to his phone and social media accounts; however, Kline denied that accusation, reportedly saying, "I wouldn't let my dad have my phone for long periods of time or nothing like that."[10]

When Becky first heard of Kline's potential involvement, her heart sank. She'd believed the investigators when they'd initially told her they didn't think the murders were connected to Snapchat or possible catfishing.

"I hung my hat on that," Becky said and grimaced. "I feel like I let Libby down. I didn't protect her. I didn't check her phone."

When she later expressed this guilt to Paul Holes, he reassured her that she had done nothing wrong and neither had the girls. After all, as a former investigator himself, he knew what went into the grooming process.

"It is not your fault," Holes told her sincerely. "Abby and Libby did nothing wrong. They are young girls who were maybe trying to meet up with someone they thought was their own age. The sick people that do this are experts at grooming."

WHEN INVESTIGATORS HAD FIRST ANNOUNCED THE NAME OF THIS ACCOUNT TO THE PUBLIC, THEY didn't specify whether they believed that the person behind @anthony_shots was directly linked to the girls' deaths, or whether either girl had ever interacted with the account.

They also made it clear that they didn't think the man in the photos that Kline pretended to be was responsible in any way for the murders. The man was later identified as police officer Vincent Kowalski; the pictures had been taken during his modeling days in high school. This wasn't the first time his pictures, or even his name, had been linked to a catfishing scheme either.

"It's been happening since 2014. . . . You just search my name, there's a hundred accounts, fake accounts, of me," Kowalski said. "For a long time, I . . . reported every single account I came across. But then I just eventually just stopped because . . . because these social media websites aren't here to help anyone right now and they gotta do better. I don't know why there's not a verification process before you're even able to make your account."[11]

Kowalski was now a father himself of two daughters, which made the fact that his pictures had been linked in any way with the crime even more despicable.

"Soliciting videos from young girls, that's disgusting. Makes me sick. But to know that two young girls possibly lost their life because of my picture—it's the worst of the worst. It keeps you up at night, as a parent, knowing that people out there are like that.

"At the end of the day, it breaks my heart. Couldn't imagine losing my girls so they have all my love and support and I just wish I could support them more."[12]

It was eventually revealed that Kline had "allegedly communicated via social media with Libby the night before her death," but that seemed to be the extent of his interaction with the victim. Did that interaction with Libby lead Indiana State Police back to Kegan Kline three years after they had seized property from his home?

Kline's property was initially searched, back in February 2017, twelve days after Abby and Libby were killed, but he wasn't arrested for possession of child pornography until August 2020. Why did it take more than three years? Local and national media outlets pushed back and demanded answers from the Indiana State Police. In a rare move, ISP responded and issued a statement on December 13, 2021, explaining the delay.

> The Indiana state Police has received many media inquiries since our December 6th press release concerning "anthony_ shots" and eventually the identification of Kegan Kline. Your questions are certainly relevant as they relate to a long complex and extremely complicated murder investigation. During the last nearly five years, we have conducted dozens of secondary investigations based on information we received. One of those investigations included a Possession of Child Pornography case resulting in the arrest of Kegan Kline. The information we had, have, and continue to receive concerning Kline has ebbed and flowed over these last few years. We understand there was a period of time that passed between 2017 and 2020 when Kline was not arrested and incarcerated for possession of Child pornography. Once the Indiana State Police presented the criminal case to the Miami County Prosecutor in June of 2020, immediate action was taken by both Indiana State Police and the Miami County Prosecutor's Office, which ultimately

resulted in Kline's arrest. Like so many other pieces of this investigation, we will always review, learn from, and make any necessary adjustments. We do not believe that any person has done anything intentionally wrong, but we will continue to critically evaluate our efforts. We know there is enormous interest in the "Why" of everything we do, but we cannot and will not speculate. One day you will have the opportunity to see and know what we do, and we look forward to that day.—Indiana State Police[13]

Kline maintained that he was not responsible for harming Libby or Abby, but he did admit to soliciting nude pictures from underage girls. Consequently, he was "accused of at least 25 counts of child exploitation, child pornography, and other charges" relating to the other young girls he'd preyed on via social media. In March 2022, the podcast *Murder Sheet* obtained and released a transcript of a police interview with Kline. According to the transcript, when he was asked about Libby, Kline stated, "I don't remember talking to her really. I don't even know who she really was until after I saw that on the news." After failing a polygraph, Kline then deleted his Snapchat and Instagram accounts and searched online "how long does DNA last." The Indiana State Police responded to media questions with a statement essentially saying the information released did *not* come from the Indiana State Police and "the investigation is ongoing."

Then, five months later, in August 2022, it seemed as though the investigation picked up steam. Kegan Kline was taken out of the Miami County Jail and placed in the temporary custody of Indiana State Police.

But why? They obviously needed him for something. Why did Kegan Kline have to be physically present?

A court document showed the prosecutor and Kline's defense attorney agreed to have him released and returned to the Miami County Jail.

Why did they want to meet with Kegan Kline and where did they take him? It was a nagging question that even Abby's and Libby's family members didn't know the answer to. Investigators had searched sections of the Wabash River, which ran close to Kline's residence, for several weeks in August 2022.

Could the lengthy search of the Wabash River in Peru, Indiana, be connected to Kline's jail transfer? It was never publicly disclosed what they were looking for, let alone whether they found it, but Kline was *never* formally connected or charged with the murders.[14]

During this time Kline's defense attorney filed a motion to delay a scheduled pretrial conference set for September 1, citing the parties are "currently engaged in negotiations." Kline's trial date had been moved from January 2023 to May 2023.

After back-and-forth discussions, Klein's attorney and the prosecution did not reach a plea deal and, in March 2023, Kegan Kline pleaded guilty to twenty-five counts of child pornography, child solicitation, child exploitation, synthetic identity deception, and obstruction of justice (as the result of an investigation undertaken by detectives attempting to solve the murders of Abby Williams and Liberty German near Delphi in February 2017). His guilty plea meant he was waiving his right to a jury trial. Kline's sentence would now be decided by the judge on May 18.

Then, another holdup. Just as the sentencing hearing was about to begin, Kline's defense team asked for a last-minute continuance, claiming their client needed more time to review evidence that Kline claimed he hadn't seen and that Kline may want to withdraw his guilty plea based on that evidence. The prosecution argued against this, stating they "vehemently objected to the continuance" and called it a delay tactic.

Miami County Circuit Court judge Timothy Spahr ruled in favor of the defense, and a new hearing date was set for July 27. Judge Spahr also told Kline's defense team that they had until May 26 to file any new motions, including withdrawal of a guilty plea. That date was moved to May 31 after Kline fired his defense attorney and two new attorneys were assigned to his case.

Immediately after the news broke indicating Kline may be changing his plea, the conspiracy theories and rumors connecting Kline to the murders of Abby and Libby reignited with renewed furor. Then, on May 31, Kline and his new representation elected *not* to withdraw his guilty plea.

During the summer months of 2020, it appeared that the cards were stacked against Kegan Kline. His transfer out of Miami County Jail and into the custody of the Indiana State Police, his alleged failed polygraph, his communication with Libby, court delays, his defense attorney possibly negotiating with the prosecution, the lengthy search of the Wabash River: based on all of those considerations, it's easy to understand why so many people thought it was only a matter of time before the Indiana State Police announced charges connected to the murders of Abby and Libby.

But that didn't happen, and once again, in the absence of clear information, the investigators were criticized.

Still, I believe the continued silence from law enforcement *did* tell us something in the end. For more than five years, the multi-agency task force working to solve the case *never* named an official person of interest—not Daniel Nations, not Paul Etter, not James Chadwell, not Ron Logan, and not Kegan Kline—until they finally made an arrest. And that arrest involved a man that no one had ever heard of.

12

"Today Is the Day"

It was just past noon on a sunny Friday—October 28, 2022, to be exact. I was driving around Atlanta, running errands (my typical end-of-the-week routine, since it was the day before my two o'clock Saturday-morning wake-up call for *Weekend Express*). I was walking out of a store, holding my dry cleaning, when I looked down at my phone and noticed I'd missed a call from Bryan Bell, my programming director. I knew he'd call only if there was breaking news, so I tapped my screen to see whether he'd left a voice mail.

Instead, I noticed a new text from Dan Szematowicz, a close friend and coworker who had been to Delphi several times. It was just two words.

"Delphi arrest."

I immediately called him.

"What? Who?" I asked. I could barely contain myself.

"A guy named Richard Allen," he answered.

"Who?" I responded, confused. I'd never heard of him before.

"Yeah, he works at CVS and wasn't on anyone's radar."

"Are we sure?"

"I think so."

I could feel that familiar mix of excitement and anticipation rising in my chest. Could this be the one? Could it really be him?

Then again, we'd had similar conversations in the past about different persons of interest.

"You've felt this way before," I mumbled to myself, trying desperately to remain calm and levelheaded.

As bad as it was for me, it was thousands of times worse for the families each and every time there were reports circulating around a certain name, only to be proven wrong.

"Susan, I've been down that road," I remembered Mike saying to me back when we'd talked in his kitchen. "I have learned to wait. I need to hear from law enforcement before letting myself even think about what we are all waiting for . . . It's a roller coaster I'm not getting back on."

I thought back to how Mike had initially felt when Daniel Nations's name first came up, only to be disappointed when it turned out that he had nothing to do with the crime. At the time of the murders, Nations had spent ten months in prison for various crimes in Colorado and Indiana, and the circumstantial evidence seemed stacked up against him. But even though he lived only two hours away from Delphi and clearly resembled the sketch of the bridge guy, he'd told authorities that he didn't know where Delphi was—that he couldn't even point it out on a map. He'd denied any involvement. Later on, Nations told a local reporter he'd only heard about the double murder from three inmates when the news broke that Indiana State Police were on their way to question him about it.

At the one-year-anniversary press conference, which was held feet from the Monon High Bridge, Superintendent Carter had admitted that Nations at one point had been "a person of interest," but he also said, "We feel confident there was no involvement," adding that the arrest warrant connected to the crimes he'd confessed to doing was sealed. Ultimately, Nations was just one of many persons of interest who were later let off the hook after police had looked into them.

But this?

This was different.

Finally—*finally*—someone had been *arrested*.

On the drive home, I kept glancing down at the image of Richard Allen on my phone.

Is this you? I wondered. *Are you the man on the bridge?*

Then, another text from Dan came through.

"He has a daughter."

Richard Allen was a father. There was an image circulating online of his daughter sitting on the bridge very close to where Abby and Libby had last been seen.

My mind immediately went to Kerri Rawson.

I'D FIRST MET KERRI RAWSON AT THE 2021 CRIMECON IN AUSTIN, TEXAS. KELSI HAD FACILITATED our connection, calling me a few months before the event.

"Would you be interested in interviewing Kerri Rawson, the daughter of BTK?" Kelsi asked me. "I said you were someone I trusted."

"Absolutely." I knew who BTK was, but not much about his daughter, Kerri.

Dennis Rader—now known as the notorious serial killer BTK (bind, torture, kill)—terrorized Wichita, Kansas, for over three decades until he was finally apprehended by authorities on February 25, 2005. He was charged with ten counts of first-degree murder and shocked everyone by pleading guilty to all charges just a few months later, in June. I had covered the story several times during my tenure as a journalist—not just the original arrest and charges but also his trial and conviction.

Kerri Rawson, Rader's daughter, was only twenty-six years old when the FBI informed her that her father was BTK.

Sitting next to Kerri on stage at CrimeCon, I could tell that she was still grappling with all the implications of her father's incomprehensible past. "I was Kerri; he was Dad. Then, all of a sudden, he was BTK, and I was BTK's daughter."

It had seemed impossible at first. *Her* dad? Her Boy Scout–leading, church-ushering, stamp-collecting dad?

But then, within hours of his arrest, her father actually confessed to the crimes. And the more Kerri reflected on the time she'd spent with her father as a kid, the more she started seeing signs everywhere, embedded in more than a few of her memories.[1] In the years since his arrest, she's been constantly plagued by questions from the media about his crime spree that she knew *nothing* about. There weren't any obvious signs.

"I grew up with a pretty normal childhood. He was just my dad, and I loved him; he was like my best friend. We went camping and fishing together, hiking . . . he moved me up and back from college a million times, moved me after I got married. I was on the phone with him the night before he was arrested."

"Just a normal dad," I murmured.

"A normal dad," she echoed, "asking me about the tire tread and oil change. That was our last convo."

And then the FBI knocked on her door, and her life changed forever.

"I was home from substitute teaching. I was living outside of Detroit, Michigan. I'm twenty-six years [old; I've] been married eighteen months. The FBI [was] sitting outside of my door, in a car, waiting to arrest my dad. So they were waiting to arrest my dad; [then they would] notify my mother in Park City, Kansas; notify my brother in Connecticut; and notify me. They didn't know *what* they were walking into; they had just confirmed Dad was BTK the night before, with DNA. The FBI guy knocks on my door, [and I remembered that] my dad had always told me [to] make them prove who they are, check their badge. I found out later [that my dad] used these [same] ruses; he would dress up like a maintenance man or pretend to be a policeman to get into these homes and murder these women. So I was already on high alert."

"Did you process that, when he said your dad was BTK?" I wondered.

"Well, I let [the officer] into my kitchen, and he said, 'Have you heard of BTK?' I thought my grandma, my dad's mom, had been murdered. So I said, 'Is my grandma OK?' He said, 'Yeah, your grandma's fine.' Then, he just—*boom*—lays it on me: 'Your dad is BTK.' Not that 'we suspect he is,' not that we're looking at him. I mean, they *literally* arrested him on seven of the ten murders, and that's when everything changed."

Kerri and I hugged after we first met, and she'd been warm and open, something I really admired, especially considering I'd read her memoir, *A Serial Killer's Daughter: My Story of Faith, Love, and Overcoming*, twice. I still shuddered thinking back on everything she'd gone through. When the news first broke, she felt as if she were on trial too, even though she was just as horrified as the rest of the world—if not more so. Suddenly, her name was everywhere, and journalists kept coming out of the woodwork, begging her for quotes on what it was like to grow up with the infamous BTK as a dad. It took a long time, and a lot of healing, before Kerri no longer felt responsible for her father's crimes, even though she knew logically there was nothing she could've done to stop him. Kerri now had two kids of her own, a daughter and a son, and she still struggled with how much to tell them about their grandfather.[2]

I wondered what it would be like for Richard Allen's daughter now. Would the rest of her life be defined by this moment, this arrest—like Kerri's had been?

LOST IN THOUGHT, I SLAMMED ON MY BRAKES, ALMOST HITTING THE CAR IN FRONT OF ME.

"OK, focus!" I whispered to myself as I finally pulled into my driveway. As soon as I parked, I immediately refreshed my email. The police department in Delphi had just announced that a press conference was to be held on Monday, October 31.

Just three days away.

Hands shaking, I ran inside my house to call Becky. I wasn't quite sure what to say; I just knew I had to talk to her. When no one answered, I hung up without leaving a voice mail, my hands still shaking. Seconds later, I saw Becky's name flashing across my phone screen.

"Hi!" I answered. "Oh my gosh."

"Can you believe it?" Becky said. "Wait a second—I'm walking out in the hall. I'm at my nephew's wedding in Ohio. I don't want to ruin his wedding, but it's all people are talking about."

I heard music and laughter fading into the background, accompanied by her steps. What a strange juxtaposition it must have been, to be at a wedding filled with the joy of new beginnings, only to learn that the thing that had been haunting you for the past several years might finally be over.

"OK, that's better," Becky said after a few moments. "They told us on Wednesday but never gave us a name. They said they would call us back, but they never did. I was up all night."

"Becky, they never called you back?"

I was suddenly infuriated. After more than five years of searching for the killer, no one had the decency to call the families back once someone had finally been arrested for the crimes. It seemed inconceivable. But I kept that thought to myself.

"No, I found out from you guys, watching the news."

"What did Mike say?"

"Well, he's waiting to hear it from Doug Carter," Becky replied. "He worked at CVS, and you know what, Susan? Tara remembers him."

At this point, we were both whispering. I'm not sure why, but it felt like we should be.

"She does? What? How?"

"Yes, Tara went into CVS the day before the girls' funeral to develop pictures of Libby to put near the casket. Tara was crying, and Richard Allen said, 'It's on me.' He didn't let her pay. She remembers him!"

My mind was buzzing. He'd been hiding in plain sight the whole time—just like Superintendent Carter had said three and a half years ago, on April 22, 2019.

"You know what, Susan? I think I'm ready to walk on the bridge. To go back," Becky said at last. "I haven't been able before, but I told Kelsi I was ready."

I started to cry, and this time I just couldn't hold back my tears. I knew I was supposed to keep my composure as a journalist, but this whole case had become so much more to me.

"I'm so sorry that I'm crying," I said, "but you are like family to me. This is not just an unsolved case to me."

"I know it's not," she said reassuringly.

"I shouldn't be crying," I said, chastising myself. "Becky, how are you feeling?"

"Well, remember, Susan, when I used to say that I would scream from the rooftops when someone was arrested? I don't feel that way." At this, Becky's voice lowered to a whisper again. "I don't know what my purpose is anymore."

"Becky, I know what it is, because I've seen it. I see how much you do for everyone at CrimeCon. You have helped countless families."

Becky asked whether I'd be able to come back to Delphi for the press conference. I told her that I wished I could, but the network wanted me to anchor the show following the event, from the desk. I told her I'd talk to her afterward and that I'd be thinking of her and the rest of the families.

"Please tell everyone I said hello," I said, "and I'm sending my love."

"I will."

Shortly after that, we hung up.

I don't know how long I sat there, on the floor of my room, after the call. I remember it was dark; in the excitement of the conversation, I hadn't even turned the lights on. I just sat in silence, completely still. It could've been minutes or hours. I lost track of time.

That night, I couldn't stop looking at my daughter, who had just turned thirteen—the same age as Abby—and my sweet son, still so much younger. I watched them eat dinner and get ready for bed and continued to stare as I tucked them in.

All routine things, yes, but things I realized could be gone in an instant. Hadn't February 12, 2017, been like that for the girls' families? Routine. We just never know the time we've been gifted with the people we love most. I squeezed my kids a little tighter.

Libby's and Abby's families had been in a holding pattern, a Groundhog Day from hell, for the past five and a half, almost six, years. I hoped that they would soon be able to get the justice that had so long evaded their grasp.

I didn't get much sleep that night, if I got any at all. My alarm was set for 2 a.m., like it had been every Saturday and Sunday for the last seven years. I couldn't wait to talk to the weekend team. The arrest, of course, was set to be our lead story. I quickly took a shower, got ready, and got in my car. I pulled down the visor and noticed my eyes were bloodshot and puffy. After taking a deep breath, I headed south toward the CNN Center.

During our hourlong break in between shows, I checked my phone. It was filled with text messages from my family and friends who had been following the case and now knew of the arrest. I also had several messages on Facebook from viewers who had been hoping and praying for this day. I immediately noticed something new on Becky Patty's profile; her picture had changed. I was staring at the sketch of the suspect from the original wanted poster, only this time, stamped diagonally across his face in bold red letters was a new word: ARRESTED.

13

———

Captured, the Press Conference

The press conference was scheduled for Monday morning, October 31, 2022—Halloween—at the Delphi United Methodist Church. That morning, I sent Kelsi a text, letting her know we were watching and ready to share the news with the world. It was difficult to describe how I was feeling, excited and nervous but still somber, all at once.

At 10:00 a.m. sharp, the public information officer, Sergeant Jeremy Piers, approached the podium and laid the ground rules, so to speak—basically telling us what we would be hearing as well as what we would *not* be hearing. He said there would be time for limited questions following the presser, but he reminded everyone that "this continues to be an active and ongoing investigation." Likewise, evidence would not be discussed at this time. Piers then took a moment to introduce Superintendent Doug Carter, inviting him up to the podium.

Carter took a deep breath and a second to gather his thoughts before speaking. I could hear him sniffing and muttering "man" under his breath, like he just couldn't believe what was happening. He cleared his throat and rubbed his palms together.

"Seldom do I have remarks, but today is different, because I do not want there to be any confusion or ambiguity with what I will say.

"Today is not a day to celebrate, but the arrest of Richard M. Allen of Delphi on two counts of murder is sure a major step in leading to a conclusion of this long-term and complex investigation."

The superintendent then addressed the family. "First, I'd like to speak directly to Anna, Mike, Becky, Kelsi, your extended families, along with the entire Delphi community that certainly has grown and now includes our nation and even many countries around the world.

"I am proud to report to you that today—actually, last Friday—was the day.

"And an arrest has been made thanks to literally hundreds of media outlets that have been steadfast in reporting and keeping the memories of Abby and Libby front and center. Many of you in the room have developed relationships with me personally, and you know I always have a personal perspective, and today's no different, but from a very personal perspective, you have provided—you all have provided—inspiration and support, even while oftentimes frustrated with us and me. But you continued to encourage the efforts, and you too believed that one day we would all be here participating and sharing this news."

He took another deep breath. "To the entire law enforcement community, which includes all local, state, and federal agencies, which are far too many to specifically mention today: thank you, thank you, thank you. We are going to continue a very methodical and committed approach to ensure that if *any* other person had any involvement in these murders in *any* way, that person or persons will be held accountable.

"Since the murders of Abby and Libby 2,086 days ago, the daily investigative team has worked tirelessly and is certainly worthy of mention today. Specifically, Sheriff Leazenby, the sheriff of Carroll County; Detective Tony Liggett; Detective (retired) Kevin Hammond; former Delphi chief, and now the prosecutor's investigator, Steve Mullin; state police first sergeant Jerry Holeman; Detectives Jay Harper, Dave Vito, and Brian Harshman; along with members of the United States Marshals Service, specifically Agent Jeremy Clinton and Agent Bill Colffers. With them today is Dan McClain, appointed US Marshal.

"Our state police analysts, our scientists from many different disciplines within our laboratory division. Mrs. Kathy Shank, for your incredible dedication to detail, and to so many others that I know I've missed, I really believe that Abby and Libby would be proud of you for standing strong, even in the face of immense pressure and perpetual criticism. Some of these individuals have postponed retirement, passed on promotional opportunities, have dedicated personal time away from their families, given up nights, weekends, and holidays—all while in the pursuit of accountability for Abby and Libby.

"I know that today's announcement will not diminish your resolve, and I hope you have found just a bit of peace in this most complicated world." Carter then stopped to look up at the media and the crowd gathered before him. "This is *really important.* While I know you are all expecting final details today concerning this arrest, today is not that day. Today is *not* that day. This investigation is far from complete, and we will not jeopardize its integrity by releasing or discussing documents or information before the appropriate time. Prosecutor Nick McLeland, of course, will share additional information about what we can and cannot say, and also explain to you why the probable cause affidavit is temporarily sealed by the court and not available. And by the way, he has been a *tremendous, tremendous* asset to this team.

"I am yet again asking you for your patience and, please, your understanding while our system of due process works. Also, remember that all persons arrested are presumed innocent. *All persons arrested are presumed innocent.*

"You all will have an innate desire to subjectively interpret and then report what you think. We in the law enforcement realm cannot, and you should never allow us to, talk about what we think concerning facts, but rather discuss and share at the right time what it is we *know*. The time will come when additional details can be released, but again, today is *not* that day. It's about Abby and Libby, their families, and this community, this nation, and even our planet." Carter paused then continued.

"The prosecutor has been very clear with law enforcement about what his expectations are about what can and cannot be released, shared, or discussed, so we will of course comply. If you choose to be critical of our silence, be critical of me, *not* the front line. These are the folks that have committed their entire lives to a successful conclusion—in other words, a guilty verdict. As we move to the next phase of this investigation, I will continue to offer all resources that the ISP has to not only the investigative team that I anticipate growing but also to prosecutor McLeland as we prepare for the coming months. Again, Nick has been very resolute and very clear, and I'm most grateful for his leadership, and it's going to be really important as we move forward. Please continue offering tips that you would like to share. The many avenues to report will remain open and will be available to all. *Please* continue doing that."

The tip line was still open? Why? By this point, there had been more than seventy thousand tips, and a man was now in custody, charged with the murders. Why would the tip line still be open? Nick McLeland would later explain in court that he believed "other actors may be involved." So did they have evidence indicating someone else was involved? If so, who? Keeping in line with the rest of the investigative process over the past few years, they weren't saying anything. At least not for now. Not today.

"In closing, I stand before you in this church and very place where we held our first briefing nearly six years ago, and just hours after the murders of Abby and Libby . . . right here." Carter's lips remained tight, pulled in a straight line, and it seemed like he was doing everything he could not to cry. "Pulling in today, I wasn't really sure what emotion I would experience, but peace came over me, and I didn't expect that to happen. And I hope all of you, with all the different responsibilities you have from around the planet today, have felt some of that as well, but remember—we're not done. I think what we all have experienced proves that, together, there is *nothing* we cannot do. But more importantly, giving of ourselves, all of us, *all of us*, giving of ourselves, matters more than what we could ever receive. Abby and Libby, though in death, have had a profound effect on *so many of us*—on how we live and, as importantly, who we all should be."

Next up, Carter introduced Sheriff Leazenby, inviting him up to the podium to say his remarks. Leazenby opened up his folder and looked out at the audience before him.

"I believe in a God of justice and righteousness," he began. "Today I believe that same God has provided us with justice for Abby and Libby. As sheriff of Carroll County, Indiana, I want to publicly and sincerely thank each individual who played a role in helping us during this five-and-a-half-year investigation. Whether it was in an investigative capacity; providing tips, cards, or letters of suggestions or encouragement; phone calls; and thousands of other countless ways of communicating. I earnestly thank those who prayed for this moment in time. We now move forward through the Indiana criminal justice system, allowing the system to provide its due diligence and process, and providing that justice which is owed to Abby and Libby, their families, and this community. Thank you."

The person following Leazenby was the prosecutor who Doug Carter had said several times was pivotal to this case. Up at the mic, he seemed nervous, hesitant. Wearing a soft gray suit and a light pink shirt with a navy tie, his hair slicked back and beard neatly trimmed, he introduced himself to the crowd.

"Welcome, everybody. My name is Nicholas McLeland," he said firmly but calmly. "I'm the Carroll County prosecutor. And before we get started, I want to reiterate some of the things that Sheriff Leazenby and Superintendent Carter stated. I first want to thank both of them. They've been a great support to my office throughout this investigation. They've always been there for a phone call and always been willing to lend a hand or line of assistance to me and my office during this investigation. I want to thank the team behind me. This is the homicide task force team that we've put together. Thank them and thank their families for being so understanding for the many nights they've worked away from their families, away from their children." He took a breath and continued.

"There are many dates in a lifetime that you're going to remember: The dates your children are born. The date you're married. The date you buy a first house. The date Abby and Libby went missing. One of those dates was last Friday, October 28, 2022. At that time, we had gathered evidence to formulate a PC [probable cause] that we submitted to the court, and the judge did find probable cause for the arrest of Richard Allen. He's been charged with two counts of murder for the murder of Abigail Williams and Liberty German. This investigation is still very ongoing. We're keeping the tip line open, the tip email open. We encourage everybody to continue to call in tips, not only about Richard Allen but about any other person that you may have. For that reason, and for the nature of this case, the probable cause and the charging information has been sealed by the court."

I stopped to wonder, *Is this even legal?*

"I've been very clear to everybody that, per the court order, we *cannot* talk about the evidence that's in the probable cause or the evidence that's in the charging information. That will become evident to you at some point, and it will be released, but right now is *not* that day. Today is about Abby and Libby, focusing on them. Mr. Allen has had his initial hearing. He's entered a preliminary plea of not guilty. The matter has been set for a pretrial on January 13, at 9:00 a.m., 2023, and a trial date of March 20, 2023, at 9:00 a.m. He is presumed innocent. We will have our opportunity and day in court where we can present the evidence that we have against him. But until that day, he is presumed innocent."

McLeland then opened up the floor to a few questions from the audience, reiterating that the evidence would not be discussed. During questioning, McLeland added that Allen was currently being held in jail without bond, but he refused to disclose much more than that. Reporters became visibly frustrated as their questions were continuously shut down—something that McLeland acknowledged was frustrating, but he said again he wouldn't do anything to jeopardize the integrity of the investigation. He also admitted that their refusal to disclose documents wasn't something they did very often but that it was necessary in this case because it was still open. He told the audience that there would be a public hearing in regard to whether the sealed records would remain sealed, but until then, they weren't sharing any extra details.

At last, a reporter asked the superintendent what he'd learned from the case and from Abby and Libby.

"Man," he said, stepping toward the mic. "I think probably resilience. And understanding the value of each and every day. That today was the day, but I didn't anticipate they ever thought today would be their day. And I feel like I've known them for a long time."[1]

At about one o'clock that afternoon, I drove home to quickly check in with my family before heading back into the CNN Center to prepare for the hour special.

I'd almost forgotten it was Halloween, until I saw my son, Jack, dressed in a costume, laughing, and running around the house. My thirteen-year-old daughter, Emery, was excited to meet up with her friends at a Halloween party. She was dressing up as a Powerpuff Girl.

"Mom, do you know where my blue top is?" she asked as she ran by.

"Check the dryer . . . and slow down."

I was able to give her a quick hug before returning to my room to rewatch the press conference. Before I knew it, it was already time to head back downstairs.

I pulled into the parking deck and walked toward the bridge, past security, to my office. On the left side of my door, above my nameplate, was a pink sticky note inscribed with Kelsi's handwriting and a small heart at the bottom. "We were here, you were not. Sorry we missed you. Becky, Kelsi, Tara & Tribe." A few months earlier, on their drive down to Florida, the family had stopped by the CNN Center. I wasn't in that day, but I've kept that note on my door ever since, and I think of them every time I see it.

As I headed toward my office, past an empty newsroom with lines of empty chairs, I began thinking of all of the cases, stories, and trials I had covered at CNN and HLN. Six months prior, our parent company, Warner Media, had merged with Discovery, creating what was described as "a new streaming-centric media company" that promised to "reshape the media landscape." What would this change mean for HLN? I tried not to believe every speculation and rumor that was spreading fiercely and ferociously through the newsroom, but we all knew, or at least suspected, that change was coming. At least I did.

I pulled the note off my door and stuck it to the top of my computer. Eager to start preparing, I opened the rundown in the 8 p.m. hour. At the top of the A block was a list of the guests and the name of the special: "The Delphi Murders: Is the Killer In Custody?"

I still had a few hours before our eight o'clock show. I'd be reporting from the flash studio, and I'd be talking with Mike and Becky first. Considering the number of guests that we had scheduled for the hour, I knew they probably wouldn't have a monitor set up at their location, so I sent a text in advance letting them know I'd be able to see and hear them and they'd be able to hear me but not see me. I knew well how very awkward it can feel if you are not used to the setup.

I scrolled through the A, B, C, and D blocks of the rundown. The show was packed. At our afternoon meeting, I learned there would be many familiar faces on the panel, including criminal defense attorney Joey Jackson, HLN contributor and attorney Jean Casarez, criminologist Casey Jordan, and Paul Holes. This always made it easier. Superintendent Doug Carter would join me in the B block after the first commercial. For the next few hours, I rewatched and studied the press conference and read every article about the arrest of Richard Allen.

The show began with images of Abby and Libby, that infamous picture of the man on the bridge, and then a graphic with the words, "The Delphi Murders. Is the Killer in Custody?" covering the screen across an image of the bridge. I saw my face in the monitor below the camera and began.

"I'm Susan Hendricks. A blockbuster development in the double murder case of two young girls from Delphi, Indiana. Liberty German and Abigail Williams, Abby and Libby. Brutally murdered in the middle of the day. A day off from school in 2017. A crime that shocked the nation, leading investigators down a winding road of evidence with the ever-present question, "Who killed Abby and Libby?" And now we move one step closer to possibly finding the answer. The Indiana State Police are announcing they have this man in custody"—the mug shot of Richard Allen appeared on the screen—"and have charged him with two counts of murder. Fifty-year-old Richard Allen of Delphi. Here is State Police Superintendent Doug Carter." We then proceeded to a clip of Carter from that morning at Delphi United Methodist Church, the same place where the superintendent stood at the first press conference on February 22, 2017. Two thousand seventy-seven days before.

"I am proud to report to you that today, actually last Friday, was the day," Carter announced. Along with the viewing audience, I watched Carter's speech again before the camera turned back to me, live in the studio. I continued, "Certainly a stunning news conference, [with] what was said and what was left out. We're going to break down today's major and many questions with our expert panel, but first I do want to bring in Mike and Becky Patty, Libby's grandparents, who I've been lucky enough to have gotten to know through the years."

Just then, Mike and Becky appeared on screen. It was clear that Becky was distraught, now that her mission to track down the killer had been halted so abruptly. At that moment, I wished I could be there, right next to her, next to the families. Not in a studio, asking questions I already knew the answer to. "We've discussed many times on maybe what this day would be like for you. What did it feel like? Was it different from what you thought?"

"Oh, much different," Becky told me. "I've always told people that when we were told, they'd hear me yelling from the rooftops. And when they told us, it was really just kind of like, 'Oh, reality.' It was much different than what I expected. I got up the next morning, got my coffee, and got ready to post my 'Today is the day' [on Facebook] and realized . . . well, I don't have to do this anymore. Reality set in. Then I thought, *Now what is my purpose?* We are finding our feet there, figuring out what it is we have to do."

"The reality *is* setting in," Mike agreed, "and we are trying to figure out our path forward, which is the prosecution. We are still big advocates of law enforcement, and the case is not over."

Mike had always been a doer—someone who was most comfortable taking action.

"Susan, there is a face with the bridge guy and a name with the bridge guy, so if anyone knows anything, the case is not closed. We want to make sure that we look under every rock and check every lead, [for] any information that's out there. I've said this before: police don't know what they don't know, and I'm again asking for the public's help. Let's just keep the pressure on this, you know? Keep our foot on the accelerator. Let's drive this *all the way* to a closure. I mean, we've got another hill to climb in front of us, you know . . . We've made it to the top of one; now we've got another one in front of us, and we're not going anywhere. We're gonna make it to the top of the next hill as well."

When I asked about Anna and Tara and other family members, Becky responded, "We're all a united front. We're all in this together. We are all after the same thing." She spoke softly, almost whispering.

They'd always told me they felt like Libby was with them. Always. I asked whether they felt that these last couple of days.

"I know Libby knows we are down here working hard," Mike affirmed.

"I feel that too, Mike, and thank you. It's been such an honor getting to know you both, and I know your strength has to continue, and we are thinking about you constantly."

I felt helpless behind a desk. During the commercial break, I sent Mike and Becky a quick text: "Thinking of you." The interview had felt so formal, distant. I should be there.

"We are ten seconds out," I heard Brian Bell buzzing in my ear from the control room. Could he tell my mind was drifting?

"Welcome back." I snapped back into host mode, ready to talk to our next guest. "At the center of this investigation is Superintendent Doug Carter. Superintendent, it's good to see you. I know you have been working tirelessly to get this solved, but you say it's not a day to celebrate even though someone is in custody."

"Susan, I appreciate you taking the time to talk to me, and I would also like to recognize Becky and Mike, Kelsi, and Anna. I heard part of the interview, and I just love them dearly, and I'm so proud of them [for] the way in which they are handling this." It was obvious that Carter meant every single word he was saying.

I then pivoted to the press conference earlier that day. "You said that while you were driving in to make this announcement that everyone has been waiting for, someone in custody, that you felt a sense of peace come over you. When I heard that, I thought it was very profound."

The superintendent confessed that he hadn't expected that to happen. "I didn't really know what I would feel, but quite frankly, I pulled in that parking lot, and I saw news outlets from around the country, and I just thought to myself, *My gosh, they've stuck with us for all these years.* And I realize today was a somber day, but today was [also] a good day, and frankly, it was very peaceful."

Next, I wanted to talk with him about the "new direction" press conference back in April 2019. It still played heavily in my mind. "I was there," I reminded him, "and you said, 'We have changed direction, we believe that you are local, we believe that you are hiding in plain sight.' It appeared that you were right. I know you can't talk about specifics or particulars of the investigation, but *wow.*"

His answer didn't surprise me, but, still, I had to at least ask.

"Susan, I look forward to telling the country the story by presenting the facts to what we know versus what we think, and I say that all the time, but one day I'll be able to talk about my personal feelings about that. . . . Today is a good day for the city of Delphi and for the county and for the state of the nation. I really hope that after today, people start healing just a bit and start trusting again."

I was impressed by his composure and his steadfast leadership amid all the ups and downs of the previous years.

"Superintendent, something stood out to me. You did say at the presser that you believe that good outweighs evil. Do you still believe that?"

"I do," he said simply. "You know, very personally, before my dad died, he made me *promise* not to become cynical like him, and I was proud to report to him in 2018 that I'm not, and still, to this day, I'm not. I really do believe after all of these years in this business and seeing such horror and tragedy—and the list goes on and on—that good always, always comes through evil. And today's an example of that."

To wrap up the interview, I asked Doug Carter to elaborate more on how he was able to stay above the fray and remain positive.

"I have a great seat on the bus, Susan, to watch so many incredible people giving themselves for so many years," he told me. "And I don't want anybody to think this was all because of me because it's not, not even close. But I'm the luckiest guy in the world to be able to represent them."

Carter then addressed the frustration he knew everyone was still feeling, now that someone had been arrested but there were still so many questions left unanswered, details left undisclosed. "I don't blame them—the media—for wanting to know answers, but I think of the families of Abby and Libby, and I'm not about to jeopardize the integrity of this. . . . I want to maintain this partnership with our news outlets, and they have been wonderful, they really, really, really have."

I thanked him for his time and moved on to our next guest, Paul Holes. I was particularly interested to hear what he thought about the press conference.

"Well, obviously this is an amazing moment in this case; it's been a long time coming," Paul started. "Kudos needs to go to

Superintendent Carter, Indiana State Police, [and] Carroll County sheriff's office for staying on top of it.

"You know," he continued, "listening to Superintendent Carter, he obviously has a personal connection with the families of Libby and Abby. I completely understand the emotions he's going through . . . even though this is a good moment in the case, in many ways it's just the beginning. I've experienced that with the Golden State Killer. With the trial coming up, there is going to be a lot of challenges for Carter, his staff, and the family moving forward."

It appeared that those challenges had already started to surface in different ways.

The following day, Becky elaborated a bit more on her feelings via a public post on Facebook:

Yesterday was a long hard day, and I am glad it is finally over . . . When we were called in and told [law enforcement] had someone in custody, I thought I would be elated—but then you stop and think about all the new lives that will be affected by this person being arrested and realize it really is sad. The next phase then starts—society mandates that anyone arrested is only accused innocent until proven guilty. So, in that case—if he is still innocent, how am I supposed to be mad, angry, and hate this person? . . . But then I think—what about Abby and Libby's rights? I feel like in all this chaos, the focus on doing what is best for their rights and attaining justice are being trampled and forgotten. So, when he walked into the courtroom, and I saw him for the first time—all these emotions and thoughts were running through my mind at the same time and I didn't know how to feel. I guess my answer to that question is confused. I am just confused.

Kelsi understandably kept her feelings a bit closer to the vest, but on November 2, she pinned a tweet on Twitter reminding everyone that "all parties are innocent until proven guilty. Please do not wish harm on anyone or convict anyone before there is a trial.

"At this point there has been an arrest," she added, "but the investigation is not over." It had been almost six years. If this was the guy, Kelsi didn't want *anyone* or *anything* interfering with the many legal steps that lay ahead.

14

"Bloodlust"

Immediately after Richard Allen was announced as a suspect and taken into custody, the media at large was on the hunt to find out everything they possibly could about this man who had seemingly managed to evade suspicion for so long. Many details still were not yet clear, but it was immediately evident that as far as the media was concerned, anything and anyone in proximity to this case was considered fair game.

On November 3, six days after Richard Allen was charged with the girls' murders, Sheriff Tobe Leazenby filed a motion requesting a transfer from county jail to Indiana state prison for "safe keeping." In the motion, Leazenby stated that "his department could not provide the supervision to jail Mr. Allen due to safety concerns fueled by extensive coverage from an array of various media platforms both mainstream and social, throughout this state, the United States and the world."[1]

Carroll County judge Benjamin A. Diener signed off on that request and condemned the public's "bloodlust" and morbid "interest" in the case in no uncertain terms. Diener considered this bloodlust to be "extremely dangerous," noting that the public servants who were now pestered for information "do not feel safe and are not protected," even though they were "simply people doing their jobs" and, on top of that, "woefully underpaid." The judge himself expressed concern that his court could not keep up with "a storm of requests" to unseal the probable cause affidavit. He also said he'd become aware of widely circulated YouTube videos, including photos of his family members' faces, which, understandably, he found extremely troubling. Judge Diener issued a dire warning to anyone who might come into contact with the case in the future: "When the public peddles misinformation with reckless abandon, we all are not safe."[2]

On that same day, Diener recused himself from the case; the Indiana Supreme Court appointed Allen County judge Fran Gull as a special judge to serve in his place.[3]

A few days later, Richard Allen penned a handwritten note to the Carroll Circuit Court, "throw[ing] [himself] at the mercy of the court" and "begging to be provided with legal assistance in a public defender or whatever help is available."

Even though he'd originally stated at his hearing on October 28 that he would seek his own representation, Allen admitted in the letter that he hadn't realized then how expensive it would be to find someone, as well as how much it would imperil his family's immediate financial situation. He added that he and his wife had been forced to quit their jobs, and "she has had to abandon our house for her own safety." Allen closed by repeating that he was throwing himself at the mercy of the court, and he thanked them for their time.[4]

The following Monday, November 14, Allen received two court-appointed lawyers. According to local paper *Journal and Courier*, "Andrew J. Baldwin, of the firm Baldwin Perry & Kamish, filed his appearance just before 2 p.m." while "just before 3 p.m . . . Bradley A. Rozzi from Logansport entered his appearance on behalf of Allen."[5] The article added that Rozzi was listed as counsel while Baldwin would be cocounsel.

WHAT DID WE REALLY KNOW ABOUT THE MAN WHO WAS NOW LAWYERED UP? AT THE TIME OF HIS arrest, Richard Matthew Allen was fifty years old, but he would have been forty-four at the time of the murders. According to online records consulted by the *Independent*, Allen "has lived in Delphi since at least 2006, and in Indiana his whole adult life."[6] He lived with his wife, Kathy; the couple also shared one daughter, now an adult.

He worked as a pharmacy technician—his most recent license was issued in 2018, a little over a year after the girls were murdered—and was employed by the local CVS; several members of Libby's family remembered interacting with him at that location, even getting photos printed by him.[7] When asked, neighbors and coworkers just kept saying he seemed like "a normal guy," if a bit reserved and quiet.[8]

I thought back to what Paul Holes said on the day that he learned they had a DNA match and Joseph DeAngelo was the Golden State Killer.

"Evil finally had a name. The vicious serial rapist and killer was a father and grandfather with a fishing boat in the driveway and a Volvo in the garage; a regular guy who passed the time building model airplanes; a proud homeowner who liked his grass nice and short."[9]

During my twenty-plus years as a journalist, I have learned that rarely, if ever, do the most despicable, deplorable criminals look like the monsters they truly are. They blend in, often hiding in plain sight.

Richard Allen lived right there, in the small community of Delphi. Just a couple miles from the bridge.

Could this really be the person we'd been looking for all this time?

Several media outlets, including CNN, continued their efforts to access the charging information, something the public was supposed to have access to, thanks to Indiana's Open Records Act. However, the families still sided with the prosecutor and wanted to err on the side of caution. They had come this far; they trusted in the process. Plus, Becky wasn't willing to risk *anything* interfering with a fair trial. I understood.

Becky created a petition for people to sign to keep the details under wraps and posted it to Facebook with the following explanation:

> I have had several people ask me why I support this petition, so I have taken some time to discuss it with people that have varying views on the petition. I understand what you are saying and why—and I respect everyone's opinion—but in the end, a fair trial is my first priority. I do not believe our prosecutor would ask for this to happen without a good and justifiable reason. This case is already complex and hard enough—why would he add to the challenges he is already facing? He is doing something rarely ever done and shining the spotlight even brighter on him

and the investigative team. I am sure he looked at all alternatives and felt this was necessary for the integrity of the trial. I commend him for doing what he felt needed to be done despite the backlash he knew he would receive. First, some have said this petition would be no help, which I have to disagree with. According to the rule 6 which was cited—there is to be an open hearing in which the public may attend and speak, which in my thinking means the judge wants to hear what the people think and have to say. I am the public—and every signature on this petition is the public—so I am hopeful it will make a difference. Some say keeping it sealed goes against their constitutional rights—freedom of access—and against the law. Again, I disagree. When our forefathers wrote the constitution and made our laws fortunately, they had the foresight to include exceptions. They knew there would come a time when it might become necessary for certain case documents to remain sealed for a time hence the rule 6 our prosecutor cited. He is not breaking the law—he is utilizing all necessary tools for a fair trial. Those documents will be unsealed when the time is right—which will be during the trial—it just won't be unsealed on your time. All parties involved in the trial will have the entire probable cause affidavit—this includes the judge, prosecutor, and defense attorney. Who else truly needs those documents? It was said transparency is a checks and balance, ensuring the defendants' rights are being upheld. I am sure every LE that has been in contact with the defendant has gone out of their way to make sure everything is being done strictly by the book. I do not believe they would take a chance of jeopardizing the case by not doing so. I am sure the defendant's lawyer would not hesitate to immediately share with the public if he felt his clients' rights were not being met. His lawyer is there to defend him not only in court—but to ensure his rights are being upheld. Who knows—his lawyer may even agree with the prosecutor on this. Someone stated that by keeping the records sealed it defends the defendant. They are right. It defends him in being able to receive a fair trial by being able to select an unprejudiced jury. Can you imagine how hard it will be to select an impartial juror if they were read or hear what's in the document?

Becky continued with something that, in my opinion, she had wanted to say for some time. The accusations and lies that had been slung against these families for years were despicable. Not only did they have to mourn the loss of Abby and Libby, but they had also been forced to endure hateful accusatory posts from random people on the internet, who experienced few, if any, consequences.

This wasn't the first time the family had tried to fight back against these internet trolls. Three years before the arrest, in July 2019, Kelsi tried to debunk the rumors and lies about her family by hosting a live chat online. She talked about some of the rumors circulating and reiterated the trust they had in law enforcement. "Contrary to what most people seem to think, we really like our law enforcement. They're super encouraging, they're very honest with us, they're amazing, and I'm so proud of their work."[10]

Sadly, the misinformation and lies strewn across the internet did not slow down; they got even worse.

When it came to her thoughts on the sealed probable cause affidavit, Becky wasn't willing to stand down. As she finished her post, she made every effort to be as clear as possible:

You know once media and social media gets a hold of the information it will be broadcast all around the world. Where is the value if that happens for the case or the defendant? It defends the prosecution again by being able to provide a fair trial and aide in the selection of an unprejudiced jury. It defends all those witnesses contained within the report from having their lives scrutinized under a microscope and personal lives splashed all over the internet. Please—don't say we can just redact names and addresses—don't ever underestimate the determination of some of those internet sleuths and reporters—they are relentless and capable of coming up with information you would never expect them to uncover. Those lines you say to draw through the names won't stop them from finding out who those people are. We have seen throughout the last five and a half years the many innocent people that have had their lives turned upside down, pictures splattered all over and accusations thrown out with no evidence to back them. Those same people—who after this case is over will move on to the next case to spread havoc on the next bunch of innocents. While they move on with no consideration to the damage they have done—those innocent people are left picking up the pieces and trying to move on with their lives. Those witnesses also have rights— and they need to be defended also. We have just had our judge recuse himself from the case stating he felt unsafe for himself and his family, yet you want to unseal those documents and throw those witnesses to the wolves. I understand people want to know—and they will know—in time. We need to let those people that have all the evidence and realize the consequences of releasing the documents do whatever it takes to ensure a fair trial for all parties—to allow us to have our day in court—to let the justice system work. In the end—Isn't that what we all want? This is why I support keeping the probable cause affidavit sealed at this time.

Personally, I was on the side of the families. Yes, I wanted to know the details of the PCA, but *they* were the ones who were suffering. They were told by investigators that keeping it sealed was the best path, so that's what they went with. As a member of the media, I couldn't sign Becky's petition, but I would have if I could have.

Becky and Kelsi were far from the only members of the family who felt that it was important to keep this information close to the vest. In fact, all of Abby's and Libby's family members agreed with Becky, including Libby's mom, Carrie Timmons, who told the *US Sun*, "What's waiting a little longer going to do? I don't want anything to happen that would jeopardize the case in any way."[11]

———

ON NOVEMBER 22, MORE THAN THREE WEEKS AFTER RICHARD ALLEN WAS ARRESTED, HE WAS LED into court surrounded by several deputies. Wearing an orange prison jumpsuit and a bulletproof vest, Allen shuffled to the defense table, his wrists and ankles shackled.

Judge Fran Gull listened patiently as the prosecution and the defense argued about the consequences of unsealing the probable cause affidavit. Prosecutor Nick McLeland claimed that if it was unsealed, it could jeopardize the integrity of the investigation. He pointed to the families' wishes and the online petition, which by now had been signed more than forty thousand times.

For the first time, McLeland also mentioned the possibility that other people may have been involved. "We have good reason to believe that Allen was not alone, that there could be other actors." In addition, McLeland was concerned for those on the witness list who were considering testifying against Allen.

Allen's defense team, however, was adamant in their desire to release the affidavit to the public. His attorney, Bradley Rozzi, argued that "the public needs the truth" and added that keeping the documents secret only heightened the public's curiosity about the case.[12]

"The public has an absolute right to the information," McLeland agreed, "but at what cost? They [the public] already forced his wife to abandon their house." He didn't need to mention that Allen's wife and mother were at the hearing, sitting in the very same courtroom.

A day after presenting their case in front of the judge, the prosecutor's office released a statement to the media. "The Carroll County Prosecutor's office appreciates the Judge hearing our arguments yesterday morning and looks forward to her ruling. As I stated in court yesterday, we strongly believe the evidence shows Richard Allen was involved in the murder of Libby and Abby. Because the investigation is ongoing and given the intense public interest in this case, we think it would be best if the documents remain sealed. Regardless, we believe we have a very solid case against Mr. Allen and look forward to making our argument in trial."

On November 29, Judge Gull finally came to a decision and issued a written ruling, stating that the prosecutors had "failed to prove clear and convincing evidence that the Affidavit of Probable Cause and the Charging Information should be excluded from public access." Immediately afterward, seven of the eight pages of the document were finally released to the public.[13] And, as expected, the redacted document contained more than its fair share of bombshells—while still leaving many questions unanswered.

The first part of the affidavit focused on the girls—Victims 1 and 2—and reiterated the timeline of events, according to investigators.[14] It confirmed that the girls had been dropped off at the trailhead at 1:49 p.m. on February 13, and also that "Victim 2's phone shows that at 2:13 pm, Victim 1 and Victim 2 encountered a male subject on the southeast portion of the Monon High Bridge." According to the affidavit, no witnesses saw the girls after this encounter, and neither were there outgoing calls or texts from the girls' electronic devices. It also said that one of the victims mentioned the word *gun* before the girls were instructed to go down the hill and confirmed that there was "a .40 caliber unspent round less than two feet away" from the girls' bodies, with extraction marks on it.

The affidavit went on to include a series of interviews that painted a damning picture of what had happened next. Three juveniles who had been at the bridge around the time of the murders remembered coming across a man one of them described as "kind of creepy"; their descriptions of his clothing differed slightly, but they all agreed that he was wearing dark clothing (blue or black) and that he "glared" at them when they greeted him. He also apparently had "something covering his mouth" and "did not really show his face." The data on the juveniles' phones confirmed that they had been on the trail at the time they'd stated.

Another witness reported that she'd seen a group of four girls walking toward the bridge and that she'd come across the "white male, wearing blue jeans and a blue jean jacket," who was "standing on the first platform of the Monon High Bridge." She also reported seeing two girls who she believed to be the victims walking toward the bridge. As she was leaving, she noticed "a vehicle parked in an odd manner at the old Child Protective Services [CPS] building." Another witness confirmed seeing a "smaller dark colored car" parked in the same location, and his diagram of the scene matched up with the other witness's account.

A final witness account described a man "wearing a blue colored jacket and blue jeans" who was "muddy and bloody," appearing as if "he had gotten into a fight." This witness had seen the man while driving across CR 300 North, with a time stamp around 3:57 p.m. Though law enforcement interviewed other people who had been on and around the bridge that day, no one reported seeing the girls or the suspicious-looking man. In fact, none of the other individuals who were on the trail between 2:30 p.m. and 4:11 p.m. noted seeing a man who matched Richard Allen's description.

The affidavit also revealed that investigators had officially interviewed Allen back in 2017, during the initial rounds of interviews. He'd confirmed that he'd parked his car "at the old Farm Bureau building" (investigators believe this must have been the former CPS building, since there wasn't, and had never been, a Farm Bureau building in this location), and that he was on the trail between 1:30 and 3:30 p.m. He admitted to running into "three females" while he was at the bridge but denied ever running into the victims. I couldn't believe what I was seeing. He came forward in 2017. And he'd told an officer that he was there? Was *this* the reason the affidavit was sealed until now? I continued to read.

Investigators noted that his phone did not have an IMEI (i.e., international mobile equipment identity, which is basically a unique identification number), but they did record his MEID (i.e., mobile equipment identifier, which is a digit shorter).

Underneath his statement on the original report was a follow-up question, seeking to verify the identity of the three girls he'd encountered; it was unclear whether anyone had been able to confirm this, or had even tried to do so. Furthermore, it was revealed that at the time of the murders, Allen owned two cars, including a 2016 black Ford Focus that resembled the car other witnesses had reported seeing.

After this initial interview, there was a significant time gap right up to October 13, 2022, or shortly before Allen was taken into custody. He confirmed again that he had been on the trails on the day of the girls' disappearance and said that he'd been wearing "blue jeans and a blue or black Carhartt jacket with a hood." He admitted to owning firearms, but not to carrying them with him at the time, and said he had gone out to the bridge only to "watch the fish." In 2022, investigators also spoke to his wife, who verified that he owned both weapons (including knives and guns) and a blue Carhartt jacket, which he still had.

After issuing a search warrant of Allen's residence, law enforcement recovered several potentially important weapons, including a .40-caliber SIG Sauer P226 pistol—a handgun that Allen himself admitted "he never allowed anyone [else] to use or borrow." The laboratory performed testing on the gun the following week, and it was revealed that the unspent round located near the victims' bodies had been fired not just by a similar gun but by Allen's *exact* gun, which had been purchased back in 2001. Though the report acknowledged that such testing was by nature subjective, it justified the verification by noting that there was a "significant duplication of random striated/impressed marks," enough to confirm that there was "a sufficient agreement of individual marks."

TAKEN ALL TOGETHER, THE COLLECTION OF EVIDENCE AS PUT FORTH IN THE AFFIDAVIT—AT LEAST THE pages that had been revealed to the public—was damning. And yet so many questions were left unanswered.

During the course of this almost six-year-long investigation, bushels of armchair detectives, podcast hosts, and even some journalists had zeroed in on the presumed culpability of Ron Logan, or Kegan Kline, and in some instances both. Now Richard Allen, a man virtually *no one* had heard of up until this point, had been officially charged with the murders of Abby and Libby. Why hadn't he come up earlier?

The day I heard about Allen's arrest, I thought about a conversation I'd once had with Paul Holes about what he dubbed "criminal investigative failures."

"Susan, there is a great article written by Dr. Kim Rossmo, a twenty-one-year police veteran and university research professor, where he talks all about investigative traps and, in particular, confirmation bias. It's when you pick a suspect [first] and try to make the evidence fit, when what you [really] need to do is see if the suspect fits the evidence."

Paul Holes himself had been a victim of his own confirmation bias years earlier while he was investigating the Golden State Killer. Paul was laser focused on one particular suspect—so convinced of this person's guilt that "details [from the crime] that didn't fit [this suspect] I excused away. I came up with a reason why it didn't work, and then, ultimately, DNA evidence showed I was wrong. That's when I stepped back and reassessed."

I admired Paul Holes's ability to step back in that instance, particularly when so much was on the line, in order to try to regain as much objectivity as he could. But in the case of identifying Abby and Libby's killer, it wasn't like these presumptions of guilt the public was hearing about were coming from skilled investigators who were assessing all the components of the case. Instead, they were coming from self-proclaimed armchair detectives and even journalists who were making and posting false claims online based on a suspect that *they* had already decided was the killer. And though much remained up in the air after Allen's eventual arrest, it became even more apparent that many of the narratives and theories that had been posted on the internet were simply not true. I wondered how many details from the case had been conveniently disregarded in order to make these other potential suspects fit better. What else had we, as the public, missed for so many years?

The other big question that plagued me, as it had so many times before, was "Why?" If Richard Allen was in fact the person who had done this, what had been his motive for killing Abby and Libby? Was it premeditated, or was it simply a crime of opportunity? Allen claimed that he'd been on the bridge because he wanted to "watch the fish," but were there more sinister intentions lurking beneath that explanation?

Again, I questioned why the investigators hadn't pursued Richard Allen as a suspect after his initial interview in 2017. Is that why the prosecutor fought to keep the probable cause affidavit sealed? Was that an attempt to cover up a major screw-up?

And perhaps most mind-boggling of all, what had happened in the fall of 2022 that reignited interest in Allen as a potential suspect—thus bringing about his arrest in the first place?

As expected, investigators weren't saying, for now.

15

Investigative Insights with
Paul Holes

Though law enforcement insisted that the tip line was still open, and Richard Allen is presumed innocent until proven guilty, I found myself getting restless as the winter months wore on. There were still so many unanswered questions.

Perhaps the most glaring one was the reason no one was arrested for close to six years. How could it be that Richard Allen inserted himself into the investigation soon after the murders by telling a law enforcement official he was on the bridge that day, yet *no one ever followed up?*

The explanation swirling around the internet was that it had been a "clerical error," that an FBI civilian employee had "mislabeled" or "misfiled" Richard Allen's interview information.

But almost immediately the FBI responded to those claims, explaining that "the implication that an alleged clerical error by an FBI employee caused years of delay in identifying this defendant is misleading. Our review of the matter shows FBI employees correctly followed established procedures."[1]

With law enforcement's wall of silence reinforced post arrest, I felt compelled to reach out to Paul Holes, an expert who knew the ins and outs of how these kinds of investigations worked, to figure out just how likely it was that the family would finally get the justice they'd been deprived of for so long.

Paul had also met with Abby's and Libby's families several times; we'd even done a panel with them onstage about six months before Allen was taken into custody. He felt as invested in the case as I did, and early on he had personally reached out to Detective Holeman, offering his help if law enforcement should ever need it. With his impressive track record as a cold case investigator back in Contra Costa, I thought they'd be foolish not to take him up on it. Since retiring from active duty, Holes has connected with victims and families across the country, like Libby's and Abby's, who are still seeking answers and resolutions in their own cases. He understands more than most how the various components of a crime—the investigative element, the clinical element, even the emotional element—can overlap and butt heads with one another. I knew he'd have a levelheaded theory about what could've possibly led to Allen's arrest and what the long legal process ahead might look like.

I reached out to Paul in January, eighty-five days after Richard Allen's arrest, and asked him what he thought about the man in custody, someone who had apparently been hiding in plain sight for close to six years by that point.

"Paul, I'm so eager to hear your opinion about things, considering your expertise, everything you've been involved with, the investigation process, forensics, DNA," I began. "With the Delphi case, right now, where we are, it's still early on, and as you know Richard Allen is considered innocent until proven guilty. There's still so little we know about the crime scene, even the cause of death, with Abby and Libby. What do you think it was that finally led to an arrest?"

"Well," Paul replied, "what we do know is that Allen's name came up early on in the investigation. He admitted to having been at the location—not necessarily where Abby's and Libby's bodies were found but at the location near the bridge. And the strongest evidence that they have publicly released is the live round that had been chambered through a gun, and a firearms examination showed that that live round was chambered through Allen's gun, a SIG 226 gun, one that I'm familiar with. They obviously have more than that, and at this point in time, I think that's the one thing that I want to emphasize is that people are looking at the affidavit, the probable cause statement, to get an arrest warrant, going, 'Is that all they've got?' Well, no, it's not. They just need to be able to present enough information to a magistrate in order for him to be convinced that there is probable cause to order a peace officer to go arrest Allen, and that's what they did in the affidavit.

"I do believe that they have other information—most likely electronic information—because Allen did say he was at this location, with his cell phone, and there is technology available to authorities that is not cellular based but Google locational based. That can really finely pinpoint Allen's cell phone, within this park area, up on the bridge, possibly out to where the girls' bodies were found. And I do think that they likely have that kind of information, that contradicts Allen's statements of what he was doing, or what he said he was doing at the park. This type of technology can literally show Allen's cell phone coming up and meeting up with the smart device that Abby and Libby were carrying, and I believe it was a cell phone."

"It was," I said.

"And then," Paul continued, "watching these two phones move to the location, to where Abby's and Libby's bodies were found, if they have that kind of information, coupled with the physical evidence of the firearm. And, likely, they will get more evidence, now that he has been arrested; DNA testing is under way, I'm sure, plus other types of investigative processes. They're building a very strong case against Allen is my best estimate at this point."

"So even though the crime took place in 2017, the technology they can use now could bring those cell phones together and track Richard Allen, if it was him, to Libby and Abby?" I asked.

"Yes," he said and nodded. "In this technology, it's called a geofence. This is a technology that relies on Google location services. So if these cell phones have their location services turned on, and if you're using something like Google Maps, or other types of apps, that require it to be placed within the geography of wherever you're at, that is something that Google has kept, all the way back to about the 2008–2009 time frame. So it is a technology that they could look at, even if they didn't think to use it in 2017, and then, in 2022, they're going, 'Oh jeez. We could use that.' Very likely, that data was still present, and when I think about it, [Allen] all of a sudden just came to light. Well, it wasn't based on the firearm's round at the scene. There's something *else* that happened, and it likely wasn't DNA, because he wasn't in the FBI's CODIS system. That's where I believe it's the high-tech information."

"I think you might be on to something," I said. "Just thinking back—and this is just speculation, considering how little we know—but when I was at the bridge, for the first time, with Kelsi, she looked to the left and said, 'Oh my gosh. This might be from Libby.' It was a little box with a treasure inside. It was this little baby, and she told me they used to go geocaching. Is that similar at all with the technology in geocaching, in terms of location?"

"To a point, yes," Holes replied. "Now, I'm not real familiar with how individuals are utilizing their smart devices to do this geocaching process. I'm kind of familiar with the game, in terms of how that particular thing works, but in essence, we used to do this when I was on the FBI task force before I retired. We had a crime analyst, who was formerly out of the military, highly skilled, and he would be able to get this locational information from victims' phones, suspect phones, and then map that. And you'd literally see the victim driving around, stopping, getting out to a certain location in a city, and the suspect driving around, and getting out and moving up, and meeting up with the victim. And then there's date and time stamps with this information, and for these types of cases, they were typically gang-related cases with shootings.

"And so now, in a particular city, we had the shot spotter. So when shots are fired, the loud report of a gun, this system would immediately register a gunshot was fired. So we have a date and time stamp there, and that can now be all married up into a visual map that could be presented in court or for the investigators.

"And so, I would imagine, if I'm correct, and they did do a geofence, [there might be] Abby and Libby walking up to one end of the bridge, and going onto the bridge, and then Allen's cell phone possibly going on the bridge. And we also had the video, with the date and time stamp on that, and so they could merge all this together, and it would be absolutely compelling to show he is the man on the bridge, and he is the one responsible for their homicides."

I nodded, fully engrossed in what he was saying, trying to take everything in. Maybe this would prove to be the key? Richard Allen had admitted to having his cell phone with him. According to the probable cause affidavit, Allen stated he was watching a stock ticker on his phone as he walked.

Then I thought about the video that Libby had taken, as well as a conversation I'd had with her grandfather Mike. He always thought that she might've taken the video so she could show it to him later on, like "Look at this creepy guy on the bridge." I asked Paul what he thought about that.

"Well, [the video] is absolutely key. In part because you know they do have the date and time stamp, in which now you have this man who's approaching Libby and Abby on the bridge. You hear his voice ordering them down the hill. Now, law enforcement only released so much of that video. There's more to that video—is what I have been told—and I believe that there's enough there that supports that the man that they are recording on the bridge is their killer."

"And with the Golden State Killer, of course, all of that data and evidence had been analyzed and looked at for so many years," I said. "So, with technology, it's those advances—whether forensics or electronics—that can bring together the solution to this case, no matter what year it occurs?"

"It absolutely *can*," Holes said. "Having worked cold cases now for thirty-plus years, evidence is deposited when the crime occurs, but as time goes on, sometimes that evidence is not available to be utilized by the [current] technology, when the crime occurred. But the technology has improved [over time]. Most notably, of course, the DNA technology—which, at this moment in time, I don't know if they have DNA evidence in Abby and Libby's cases. But the technology has advanced to a point, now that they've identified Allen, [where] if they had developed, let's say, partial DNA profiles from their bodies or from their clothing that they couldn't search in a database, they can now do a direct comparison and possibly show that, yes, he is likely the contributor of this DNA, further strengthening their case. So that's an example of how just the advancement of the technology is allowing them to go after low levels of DNA. And the investigative process relying on a different technology, I believe, the high-tech side, identifies him, and then they can exploit that and go, 'Now we can get a direct sample from him and compare it directly to the evidence in the case.'"

I thought about Paul Holes's memoir, *Unmasked*, which I'd finished in record time as soon as I got my hands on a copy. I wondered whether there was anything else we could glean from the murderer that didn't come from DNA or forensic evidence recovered at the scene.

"You have a phrase that stood out to me when I was reading about in your book," I said. "'Know thy enemy'—not just about the crime that is committed, like the one that led to the deaths of Abby and Libby, let's say, but what the perpetrator did that *didn't* need to be done. Could you explain that?"

"So," he said, "when you have an offender that is interacting with the victims . . . OK, when I'm evaluating a crime scene—and let's say it's a homicide scene and it's a sexually motivated scene. First, I'm evaluating the offender's actions and behaviors in order to accomplish those crimes. However, when you have an offender that has certain fantasies, this is where that 'Know thy enemy' comes in, because the average person is aware of normal, socially accepted behaviors, whether it be sexually or how you interact with people, how you interact within somebody's house.

"Some of these offenders develop these paraphilias. They develop oddities in their sexual behavior, and they fantasize about those, and so, when they start interacting with their victims, they want to live out those fantasies, and those oddities come out during their interactions with the victims. And that's where oftentimes law enforcement is inexperienced at assessing these oddities that the offender's doing at the scene, not recognizing 'Oh, this is fantasy.' And so often these oddities are things that are not necessary to commit the crime. And that's why when I'm evaluating a scene, and I'm looking at the injuries to the victims, I'm looking at how the offender is interacting within that crime scene. I am looking for those types of oddities, where I go, 'OK, he's doing something that is unnecessary but that is important to him.' So that is what you have to focus on when you start assessing—what is the *true* motivation of this crime?"

I remembered reading a lot about these behavioral "oddities" in Paul's book; criminal profilers, like him, called them *signatures*.

"And the former prosecutor has come out and said that there were signatures left at the scene—signatures that we wouldn't think of," I said. "Would that be an example of that?"

"So let's go back to the early beginning of behavioral analysis, the FBI's Behavioral Analysis Unit, which the Netflix series *Mindhunter* is sort of based on," Holes explained. "They developed a category, a way to categorize behaviors of a crime, and so you have what everybody's now heard of: your MO, or modus operandi. OK, this is what the offender does in order to commit the crime, and offenders learn how to improve on it to commit more crimes. DeAngelo [the Golden State Killer], initially, when he first started, he was not very good at breaking into houses, but then he became better; his MO improved as a burglar to break into houses. So an MO can change, but then when you get into these oddities—I was talking about fantasy aspects that these offenders have. And *this* is where you see a signature—it's how the FBI categorized these oddities—and that signature, they would say it's unique. Really, I wouldn't necessarily say it's *always* unique, because a lot of these offenders have the same types of fantasies, and you see the same types of behaviors, but this type of signature is something that is relatively stable.

"This is one way that, using this behavioral analysis, crimes can be linked, because that offender, each time he's attacking, he's wanting to experience that fantasy, and he's possibly leaving behind the physical clues, that signature, that can be interpreted by somebody like me, looking at the crime scene, looking at what was done to the victims."

"I'm generalizing here," I said before going into my next question, "but do criminals necessarily go in *knowing* that murder will be the outcome, or are they going in just thinking of that fantasy, and that becomes the outcome?"

"It is so dependent on the offender," Holes said. "When I start talking about, let's say, a serial predator, that's sexually motivated. This type of offender has a fantasy in terms of how he wants to carry out the sexual assault. Now, many of these predators—they're typically called *serial rapists*, right? Their intent is to do this sexual assault in the way that they need to. Sometimes it's to dominate the victim. It's very angry. Other times it's trying to experience something, almost like a consensual type of interaction. These types of offenders are there to commit the sexual assault without the intent to kill. That's *not* part of their fantasy.

"Some of these offenders will kill just to eliminate the witness, and this is where you go, 'Well, is that act of homicide core to the signature of the offender?' If it is, now you're dealing with somebody who goes into the attack, into victim selection, where the attack's going to occur, with the *intent* to kill, because that's part of their signature. That's part of the fantasy. That's what they enjoy. And then other types of these offenders, somebody like Sam Little [a serial killer who murdered nearly one hundred women across three decades], they have what I call—it's like a God complex. They determine when the victim dies, and somebody like Sam Little would strangle his victims to the point of unconsciousness, only to allow them to come back to life and then strangle them again. He's playing God. So this is where, now, that type of offender goes into the attack with the intent to kill."

"And with Richard Allen," I said, pivoting the conversation back to Delphi, "if we *do* find that it was him, yes, that he was at the bridge that day, could it just be random that he was waiting for someone that fit into that category? If it was someone older, two women, would he have attacked them as well? Or was he looking for younger girls like Abby and Libby?"

"At this point in time, I don't know enough about Allen in terms of what his particular victim preference might be," Holes said. "So it's really hard to pinpoint because we have so many examples of what are called *crossover offenders*. So people think that if somebody is sexually interested in younger girls, they will *only* go after younger girls, and that's not the case. They will also attack adult women. Sometimes they will go after males as well, but their preference is that younger girl. Many of these offenders, and I think possibly in Allen's case—but I can't pin down his preference—I do believe that Abby and Libby were victims of opportunity, and whether or not he went there with the intent to go after younger girls, I don't know.

"What the perpetrator did see is he saw Abby and Libby isolate themselves on that bridge, and now, he recognized, because he knew the terrain out there, that he would be able to keep them and force them—just through his physical presence—force them off that end of the other side of the bridge. And then he purposely took them away from the neighborhood that was just south of that bridge into that isolated location across the creek. This is when I went out there, I was like, 'This person is a local. No question about it.'"

My mind went back to the bridge, thinking about the view from the first wooden plank. Paul was right. The other side of the bridge was isolated and far from the trails, where there wasn't really a chance of seeing someone or anyone seeing you. The bridge really was the perfect place to commit a crime, and I wondered whether the killer had planned on using the bridge to their advantage all along. Once Abby and Libby had crossed the bridge, they would walk right into a spot that would be ideal for isolating and essentially trapping them, preventing them from running away.

I brought up Libby. "And something that I believe the offender didn't see," I said, "or he didn't know, was Libby's cell phone. That she had that phone, that she was hitting Record. Do you think, being from Delphi, knowing what he did, that he saw that and thought, *Oh no, I'm in trouble here?*"

"Yeah," Holes said. "Well, I believe that sometimes offenders will get tunnel visioned. That compulsion is overriding, and if [this offender] saw the cell phone, he may not necessarily have recognized the danger to himself. He's just now focused on 'I've got these two girls. I know what I want with these two girls. I need to get them over there so I can spend time alone with them.'

The most critical thing is, as you mentioned, he's probably from Delphi. He's seen in this video, released worldwide, shortly after the crimes. This is where, now, my expectation is that the offender would be going, 'Uh-oh,' and this is where post-offense behavior becomes key. My expectation would've been . . . he's going to get rid of those clothes, he's going to lose weight, he's going to change his facial hair, he's going to move away from the location. And the surprising thing is [Allen] really didn't do any of that. Even though it is such a small town, he must have been so paranoid that somebody walking into CVS would be going, 'Oh my God. You're on the poster outside.'"

"Considering this happened in 2017," I said, "and Allen would've been about midforties at the time, would it surprise you, and does it surprise you, that a person could just wake up one day and do this? Could he have been fantasizing about it for that many years without taking action and having priors on his record, or killing other people, killing other young girls?"

"Well, it's not surprising that his criminal history doesn't show anything," Holes replied. "Remember the Golden State Killer, Joseph DeAngelo, had no criminal history and he was very prolific as a serial rapist and a serial killer. With Allen, he's fifty years old, right? He is getting older, for an offender to be starting this type of crime. Typically, for a serial predator, we start seeing them act out in their twenties, and they are showing indications of violent fantasies, minimally, in their teenage years. So my expectation is that he likely had some desire over the course of his life. I would not be surprised if there are unsolved cases [if he did it], not necessarily homicides. There may be child-molestation cases, there could be rape cases, that he's been involved with that just have not been linked to him for one reason or another. Again, that would be my expectation.

"But part of what we are seeing now is that some of these cold cases have been solved with the genealogy tool like we used in the Golden State Killer case. There are *many* of these cases that if I'm looking at them while they're an unsolved case, I'm going, 'This looks like a fantasy-motivated offender who's likely serial.' And we're seeing a fair number of these offenders that we're now terming *one-off offenders*. They are committing what appear to be fantasy-motivated crimes, predatory-style crimes, but they never do it again. And this is an interesting category of offender that needs to be studied. And I can't say if Allen is this one-off offender or not, but . . . I do know some details in terms of what happened to Abby and Libby by the offender, and my expectation is that there was fantasy involved by the offender and he likely had fantasy for many, many years leading up to this attack. And whether or not he ever acted out on that fantasy before, I don't know, but he saw an opportunity that day when they were out on the bridge."

"And this could all be happening without [his] family members knowing at all?" I asked.

"Absolutely," Holes said. "This is where—think about BTK, Dennis Rader, and his very active fantasy life. He was into bondage, and he's binding himself up and taking pictures of himself. His wife had no clue; his kid had no clue. His church members, the president of his church—they had *no clue* that he was this killer, out there in Wichita, who had a very active fantasy life. And these offenders find those private moments in order to fantasize, and somebody like Joseph DeAngelo, he would steal souvenirs from his victims over the years. And he's finding private moments in his own home to live out fantasies while he's holding those souvenirs or looking at those souvenirs. With somebody like Allen, I know he's married, he has kids, right?"

"A daughter," I said, nodding.

"I'm sure that there were blocks of time in which he would have been able, as we all have our private moments, and he probably was able to isolate himself and start thinking about some of these types of crimes that he would like to commit."

"You bring up a great point with Kerri Rawson," I said, thinking back on my conversation with her at CrimeCon. "She had *no* idea. Talking about a trip to the Grand Canyon that she took with her father, she said, 'This was my dad. He'd make me scrambled eggs.' So these offenders get very good, Paul, at hiding this."

"They do, and that's part of your organized offender. And I'm going, again, back to what's now somewhat of an archaic FBI profiling term, but I very much like to break offenders down into *organized* and *disorganized*, just like the early FBI profilers did, because it's easy. It's very simple for a practitioner, like me, to be able to do this. And your organized offender is able to think about, and plan ahead, how they want to commit the crimes, but they're also very good at compartmentalizing their life. And this is where they can come off like Dennis Rader, and be the president of their church, be active in a Boy Scout troop, and keep the wife or their intimate partner just clueless about it. They have this very horrifying aspect to their personality."

"And you were there," I said, "in Delphi. As an outsider, I was startled by the gravity, the height of the bridge, at sixty-three feet, and just how dangerous it appeared. As a young girl, thirteen or fourteen, I'm sure I wouldn't have been afraid of it. You don't have any fear at that age, really, to walk across it. I thought that, immediately, considering how long it took us to get there, how out of sight that it was, that whoever did this, he *had* to be local. Is that what drove you to that conclusion? Was it the bridge there and the terrain?"

"In part, it was the bridge," Paul replied. "I walked out onto that bridge. And I'm scared of heights."

"Yeah, me too," I said. "I couldn't do it. I stood near the edge."

"Yeah. I got, I don't know, maybe 20 percent—"

"*Wow.*"

"—across . . . that's where my body said no. I could *not* move my feet anymore. And what I thought, that struck me, was how casually the man in the video, looking down, hands just . . . he's not trying to balance . . ."

"Just strolling."

"Yeah, he's just strolling along, and I thought, *He's walked across this bridge before.* He's very comfortable with the height, he's very comfortable with the railroad tie spacing. He knows where to step. But most significantly, to me, was the distance he took Abby and Libby away from the bridge to where their bodies were found. And to take them down the hill, and then it's about a fifteen-minute walk to that location where they were found. Across that, I call it a river. I think they technically call it a creek, but it is a substantial body of water that they would've had to cross. Why is he doing that?

"Well, he knows that's where there's the least likelihood that there's going to be witnesses that will see him with the girls. *That's* what informed me this guy knows this area, he's been here before. Now, I couldn't say if he's still living in the area, but you have people who grow up in the area, they move away, and they come back and visit family, or have other business, and of course they retain that local knowledge. And so, from my perspective, even prior to Allen being arrested, I'm going, 'This is a local guy.' No question about it. This is not a truck driver who happened to just stop off at this somewhat scenic location, just to be like a tourist. He *knows* this terrain."

"Right, 'down the hill,'" I murmured. "He knew he'd have the isolation, seclusion, and even the time, from what we've heard, to put signatures there, or do what he did during the day, the middle of the day. I never understood that, Paul, until I was there in Delphi. I thought the middle of the day, a bridge, a casual stroll where people are going back and forth? How could you get away with that without anyone seeing? Then you actually see the bridge, and you can understand that."

"No, absolutely. Where he took Abby and Libby, he had no fear that anybody would be walking by," Holes said. "The trees, the potential other types of plants that—I'm not sure exactly how high they were. When I was out there, they were quite high. But he in essence took them to a location where he was confident that he wouldn't be stumbled across. Since this was my first time visiting the bridge location, when I'm looking south, on the bridge, and you see the forest, as the railroad tracks keep going on, my naive understanding of that location was *Well, why didn't he just take them straight down the tracks and then off the side of the railroad tracks?* Well, it's because there's houses back there that you can't see from the bridge. He purposefully diverted them away from that neighborhood.

"That is part of the detail that I think many people aren't understanding, on how that informs investigators, on how investigators should be assessing *What does the offender know about this location?* Because I was new to the location, I was like, *Well, why not there? Oh, that's why.* Well, this guy must have known it because he went completely the opposite direction once he got off of the south end of the bridge."

"And based on your experience with victims' family members," I said, "and the next phase . . . what would be your thoughts, or words, to them in terms of the trial and what is next? That feeling that *Oh, once we get this guy, it's smooth sailing from here on out.* Obviously they know it's not that simple, but what is the next step, in your experience? There's no such thing as closure, really, as we both well know."

"Right," Holes said. "Again, he's innocent until proven guilty, but right now the families believe they have an answer. Authorities got them an answer as to who was responsible for killing Abby and Libby. Now comes the process which is not kind to victims or victims' families—the criminal justice system. You have a defendant that, in our system, is given all sorts of rights, and the family members want this thing over with. They want to see a conviction. They want justice served. But this is not a sprint; it is a marathon—particularly in a double-homicide case. It would not surprise me if it takes two years, four years, six years, before this actually gets to trial, just because of all the defense motions that are going to be occurring, all the antics that can be played.

"They may be marching up to trial and he decides to fire his attorneys. Well, guess what? New attorneys, who are unfamiliar with the case, get assigned to him. Well, they're going to need time to get up to speed in order to get him a fair trial. So that's an antic that sometimes is played, and this is very frustrating to the families. They are going to have to brace themselves that this is going to probably take a long time and be very frustrating. And then when the trial occurs and they're sitting in court, in the same room as him, and then listening to the witness statements and finding out new horrifying details about what happened to their loved ones . . . It's going to be a painful process.

"So this is really where having a support system, to help them through—like, out of my office, we have victim advocates that became very close to victim families—would help them through this process," Holes said, winding down. "But also, they probably would need other professional help in order to get through this because it is going to be grueling until it's finally done. And even when it's done, as I saw with the Golden State Killer case, they're not going to all of a sudden go, 'Triumph!' and the trauma is gone. That's still going to be there."

16

A Closer Look into the Criminal Mind with Dr. Ann Burgess

It was a question that had been haunting Superintendent Doug Carter for almost six years. If he could speak to the killer, he told me, that's what he would ask: "Why Abby? Why Libby?" I've asked it too, countless times. Is there ever an answer that makes sense? How can we ever begin to comprehend the mind and motivations of someone capable of such depravity?

In my continuing quest for answers, I reached out to Dr. Ann Wolbert Burgess, an internationally recognized pioneer in the field of criminal profiling. I first met Dr. Burgess in August 2020. She'd joined me as a guest on *Weekend Express*, where we discussed the time she spent interviewing and analyzing convicted serial killer Edmund Kemper (also known as the "Co-Ed Killer"). Kemper had admitted to killing ten people, including his mother.

Dr. Burgess spent hours sitting across from Kemper as he explained how he would insert himself into the investigation by following law enforcement to their regular spots, bars, and restaurants to figure out what they knew.

I knew that Dr. Burgess could help further explain the psychology of someone capable of murdering a thirteen- and fourteen-year-old in the middle of the day.

Dr. Burgess is currently a professor at Boston College, where she specializes in forensic nursing, but she's been studying the criminal mind for decades; in fact, she was the one who helped the FBI's Behavioral Science Unit (now the Behavioral Analysis Unit) standardize the process of criminal profiling, where law enforcement analyzes all the aspects of a crime—crime scene, victimology, signatures, and so forth—to create an educated profile of the offender. Though I'd watched the fictionalized Netflix series *Mindhunter* (which was based on FBI agent John Douglas's memoir) and knew the character of Wendy Carr was roughly based on her, I'd been even more fascinated by Burgess's own memoir, *A Killer by Design*, in which she chronicles her experiences as she actually lived them. I knew Dr. Burgess could help explain the psychology of someone who was capable of committing a crime as truly horrifying as this one.

When I first contacted Dr. Burgess, she mentioned that she'd been following the Delphi case a bit and she'd be happy to chat with me. I called her shortly after I spoke with Paul Holes, in January 2023.

I had about a million questions, but to start with, I asked her how she'd felt when she heard that someone had finally been arrested for the crime.

"Well," Burgess began, "first of all, my reaction was *Thank heavens they finally got someone.* My second reaction was *Now, do they have the right person?* We have to be careful here, because [Allen] only is a suspect, and certainly the trial is coming up, and that's going to be very, very interesting. This was a very tragic, absolutely tragic case, where two young teenagers were just out for an afternoon kind of thing, walking in an area that I think they had walked in before. I don't think this was anything new to them. The only things I've seen and heard about this case have been what's been revealed as public information, in terms of meeting a male on a kind of bridge around the railroad. But it doesn't sound like they knew him.

"I was curious [and wanted to] read as much [about the case] as I could. A couple things: It's interesting that law enforcement has never told us [the public] what the manner of death was. That's kind of curious, because one of the pieces of evidence that they have is a gun, so that makes me suspect. I'm not sure that [the cause of death] was a gun, or why wouldn't they have said it? That's curious, but at any rate, these were two young teenagers, and they were approached by at least one person. There's some talk that there might have been more than one person. I haven't seen that developed very well in anything that they put out, but when you look at trying to profile a case, which is what I did with the FBI Behavioral Science Unit [BSU], you look at the victimology.

"So what do we know about these two young girls that would raise their risk level, if you will, to becoming a victim or a target? It doesn't look like there was anything in their backgrounds. They were in, what . . . eighth grade? They were best friends. They had everything going for them and didn't seem to have any risk factors, outside of the fact that they were in this wooded area, walking along. That would raise their risk level if perhaps someone who was watching, having them under surveillance. That's what we don't know, and in many, many of these cases, that's of course what happens. Everybody thinks, *Oh. Well, they didn't know these people*. Well, right. These victims may *not* have known the person or persons, but that person or persons could have known them by just watching them, not necessarily any interaction. In a way, my initial view is that this was a blitz attack, that there was no prior interaction that we know of, and that the girls were ordered, evidently by a statement in one of the videos, to get down there, because they were on this bridge, and they had to go down."

"'Down the hill,' right," I said, nodding.

"Right," Burgess said. "And I don't even know, unless maybe you do, where the bodies were found. Were the bodies found down in that area? I know that they had flowers left on a certain area, so you really had a puzzling crime scene.

"Now, this is also a very small community. I think only about three thousand people [lived there], so people knew each other, probably. When we [learned the identity of the] suspect that they had arrested, I think it's interesting that he was known in the community as working at a local store.

"A lot of things are going to be hard, I think, for a prosecutor to bring forward. But we have to be open-minded and see what [evidence] he has [to tie Allen to the crime]. As far as I can see, there are two possibilities. One, this bullet or unspent bullet, as they call it, that was found near the young girls, and the other is the car."

"Absolutely," I replied.

"Yeah," Dr. Burgess said. "It's a little bit like this Idaho case [in which Bryan Kohberger allegedly stalked and killed four college students near the University of Idaho], where you have a car, and everybody gets quite excited about that, and you have something that points to a weapon."

"If it is Allen's car, Ann—and there's a lot of speculation about whether or not it is, because there's so much information that we're not privy to—would it surprise you that, if it is him, he wouldn't have gotten rid of the car? That he kept the same car?"

"Well, you would think so," Burgess said. "I mean, that's logical, so is it counterintuitive that he doesn't get rid of it if he is the suspect? I will say this. The police have solved many, many crimes with cars. I learned that so early. In fact, when I was down at the BSU, they would always try to profile anybody's car. 'What kind of a car did you drive?' 'What's your car like inside, so to speak?' So I wasn't surprised to see that the car was a possibility, but it's still not nailed down in terms of the make and model. There's a lot of speculation about that. So, to answer your question, if he *isn't* the killer, why *not* keep the car? That's one of the statements that's coming through. On the other hand, he was in plain sight, and that could have only boosted his ego or his narcissism, if indeed he is the correct person."

I shuddered to think about the mindset of someone who was capable of murdering two young girls and then continuing to live in that small community as if nothing were wrong. I was reminded again about how brazen this crime was for a multitude of reasons, including the suspected crime scene, since it was clear he would've had to have been a local to know that once those girls were on the other side of the bridge and down the hill, they would be unable to escape.

I asked Dr. Burgess what she thought about the terrain and the possibility of the killer going to the bridge and where the bodies were found on several occasions beforehand to plan it out.

"Yeah, absolutely," she replied. "That wouldn't surprise me, that the person would have been there, and it sounds like it's easy to watch people come by if you're down there. Again, you'd have to

224 | DOWN THE HILL

be at the scene to look up and to see people coming." I wondered whether he had been to the site countless times before looking for that right moment to attack.

Then I asked about motive. "Back before anyone was in custody," I said, "I asked Superintendent Doug Carter what he would want to ask the offender, and he said he'd want to know *why* this happened. Why these girls? Knowing that you have some background in this, in looking into the criminal mind, do we ever really know why these offenders do what they do? Can we look into their backgrounds and tie it into some sort of trauma, or is it not that easy?"

"Well, the only way we know *why* is if he is able to tell us," Dr. Burgess said grimly. "That's one way. But the other new area [of research] that I'm getting involved with, and I think certainly anyone in your field will, is what is being posted [online]. Social media is a new kind of feature, if you will, to the crime scene, and so sometimes that can be posted. I'm not saying that's the case here. I have no idea in this case if the suspect ever posted anything, but that gives us a window into their cognitive. Now, I worked with the BSU looking at behavior, and that was very different then, obviously. In this case, again, it's very puzzling that a fifty-year-old person, who evidently has children of his own, with no prior background in any type of crime, has been arrested." That's when Dr. Burgess brought up Richard Allen talking to an officer and putting himself at the scene.

"I will say, another curious thing—and maybe you know more about it—is that . . . when this first happened, he volunteered to the police that he had been in that area. So we don't know *what* he told the police, but, evidently, they didn't make any other inquiries over five years. They must not have had him on their radar screen, I think, until something [else happened]. Maybe something has broken in the case."

"Yes, Dr. Burgess. What we are hearing in regard to that—and they won't elaborate much—is that it was some sort of clerical error and they're not obligated to tell the media or anyone exactly how it came about. But it was a file that was misplaced, or maybe someone didn't really think it was relevant, so apparently, Allen spoke to someone in law enforcement, a conversation officer, and said, 'I was there. This is what I was wearing. This is the time that I was there. I saw three females.' Maybe, if those witnesses saw him and would recognize him or his outfit, that he was trying to get out ahead of it, saying, 'Hey, I was here,' not knowing that Libby hit record on her phone. So maybe—and I'm hoping that the missing piece that Superintendent Carter had been asking about is Libby recording that—so maybe he got out ahead of it and they misplaced it, didn't think about it until someone new came in, with a new set of eyes, and said, 'What about this file? What about this guy?'"

"Certainly, certainly," Burgess said. "Now, the other thing is they ought to be able to nail [the timing] down. If he was working at the time, do you know what day of the week [the crime] was on?"

"It was a Monday," I replied, "and I know that he was a pharmaceutical tech at CVS, but he got that job *after* the girls were found, and I believe that he worked at another store prior. I'm not sure about that particular day, but you're right—we should be able to track down if he was supposed to be at work. I know the girls had a makeup snow day, so school was off that day."

"Right, so that would be something that they could nail down to look at," Burgess said. "Anything that they can find that would support what they feel as evidence is going to be really, really important. But . . . the clothing. I think you also mentioned the clothing—that he was wearing a dark navy-blue jacket?"

"Yes."

"Well, maybe they have found some DNA, whether they've been able to confiscate it. Certainly getting his laptop would be important to see. Also, what he was doing [*after* the crime]. Was he following it?

"We do know that, at least from the study we did on our thirty-six killers [back at the FBI], is that [offenders] do insert themselves into the investigation." That's when Dr. Burgess brought up Ed Kemper. "He always identified himself as a friendly nuisance. He would sit with the cops [at bars] and listen to their talk and so forth, but it sounds like if [the suspect in this case] . . . only made one call to the police, that's only one [time]. But if he followed [the case], that would be important."

"That's true," I said. "That was, and is, of course, the talk on everyone's mind in that town. You see pictures of Abby and Libby everywhere—in all the bars, restaurants, stores, offices. You see the two sketches of the suspect."

I thought back to Allen's family, who were also living in this town, with the dark cloud of this tragedy hanging over their heads. I couldn't be sure, but it was likely they were just as unaware that they would be swept up in it years later.

"What about his wife and daughter?" I asked. "The daughter was about, I believe, eight to ten years older than Abby and Libby at the time. But as you know, in your experience, someone like BTK, they can hide their dark sides well and be two different people."

"Absolutely," Burgess said. "They usually *are* two different people if they do it well. There was just one child?"

"One daughter," I said.

"That's important," Burgess said. "And the wife. We'd want to know more about the wife, what the daughter has done, if there's anything there, possible problems. [Families can] be a stressor too."

"It looks—and, as you know, looks can be deceiving—it looks like the Allens were a happy family," I said. "Husband and wife married twenty-plus years, so probably no indication there."

I thought back to how Allen had interacted with different members of the community, including the time he'd talked with Libby's aunt, Tara, at CVS.

"Allen was apparently giving Tara pictures right before the funeral," I said, "that she was developing for the service, and she was crying, and he said, 'They're on me,' and she remembers that. Maybe, being in that CVS in such a small town, he had his eyes on everyone."

"Absolutely," Burgess said. "And you're right—that did come out that he didn't charge for the photos. That's kind of interesting too . . . Why did he do that? I mean, it *looks* like a gesture of good-will. It doesn't have to be, though."

Burgess's point about this looking like a "gesture of goodwill" hit me. If Allen *was* the perpetrator, how could we reconcile this generous act with the brutality of the murders?

"We don't know the cause of death, but we now know there was a gun involved. Law enforcement keeps talking about the fact that these were 'brutal murders,' and that word, *brutal,* suggests something else to me," I said.

The fact that Allen didn't have any priors—that we knew of—was also interesting: Did this brutality just come out of nowhere?

"If Allen is the offender here," I continued, "do you think he would have done this again, if he wasn't caught? At the time of the murders, he was forty-four, and he's nearing fifty now. Maybe he fantasized about this for years, planned it, didn't know it was going to be those particular girls? Would he have done something like this again, or would he have been sustained by the fantasy or even the memory of doing it? We've heard talk of the offender possibly taking souvenirs from the scene."

"Well," Burgess replied, "those souvenirs would certainly keep the fantasy alive, and also if there was much [reporting] in the paper about the progress of the case, again, you'd want to look at that. So how much of that was being activated here? It seems highly unusual that he wouldn't have offended again, although look at . . . the BTK killer, who went years in between crimes and definitely had two sides to him. We do have examples where this could be a possibility, but then you have to go to motive. If he didn't do anything [like this] before or after, what is the motive? Well, in this case, it would be what we would call *personal cause*. It certainly wasn't a criminal enterprise."

"The former prosecutor, Robert Ives—the one who was handling this before McLeland—has publicly come out and discussed the case," I said, pivoting. "He said that the bodies were moved and staged. He's also said that three kinds of signatures were found near the bodies."

"I'm curious about that bullet, the unspent bullet," Burgess said. "Obviously a gun was used to get them down [there]."

"Right."

"A weapon probably would've been used [to get the girls to comply], so that doesn't surprise me, but it doesn't have to be used in the commission of the crime. Wasn't there some evidence that there was a lot of blood at the scene? Do we know that?"

"Yes, that was stated in Ron Logan's probable-cause affidavit that 'a large amount of blood was lost by the victims at the crime scene.'"

"OK," Burgess said. "That's what I thought. That really implies a blade was used [in the actual crime]. So it's not *unusual* that the gun would have been used to get them to another area. It's hard to be able to control two, what, thirteen-, fourteen-year-old girls? If they were younger girls, the killer could have used the ploy of a game, like, let's go play hide-and-seek. Obviously, with two teenagers, that's not going to work. So something more than maybe just the weapon was able to control them, but you have to figure out how two young girls would be controlled by one [person], and I'm not sure if that's why they have suspected there might have been somebody else involved."

"I do know that Libby's shoe was found near at the scene," I said, thinking back on all I'd learned from interviews over the years. "I wonder if that bullet had something to do with maybe one of the girls trying to run. Or were they forced across the creek? I don't know that much about guns, but if you pull it back, could that bullet have just fallen out somehow, or was it in there earlier? I don't know much about the unspent."

"Well, that's a good point," Burgess said. "If the bullet's in there, it was ready to use. You're not supposed to hold a loaded weapon unless you're going to use it, so to speak, so that it could have popped out. I mean, one theory is it pops out when it's pulled back, and that's what they found. I understand that Richard Allen had the type of gun that they were looking for, that it matched. Well, he's got to explain that. I understand he didn't."

"You're right—he didn't. I know that investigators searched Richard Allen's home on October 13, 2022, and found the gun. They asked Richard Allen if anyone else used or had access to his gun, but he said no. Apparently the markings on the bullet, you can match it to *that* particular gun, not even just the type of gun but specifically Allen's gun. But the defense is saying it's junk science, or not reliable evidence."

"Right, right," Burgess said, nodding. "Well, they're going to."

"With defense attorneys," I said, "they're already calling him 'Rick' Allen, saying that he is a great guy and wouldn't do this. Plus, he already put himself there at the bridge that day. *And* he never moved away from Delphi. So we'll see how this plays out in the courtroom, but it is interesting to wonder what else the prosecutors have."

"Do they have a trial date yet?" Burgess asked.

"They did," I said. "It was supposed to be on March 20, and it's already been moved once. Allen's attorneys have said, 'We need more time.' They're keeping the trial in Carroll County, but a change of venue was accepted, meaning they're going to bring jurors in from a different county. I wonder if they will be sequestered. There are no hotels in Delphi, but there are some in neighboring towns, so maybe they will just bus them in and out. I understand that the judge doesn't want Libby's and Abby's families to have to spend a lot of money on travel, which is understandable."

"It's going to be quite a trial, and I can see them needing more [evidence]," Burgess said. "The defense must be getting a little concerned that they were kind of blustery in the beginning, saying, 'He's innocent,' et cetera. But they're going to need to get some experts to testify in court, certainly on guns and bullets . . . They're also probably going to need experts in terms of the death, the manner of death, and they're going to have to try to explain, I would think, how this man was able to control two young girls and how quickly. Although I will say this: in any of the cases I've looked at, [the offenders] kill very quickly. Once they get the victim under control, they kill, so that the young girls wouldn't have had much of a chance to get away."

"In your experience," I asked, "do perpetrators, serial killers, murderers work with other people, or is it more likely that he worked alone on this?"

"The latter," Burgess replied. "[It's more likely that] he worked alone. I mean, it's not *unheard* of. I can think of a very few, but they were really psychopathic and sadistic—that they would torture and so forth. So that's usually what you see when they're a pair. Usually, [the offender's] going to be single, and it's riskier the more [people] they bring in too, so that makes me think it's just one."

"I grew up in New Jersey," I said, "and behind our house, we had some woods, and we would go down there as kids, but this area—the trail the girls were on—seemed so isolated and so secluded. Like, if you screamed, no one would hear you; *that's* how deep in the woods it was. Not that no one went there, but it definitely—you could see how this could have happened in the middle of the day, how the offender must have felt comfortable he wouldn't be disturbed."

"Where was the car parked?" Burgess asked. "Do you know that?"

"It was a couple miles away, in front of the old CPS building that has since been torn down. At the press conference in 2019, the superintendent asked for tips if anyone knew about the car parked in front of that building, but he didn't say the make and the model."

"Yeah."

"We could only guess," I said and shrugged. "Now, in hindsight, I'm thinking, *How did they find out about that? Did they*

*hear about it from the person that took that interview? Does he or she
remember speaking to someone that had a car in that vicinity?"*

"Good point," Burgess said. "The killer had to walk, you're saying, several miles."

"Yeah."

"And [the] girls were dropped off by someone at the same
place?"

"Libby's sister, Kelsi, dropped them off at the trailhead," I said.
"So would they have had to pass wherever he was parked, if he
was in a car? I believe so. Did he see them get dropped off? Was
he just sitting there waiting, knowing that the kids had [the day]
off from school, so he thought this might be the day? In the
probable cause affidavit, it says that someone did spot a man
dressed as Richard Allen said he may have been dressed that day,
like the bridge guy was, and he was muddy and bloody. So, walking along this road to get back to the car, is that why he went to
the authorities?"

"Did [Allen] see the girls? Did he say he saw the girls?"

"In the probable cause affidavit, Allen said he did not see Abby
or Libby that day. I'm wondering, Dr. Burgess, because, yes, kids
do go down there, and a couple other girls were down there that
day too. Did the killer find that, with Abby and Libby, 'this is my
moment,' or was he just sitting there, waiting? Was it just random? There's so much speculation."

"Rare to be random, though," Burgess said.

I added, "I do wonder—and I'm just speculating here—if someone with a specific tip-off called in. I'm not sure, though. How do
you think the court process will go? Or does it really depend on
what else they have as far as evidence is concerned?"

"It's [about] what else they have," Burgess said. "And how concerned and worried the defense is going to be, and how they gear

up [for the trial]. They [the prosecution] *have* to have other things, obviously . . . than what they've told us."

"And someone like this—someone who commits a crime like this—do they ever confess? I mean, I'm thinking of serial killers, like Bundy, that do and then brag about it."

"Well, do they have the death penalty?"

"Yes," I said and nodded. "In Indiana."[1]

"Well, that's the only time that they usually will [consider a] plea bargain. If they think that there's so much evidence, that could happen, but that's not going to happen for a while, [at least not] until the trial gets started. Are they going to have any other charges? Certainly the prosecutor can bring other charges [forward]."

"I know that there's at least a charge in there of kidnapping," I replied. "This really is such a small town. I know early on they brought the FBI in."

"I'd be curious. It would be interesting to see if there was a profile done, because every state now has a profile coordinator."

I thought back to the earlier press conferences. "At one of the pressers, Agent Massa was talking about the offender, saying that this person is likely going to change his appearance. He might also act differently, like abuse alcohol or drugs if he hadn't before."

"Well, there *is* a change," Burgess said. "I saw a [more recent] picture where he had a beard. Am I correct?"

"Yes," I said. "There are several pictures of him, and again, it has been almost six years, but there are definitely different looks he's had over the years."

"Well, for six years, whoever did this *did* get away with it. Obviously something happened, that more evidence came in . . . We'll have to wait and see," Burgess said at last. "I hope they get the right person. When the trial finally starts . . . I'll be watching."

17

—

The Next Chapter

I have a clear, vivid memory of what it felt like to, as we would say, "go down the brook," back when I was a kid. The "brook" was a wooded area behind my childhood home in New Jersey, with a small stream that led into the Raritan River. The shallow running water, dirt paths, and vast open space hidden under a deep canopy of trees made it *the* best place to go after school. It was our own secluded oasis.

After school, around 3:30 p.m., my sister and I would meet our neighbor Kim at the corner of Jefferson Avenue and Buccleuch Place. That gave us enough time to ditch our plaid uniforms for shorts and T-shirts. We all lived on the same street, just a few doors down from each other. The meeting area looked like an empty lot or a large dirt parking space, with patches of overgrown grass and shrubs, and it served as an entryway to our beloved spot.

Lush green weeds protruding from the reddish-brown soil intertwined above, forming what appeared to be a welcoming arch at the start of the path.

The farther you walked, the thicker the brush became. To someone not familiar with the area, this would appear to be blocking the path, a deterrent to travel any farther. To us, though, they were merely location markers. An indication that we were getting closer. When we spotted a skinny, tall tree with long, claw-like branches draped over two large boulders, we knew we were almost there.

There was an easy way around the rocks: just dip your head under the branches, step over the first rock, and step onto the second one. You did have to watch your step, though; we all knew that hidden tree stumps, holes, and branches could be lurking beneath the layer of fallen leaves, and we walked accordingly. The path then veers right another ten or so yards, and that is when it finally appears.

The "first pipe" protruded through the middle of a wide-open space with dirt hills and paths, patches of sunlight glistening between the cascading trees above. It was smack-dab in the center of a neighborhood but secluded nonetheless. For us, it signified freedom.

We didn't know it at the time, but the "first pipe" was a large rusted steel sewer main, about fifteen feet off the ground with a running stream below.

We called it the "easy one," the "lower one." There were a couple of ways to get across. You could sit down and drape your legs around the pipe and use your hands and arm strength to push against it, which was the slower but less risky way to make it to the other side. The first dozen or so times I crossed, this was the mode I chose.

Once I mastered that, however, I tried the more efficient way, the second option. Walking across the pipe involved turning your feet outward ever so slightly, like a gymnast on a balance beam. But without the grace. The more you did it, the better you got. Whoever was most skilled at this maneuvering would make it to the other side first and wait for the others. It was usually just the three of us, but from time to time, our friends Suzanne and Diana would join us to meet the other kids in the neighborhood.

We had a routine: cross the first pipe, spend about fifteen or twenty minutes on the other side, climb up to a dirt path, and follow this to the "second pipe," the higher and more intimidating one. It was about twenty feet high. We would spend the most time on and around that one. If and when I crossed it, I always used the shimmy mode. The first option.

There was also a less popular way to do it. You could walk across the brook, which involved carefully stepping on rocks leading to the other side. Occasionally I would attempt to cross this way, but the slippery, slimy rocks randomly spaced made the shallow greenish-brown foaming brook water close to impossible to avoid, and almost certainly meant my scuffed white Keds would be soaked for the rest of the adventure.

Back then, it was us against the world. We were alone, but together—with no concept of time. The only thing we really paid attention to were the shadows, when the shooting rays of sun seeping through the trees above started to fade, because that was our cue to go home. As soon as we made it back to the corner of Jefferson Avenue, like clockwork, the streetlights would flicker on. And then Kim would walk right, Lynn and I left, for the short trek back home.

It had been more than twenty-five years since we played along the pipes, clueless to the dangers I'm sure an adult would see clear as day. But when I first saw that Snapchat picture of Abby in her zip-up jacket, jeans, and sneakers on the bridge, I was instantly transported back to my own childhood: the corner, the walk, the lower pipe, the higher one, my Keds, the sun, the trees, the smells. I felt an immediate connection to these girls and their innocence. But back then, when Kim, Lynn, and I had felt so invincible, we'd had our whole lives ahead of us. That endless stream of possibilities had been stolen from Abby and Libby.

And so I asked myself, again:

How could anyone do this?

And why?

———

As their families pushed for justice, it kept getting harder for them to ignore the nagging feeling that as major milestones in the girls' friends' lives kept coming up, Abby and Libby would never get to have these special moments of their own. The 2020–2021 school year was particularly heart-rending.

"This has been a *very* hard year," Becky told me, back in November 2020. "The girls are seniors this year. And I will always speak of Libby in the present tense because to me, she's always here . . . We've been seeing, on Facebook and stuff, their friends posting their senior pictures—which, by the way, they've become beautiful young women—and I realize we don't *have* senior pictures. And they were painting their parking spaces because the seniors get to customize their own parking places, and I sit there, and when I look at theirs, I wonder what Libby would've done with hers."*

---

* https://www.youtube.com/watch?v=PvRzs7PNZl0

On Libby's graduation day, the family went to the graveyard to honor her. To the right of Libby's headstone was her yellow gown, propped up behind an eighth-grade softball picture of Libby, four years younger than she would have been graduating from high school. To the left was her cap, secured to a 2021 graduation-themed wreath that Tara made, with stakes securing it into the grass below.

"We had our own graduation; we still celebrate everything with Libby. A lot of times when we are talking, people don't even know that she's gone," Becky told me a month afterward, when we talked onstage at CrimeCon.

Libby's loved ones still think of her each and every time they do anything as a family, and Becky even attempts things she may have been hesitant to do before, knowing Libby would have convinced her to try it. "I even rode a scooter last night," Becky said, smiling, looking out toward the crowd. The family burst into laughter, and so did the rest of the room.

Honoring Libby this way, she explained, doesn't let the murderer win. Libby is still with them in spirit. They just know it.

"He's already taken so much from our lives; I refuse to let him take more," Becky told the crowd.

Forgiveness was a big topic that day too. For Kelsi, in order to continue living and create her own sense of peace, she needed to find and then forgive the monster that killed her sister. She knew not everyone would understand this, but for her, it became her mission in life. In the days and months after Abby and Libby were murdered, Kelsi wasn't sure she wanted to keep going and even if she did, she didn't know how; this new mission gave her a sense of purpose and guided her forward. This mission also led her to meet and connect with her then fiancé, now husband, Kaleb.

At dinner that same night after the CrimeCon panel in Austin, I was sitting next to Kelsi at a long table filled with her family members and a few of my coworkers at HLN. We were talking about wedding planning when Kelsi brought up having kids one day.

"I won't . . . have a baby until the man that did this is found." She looked down and continued. "I can't. I need to keep looking for him. For Abby and Libby both." I didn't say anything back. I wanted to say something, but I knew by the way she spoke, it was a decision she had made months, maybe even years, before sharing it with me. I could see the determination in her eyes, and I knew that this was something she needed to do, with every fiber of her being, to keep going.

Everyone had their own way of getting through each day the best they could. For Mike, Libby's grandfather, that meant staying busy, but he knew that no matter how many tasks he added to his calendar, he couldn't prevent something or someone from triggering a memory that would allow the dark thoughts to creep back in. "Susan, I think about everything that's been lost and the impacts they [the girls] could have made. They had so much to live for. I was just getting ready to teach Libby how to drive; we just started going up and down the driveway."

Diane, Abby's grandmother and Anna's mother, tries her best not to focus on what she can't control. "I have to live every day and decide: Am I going to use my life and my breath and my energy to hate someone that I can't see, and be angry at someone I don't know, for a situation that I can't change? I can't undo it and bring Abby back. I have to decide if I'm going to do the best I can with the life I have left." Diane chose to not go down the path of hatred and anger, but she did so because it was the best thing she could do for herself and her family, and she didn't want anyone to "put [her] on a pedestal." And she acknowledged that despite her intentions, it was still a hard choice, every day. "I don't understand why this happened. I'll never pretend to. I miss Abby so much, and my heart breaks for my daughter, Anna. She lost her only child; no mother wants her own child to suffer like that."

———

In 2019, BOTH FAMILIES DECIDED TO TEAM UP TO CREATE SOMETHING THAT WOULD MEMORIALIZE THE girls, shifting their thinking from "what could have been" to "what could be."

The Abby and Libby Memorial Park started as an idea. A small one—just some bleachers and a softball field built in the girls' names. However, over time, the plans evolved and grew into something spectacular, something the girls would have loved.

The park was a true labor of love. Volunteers from across the country pitched in to make it a reality. Eric, Abby's grandfather, told me that he will never forget one man in particular who showed up at the park building site, very passionate about wanting to help.

On a Sunday afternoon, as Eric was preparing the site for construction to begin, he met the manager of an excavation company, the one who brought gravel, dump trucks, and a whole team of guys with him to help build the park. "As we're standing there, he tells me that twenty years ago, when his family lived in Alaska, his brother and his girlfriend, they were murdered . . . [and] it's an unsolved case. And so he connected with us even though we didn't know each other. It made sense; he was so passionate and . . . I think him helping [to] get us going and helping us fulfill our dream was a way for him to heal the hurt and trauma that he's lived with, because maybe at that point, he was helpless in that situation. He didn't elaborate, but there was a void, there was a gap . . . Through our journey, we have experienced some of those kind of situations with other people, so maybe some of the things that we're doing"—his voice cracked slightly—"helps other people. This man couldn't help his brother, but he *was* able to put a stamp on the Abby and Libby Memorial Park."

Ultimately, the families formed an unexpected bond with the countless people they met during and after the park's creation. Some of these strangers knew what it was like to lose a loved one; others had heard about Abby and Libby and wanted to offer their support and encouragement in any way possible. United by a shared mission, working on this park kept the family members busy and connected. There was a lot to do. Permits, electricity, fencing, bleachers, and tables . . . the list continued to grow.

Diane was dedicated to constructing the brick path that would be an integral part of the park. Each brick would convey a different message—either to the girls or the families, or "in memory of" someone close to the person supporting the park by sponsoring a personalized paver.

Once the construction officially began, the families knew this would be a long and arduous process, but the end would be worth it. It would be a lasting landmark, something tangible, a guarantee no one would forget Abby and Libby. That is what Becky feared the most—the possibility that Libby's memory, and the fourteen years she spent making her mark on the world, would slowly fade away.

Becky had long felt like this was already happening and there was nothing she could do to stop it. She had long been the rock of her family—the person both that everyone turned to, both publicly and privately—but her grief was, at times, overwhelming. As she wrote on Facebook, "It's the little things people not close to the situation don't see, like when the insurance company sends you new insurance cards and her name isn't on there; when the dentist office calls for their reminder for the girls' dentist appointments, but don't mention Libby. She is disappearing to the world; she is evaporating in front of me. I cannot let that happen. For as long as it takes, and whatever it takes . . . Libby, I love you and will fight with all I have to make sure the world never forgets you, you will never disappear."

The Abby and Libby Memorial Park was a way to guarantee that would never happen.

During the first few phases of the process, a huge colorful billboard could be seen above the site, with Abby's volleyball picture and Libby's softball picture posted right next to plans of the park. It reminded everyone volunteering why they were there.

Anna was thrilled when she first heard about plans for a park named after her daughter that everyone in Delphi would enjoy, but her enthusiasm grew substantially when she heard about *everything* that was included in the plans. "The amphitheater, that was my one thing. I said *that* would be the coolest." She smiled. "Give kids a place to play their music. She [Abby] was constantly prancing around the house. So, now she'd have a stage to do it. It's a beautiful place."*

When Mike first told me about the park in 2019, he said it would be separate from the case that focused on the girls' deaths: separate from the investigation, the panels, the news reports, the investigative updates, the rumors and criticisms online. That was his hope—that the park would purely be a celebration of their lives. But no matter where the families shifted their attentions, the absence of both Abby and Libby and the heavy burden of a killer on the loose was seeping through.

---

* https://www.wrtv.com/news/delphi/delphi-killings-abbys-mother-puts-heart
-into-memorial-park

I understood how impossible it was to compartmentalize these complicated feelings. I had trained myself to report on Delphi for HLN with as much professionalism and composure as I could muster, but there were still times when it became too much, when I couldn't help but get emotional—even after years of reporting on it.

One such occasion happened when I appeared on Emmy award–winning journalist Ana Garcia's podcast, *True Crime Daily*, in February 2021. I had long admired Ana; I used to watch her on KNBC in the early 2000s when I was a younger reporter, back in California. This particular day was a tough one; we were only a day away from the four-year anniversary of the crime, and it was difficult for the 4.3 million subscribers to understand why the case hadn't been solved. I talked with Ana at length about the case and the most recent developments, and I think I did a pretty good job of keeping my emotions separate—until fifty-eight minutes and thirty-five seconds in, right as the episode was winding down.

After Ana thanked me for coming on the show, I could feel myself beginning to break down and starting to ramble. I explained that this case was different from ones that I'd covered on set before, that being there in person and meeting the families, who generously opened their doors to me and invited me into their lives—this one just felt so different. I thanked Abby's and Libby's families as I felt the emotions bubbling up. Biting my lip wasn't working. I shifted in my chair, aware that I was spiraling fast, as I pushed my fingers through my hair and tried to regroup. After I told listeners where and when they could tune in to the *Weekend Express* special, I turned to Ana.

"Please edit out the crying," I asked, slightly embarrassed. "I'm so sorry."

I was incredibly moved by what Ana said next.

"You know, Susan, I'd rather have you sitting there and holding my hand than someone who didn't feel anything," she comforted me. "And I'm always grateful to all the families, the survivors of these crimes, because of their graciousness. People always ask me, 'Why do you cover these horrendous crime stories? How do you manage?' And I always say that I walk away with a piece of *inspiration* and *hope* because someone who is struggling lets *me* in and teaches me how to cope and how to heal. And I take that as a lesson, and I get strength from that. That is a gift."

<hr>

FOR THE FAMILIES, SOME DAYS ARE BETTER THAN OTHERS, BUT THE PAIN *NEVER* SUBSIDES. FEBRUARY 13 is especially hard. Each year, this anniversary feels different to Anna, who said that "the second year was harder than the first year, which was a blur." The families were determined to work together to celebrate who the girls *were* before February 13, 2017, not just what happened *to* them, by giving back to the community. Even before the park was finished, they'd teamed up to hold a food drive in honor of the girls, as well as "Abby's Angels," which sent much-needed items like school supplies, clothing, and toys to children in need during the holidays. And yet, despite their dedication to helping others while keeping the memory of the girls alive, their families knew that nothing would ever truly fill the hole left by their absence.

An ache still lingered in their hearts, the ever-present longing to go back to that fateful day in 2017, to undo the events that led to such tragedy. They played the "what ifs" and "if onlys" over and over in their minds, imagining different choices that could have kept Abby and Libby safe.

If only Mike stayed later that morning; if Becky told Libby that it wasn't a good time; if Kelsi said no, she couldn't drive them; if Anna said no, Abby couldn't sleep at Libby's; if Tara had driven to the house earlier; if Derrick said he couldn't pick them up. If only it had been colder that day. If, if, if.

Still, they knew they couldn't go back. Those dark thoughts were both counterproductive and soul crushing. They recognized their focus needed to be on what they *could* control.

On June 12, 2021, Tara, Becky, and Kelsi decided to get a permanent tribute to Libby; they tattooed the word *Ohana* in cursive on the inside of their wrists. In the Disney classic *Lilo & Stitch,* the main character explains that "*Ohana* means family; *family* means *nobody* gets left behind or forgotten." For them, it signified that Libby would *always* be with them, that their bond was unbreakable.

Tara proudly posted a picture of her new tattoo, right above four hearts, sitting perfectly between her "Delphi Strong" and "Abby & Libby" bracelets.

———

FOR YEARS, THE FAMILIES WOULDN'T GO THERE, OR JUST COULDN'T. VISITING THE BRIDGE WAS JUST too painful. But on the day when she heard of the arrest—Friday October 28, 2022—Kelsi decided she was strong enough to do it. She *wanted* to.

On the way to the bridge, Kelsi passed the place where she dropped off Abby and Libby more than five and a half years earlier. Everything looked different now; about a mile of the trail leading up to the bridge was newly paved, as a part of Delphi's multiphase "next level trail project." The bridge itself was to be renovated during the next phase, which would include replacing the dilapidated beams with a new walkway and railings.

Kelsi passed many makeshift memorials to Abby and Libby—stuffed animals, notes, and bouquets of flowers wrapped in the girls' favorite colors, teal and purple—as she made her way to the bridge. She wondered what Abby and Libby would think of the Memorial Park in their name.

And then she spotted it in the distance: the bridge. Once a hidden, abandoned railway known only to locals, the Monon High Bridge had become a landmark known around the world, thanks to its connection with this brutal double murder. It had become inextricable from Abby and Libby's stories.

It was *the place* they picked to spend their day off together. *The place* where Libby took the Snapchat picture of Abby. *The place* where they were when they knew something wasn't right. *The place* where Libby decided to record the man on the bridge as he walked toward them. *The place* where the girls were forced "down the hill." *The place* where they were last seen alive.

Kelsi stood on the edge and looked across at the old wooden planks that seemed to go on forever. In that moment, her perspective suddenly changed, and her long-standing fear and anxiety started to dissipate.

The bridge.

Yes, it was *the place* where a coward decided to target two young girls, forcing them off the bridge into a more secluded area. But it was also *the place* where Libby felt brave enough to press Record. *The place* where the girls banded together, refusing to leave each other's side. *The place* where the girls may have unknowingly collected enough evidence to convict the person that murdered them.

Kelsi made a promise to the girls and herself that day to not give the man on the bridge any more power. She knew it would be OK, OK for her to live, OK for her to be happy.

A few months later, I called Becky to check in on the family and heard the news. Kelsi and Kaleb were expecting a daughter, Ellie, in August 2023. I couldn't contain how thrilled I was for Kelsi, her husband Kaleb, and their entire family. And I knew in my heart that no one would've been happier for her than Libby.

———

OVER THE YEARS, THIS INVESTIGATION HAS TAKEN SO MANY TWISTS AND TURNS THAT I'M HESITANT TO even try to predict where we might end up and when. As I sit down to write this in the summer of 2023, much is still up in the air. Though an arrest was made in the fall of 2022, I remind myself that an arrest is not a conviction; this case isn't going to be over anytime soon.

In the months since Richard Allen was arrested, he has been moved to different correctional facilities because of safety concerns. The trial was originally set for March 2023 but has since been delayed for numerous reasons—which isn't surprising in a case of this magnitude. Allen's bond hearing, which was scheduled for June 15–16, was turned into a "motion to suppress" hearing. His attorneys were keen to prevent any future jurors from seeing evidence subpoenaed from the Westville Correctional Center, where he was originally held, and his former employer CVS. This means the prosecution will not have to show any of the evidence they have against the suspect.

According to a county court official, after Allen's virtual hearing in January, "Allen's attorneys told the court it would be 'shocking' if they could be ready for trial before the end of the year due to the amount of evidence they have to comb through during discovery."[1] Special Judge Fran Gull, who will be presiding over the case, was also notably "skeptical" about how long it would take the case to go to trial, because of both the amount of evidence and the logistics of bringing in jury members from another county.[2]

The Westville Correctional Facility is a maximum-security prison that's a little over eighty miles due north of Delphi, just southeast of Chicago. On April 5, 2023, Allen's attorneys appealed to the court to move Allen to a new facility, citing poor living conditions in a cell "no larger than that of a dog kennel" (six by ten feet), isolation, and deteriorating physical and mental health, likening his position to "that of a prisoner of war."[3] They submitted a picture as evidence of his poor physical state, in which Allen appears to have lost a considerable amount of weight and looks unkempt, with a pool of spittle settling into the khaki shirt beneath his prison jumpsuit.[4] His attorneys also said they had "observed a steep decline in Mr. Allen's demeanor, ability to communicate, ability to comprehend, and ability to assist in his defense," and they noted that "the significant toll of his current incarceration on his physical person" is affecting his mental health, exacerbating preexisting depression as well as delusions and schizophrenia symptoms. Allen's counsel recommended he be moved to the Cass County Jail or somewhere closer to Carroll County so he could be in proximity to both his family and his legal team. The request was approved by the judge on April 14, but Gull did not specify where Allen should be moved, only that his physical and psychological needs should be met.[5]

At the two-day hearing on June 15 and 16, prosecutor Nick McLeland announced that Allen had made shocking statements while in jail, which included telling "five or six people" that he had killed Abby and Libby. Allen's attorney, Brad Rozzi, did not deny the admission, but rather insisted once again that Allen's isolation and treatment in prison were causing a physical and mental breakdown. "'At one minute, Rick is saying one thing, and another minute, he's saying something else,'" Rozzi reportedly told the court.[6]

Rozzi also argued that two of Allen's constitutional rights were currently being restricted and urged the court to reconsider. According to Rozzi, Allen's isolation—due to a "keep safe" order—denied Allen his fourteenth amendment rights to due process, while his incarceration nearly two hours from his attorneys denied him his sixth amendment rights to legal counsel. Former Sheriff Tobe Leazenby, now Carroll County Sheriff's Chief Deputy, argued that his motion for safe keeping was requested because the case was so high profile, though the prosecution has been so far unable to prove that this was based on any tangible threats to the defendant. Special Judge Frances Gull announced that she would publish a decision after further reviewing the arguments, as well as precedent case law on safe keeping.

At the end of the hearing, the judge, the prosecution, and the defense agreed to a three-week trial starting on January 8, 2024. The first few days will consist of jury selection in Allen County, after which the remainder of the trial will take place in Delphi.

Two weeks after the hearing, previously sealed documents were released to the public for the first time via court order, documents that could significantly impact the trial. In one of these documents, it was revealed that "on April 3, 2023, Richard M Allen made a phone call to his wife Kathy Allen. In that phone call, Richard M Allen admits several times that he killed Abby and Libby . . . His wife, Kathy Allen, ends the phone call abruptly."[7]

Time will tell if this trial date stands, or if it is pushed out again to a later date.

———

Once the trial starts, the families will be there in court, no matter what. For close to six years, this is what they had hoped for—a chance to hold the culprit accountable for their actions. Kelsi is aware that this next chapter will not be an easy one. But she is ready for what lies ahead and she's proud of how far she's come. She often thinks of a phrase that Libby posted on Facebook, which is now on her memorial page: a close-up selfie with the words "shine brightest on the worst days." And that's just what Kelsi intends to do.

Kelsi now tries to help and support others who truly understand, those who are part of the club that no one wants to join. She wants them to know that eventually it does get better. A year before the arrest, Kelsi stood on stage at CrimeCon and shared with the crowd what she believes was the beginning of her healing process. During her first CrimeCon, she felt she wasn't strong enough to talk to a large crowd about her experiences. She asked herself what Libby would want her to do and knew instinctively that Libby would want her to share her story. It is in sharing that story with others that Kelsi has found strength; in her words, "as you keep going for them, you'll eventually be able to keep going for yourself as well."

Through it all, she keeps Libby close to her heart, always with her. "In all of those moments, every single moment that happens—whether it's good or it's bad. No matter what I'm going through, she's always there and I always feel her presence right there with me, every step of the way, holding my hand, giving me a hug, encouraging me to go on when I don't feel like I can."

And she's right; our loved ones never really leave us. They continue to show up again and again over the course of our lives, in beautiful and often unexpected ways.

I often think back to that moment in Libby's kitchen, right after I'd met the family in person for the first time. We'd spotted the cardinal just outside the window and Becky shared the picture she'd snapped of two cardinals on that same branch months earlier. It seemed too meaningful to be just a stroke of serendipity. In the years since, I've seen more cardinals than ever before—or maybe I just notice them more, whenever they are around. Usually, they visit alone or in pairs, though if I'm lucky, sometimes I see three sitting together. My son and daughter still get excited whenever they see them land on the tree right outside our back door.

Whether or not the cardinals we saw that day in Libby's kitchen were visitors from heaven, I take comfort in remembering the sweet serenity of those small crimson birds, huddled together to share a moment of warmth, before stretching their wings wide and soaring off, side by side, into the sky above, ready to greet the day.

Acknowledgments

First and foremost, I'd like to express my utmost gratitude to the families of Abby and Libby: Becky Patty, Anna Williams, Mike Patty, Kelsi Siebert, Tara German, Derrick German, Diane Erskine, Eric Erskine, Clif Williams, Carrie Timmons, and their extended families and friends. Thank you for teaching and showing me what strength and resilience truly looks like.

Thank you also to the many members of law enforcement, including Superintendent Doug Carter, former Carrol County Sheriff Chief Deputy Tobe Leazenby, State Police First Sergeant Jerry Holeman, retired Sergeant Kim Riley, retired Indiana State Police Captain Dave Bursten, Detective Kevin Hammond, Detective Tony Liggett, Detective Jay Harper, Detective Brian Harshman, Detective Dave Vido, Investigator Steve Mullin, members of the United States Marshall Service, and members of the FBI.

Thank you to the residents of Delphi for welcoming us into your community.

To Paul Holes, thank you for your invaluable insight. Your ability to assess and investigate a crime while connecting with victims and their loved ones is unmatched.

To Dr. Ann Burgess, a pioneer and role model, thank you for lending your expertise to the chapter in this book. I am immensely grateful and inspired by you.

To Kevin Balfe, thank you for creating a safe space for survivors to share their stories.

To Kerri Rawson, thank you for sharing yours. I consider you a friend.

Thank you to Joe Petito and family, who continue to fight to make a difference in the lives of many, all while carrying on the legacy of their daughter, Gabby.

To Deanna Thompson, thank you for sharing your unique perspective. Your dedication to helping others find justice is apparent.

To Carrie Napolitano, my editor at Hachette, your guidance and advice have been invaluable. To the entire Hachette team: Mary Ann Naples, Michelle Aielli, Michael Barrs, Amanda Kain, Terri Sirma, Monica Oluwek, Kindall Gant, Ashley Kiedrowski, and the countless people in sales who have worked so hard to get this story out to the world, I am forever grateful.

To Steve Troha and Katherine Odom-Tomchin with Folio Literary Management, thank you for leading me in the right direction.

Thank you to CNN/HLN for prioritizing this story and allowing me to share it.

Thank you to Mike Galanos, Joey Jackson, Casey Jordan, Jean Casarez, Jennifer Williams, Christi Paul, Tim Mallon, Stephanie Todd, Robin Meade, Bob VanDillen, Jennifer Westhoven, Melissa Knowles, Elizabeth Prann, Lynda Kinkade, Shyann Malone,

Brian Bell, Peter Kaplan, Kerry O'Connor, Robynn Love, Clark Goldband, Sammy Jones, Tim Melligan, Sarah Diden, and everyone at HLN that made our workplace feel like home.

To Ken Jautz, thank you for your encouragement through the years.

Thanks to my sister and best friend, Lynn, for always being there.

To Lynn, Suzanne, Diana, and Kim, I wish we could go back.

Mom and Dad, thank you for your love and unconditional support.

Lastly, I'd like to thank my family, my husband Joe, my daughter Emery, and my son Jack, for making me feel loved and supported during my time away from home.

A Note on Sources

Much of the information you'll find in this book comes directly from my own reporting, much of which was conducted during my time as a journalist and news anchor for CNN's Headlines News Network (HLN). First and foremost, I am eternally grateful to Abby's and Libby's families for welcoming us into your homes and your lives. The conversations we've had over the years, both on the air and off, have touched me to my core; I am a changed person—a *better* person. I would also like to thank law enforcement who worked tirelessly on this case for several years, working alongside family members and the media. They couldn't always tell us about the particulars of the investigation, but they were warm and welcoming when communicating what they could.

I am also immensely grateful to the colleagues I worked with during my time at HLN, interviewing the families and investigators on the ground in Delphi, or organizing specials and panels back in Atlanta. These brilliant people, whom I consider friends, inspired and supported me along the way.

In addition to our original reporting, I have benefited immensely from following the on-the-ground reporting of local news affiliates, and I have cited them as much as possible. I want to extend my gratitude to these peers of mine, whom I respect beyond measure. It is impossible to find every angle of a story from a singular viewpoint; by incorporating details from trusted sources and perspectives, I was able to get a much clearer picture of the investigation we were privy to, not to mention the various twists and turns of every lead.

I am also indebted to experts like Paul Holes and Dr. Ann Burgess, who generously talked with me at length about this case and all its implications from a variety of perspectives. Finally, I want to thank the historians and researchers online whose work allowed me to paint a more complete picture of Delphi over the years, infusing this narrative with crucial context and depth.

As of this writing, while there has been an arrest and charges filed, this case has not yet been brought to a trial; as such, all parties mentioned within these pages remain innocent until proven guilty in a court of law. I have updated the legal developments to the best of my ability, but please note that this story is still ongoing.

The pursuit of justice continues.

Notes

Chapter 2: On the Set

1. *Down the Hill: The Delphi Murders*, HLN, podcast audio, February 14, 2021, https://www.cnn.com/audio/podcasts/down-the-hill-the-delphi-murders.
2. Kim Goldman, interview with Kelsi German, "Double Murder in Delphi with Kelsi German," *Media Circus with Kim Goldman*, podcast audio, February 7, 2023, https://www.iheart.com/podcast/269-media-circus-with-kim-gold-9807 2103/episode/double-murder-in-delphi-with-kelsi-100635730/.
3. "U.S. Census Bureau QuickFacts: Carroll County, Indiana," US Census Bureau, accessed May 12, 2023, https://www.census.gov/quickfacts/fact/table/carroll countyindiana/PST045221; "Delphi Demographics," Indiana Demographics, accessed May 13, 2023, https://www.indiana-demographics.com/delphi-demo graphics.
4. "Delphi Police Conference 02.22.17 FULL | RTV6," Frank Young, February 23, 2017, video, 32:36, https://www.youtube.com/watch?v=P1uSKrtYdDw.

Chapter 3: Arrival in Delphi

1. "County History," Carroll County, Indiana, accessed May 12, 2023, https://www.carrollcountyindiana.com/information/county-history.

2. "Fire Department," City of Delphi, accessed May 13, 2023, https://www.cityof delphi.org/contact/contact-city-departments/26-fire-depsartment.

3. "U.S. Census Bureau QuickFacts: Carroll County, Indiana," US Census Bureau, accessed April 25, 2023, https://www.census.gov/quickfacts/fact/table/carroll countyindiana/PST045221.

4. "Delphi, Indiana Population 2023," World Population Review, accessed May 14, 2023, https://worldpopulationreview.com/us-cities/delphi-in-population.

5. "Population in Delphi, Indiana (Community Demographics)," Dwellics, accessed May 14, 2023, https://dwellics.com/indiana/community-in-delphi.

6. "Crime in Delphi, Indiana," Best Places, accessed May 14, 2023, https://www .bestplaces.net/crime/city/indiana/delphi; "About the City of Delphi," City of Delphi, accessed February 11, 2020, https://www.cityofdelphi.org/information /about-the-city-of-delphi; "Population in Delphi, Indiana (Community Demo- graphics)," Dwellics, accessed May 14, 2023, https://dwellics.com/indiana/com munity-in-delphi; "Industries," Carroll County Economic Development, accessed May 14, 2023, https://www.carrollcountyedc.com/information/industries.

7. "Crime in Delphi, Indiana," Best Places, accessed May 14, 2023, https://www .bestplaces.net/crime/city/indiana/delphi; "Delphi, IN Property Crime Rates and Non-Violent Crime Maps," CrimeGrade.org, accessed May 14, 2023, https:// crimegrade.org/property-crime-delphi-in/.

Chapter 4: The Bridge

1. Katie Cox and Kara Kenney, "Delphi Daughters: A 360 Tour of the Monon High Bridge," WRTV Indianapolis, February 12, 2019, https://www.wrtv.com /longform/delphi-daughters-a-360-tour-of-the-monon-high-bridge.

2. "10 Most Endangered," Indiana Landmarks, accessed December 31, 2016, https://www.indianalandmarks.org/10-most-endangered.

3. "Indiana Landmarks Announces Rescue of Monon High Bridge," Indiana Land- marks, April 11, 2017, https://www.indianalandmarks.org/2017/04/indiana-land marks-announces-rescue-of-monon-high-bridge/.

4. Dave Bangert, "$1.2M to Restore Monon High Bridge Trail, Scene in Delphi Teens' Murder," *Journal & Courier*, May 2, 2019, https://www.jconline.com /story/news/2019/05/02/1-2-m-restore-monon-high-bridge-trail-scene-delphi -teens-murder/3651327002/.

Chapter 5: A Killer in the Room

1. Logan Gay, "Family Mourns on 5 Year Anniversary of Flora House Fire That Killed 4 Young Girls," WTHR, November 21, 2021, https://www.wthr.com/article/news/local/family-of-4-girls-killed-in-flora-indiana-house-fire-search-for-answers-on-5-year-anniversary/531-546bf706-97cd-4e6b-b959-68877a04bd2f.
2. Jennie Runevitch, "Flora Fire Unsolved 6 Years Later; Family of 4 Girls Still Seeking Justice," WTHR, November 21, 2022, https://www.wthr.com/article/news/crime/deadly-flora-fire-unsolved-six-years-later-family-of-4-girls-still-seeking-justice-carroll-county-arson-indiana-investigation/531-1a9c6d70-6db1-4a4e-b92a-98b72c9b099d.
3. Travis Fedschun, "'New' Delphi Suspect Sketch Was Drawn Days After Murders of 2 Indiana Girls, Artist Says," Fox News, April 23, 2019, https://www.foxnews.com/us/new-delphi-suspect-sketch-indiana-girl-murder-video-suspect-description.
4. Ibid.
5. Vic Ryckaert and Justin L. Mack, "Delphi Murders: New Sketch of Killer, Video from Libby's Phone Released," *IndyStar*, April 22, 2019, https://www.indystar.com/story/news/2019/04/22/delphi-murders-update-2019-new-cellphone-video-sketch-released/3536773002/.

Chapter 6: Abby and Libby

1. Jessica Hayes, "Anna Williams Discusses Loss of Daughter on Delphi 2-Year Anniversary," Fox59, February 13, 2019, https://fox59.com/news/anna-williams-discusses-loss-of-daughter-on-delphi-two-year-anniversary/; Rafael Sanchez and Katie Cox, "Delphi Murders: The Families of Libby & Abby Still Believe That 'Today Is the Day,'" WRTV Indianapolis, February 12, 2019, https://www.wrtv.com/news/delphi/delphi-murders-the-families-of-libby-abby-still-believe-that-today-is-the-day.
2. "Delphi: The Life of Abby Williams—a Painter and a Photographer with a Big Heart," WRTV Indianapolis, video, 3:26, April 27, 2017, https://www.youtube.com/watch?v=9KviOxEnvZs.
3. "Abby and Libby," Abby and Libby Memorial Park, accessed May 12, 2023, https://abbyandlibbymemorialpark.org/abby-and-libby.

4. Katie Cox, "Abby Williams: 'I Still Don't Know How to Live Without Her,'" WRTV Indianapolis, February 11, 2019, https://www.wrtv.com/longform/abby -williams-i-still-dont-know-how-to-live-without-her.

5. Jason Hebert True Crime & Missing Persons, "The Delphi Murders: Anna Williams Interview," October 1, 2020, https://www.youtube.com/watch?v=p9B7B0Nv6cQ.

Chapter 7: The Hunt for "Bridge Guy"

1. "Henry C. Lee, Ph.D.," University of New Haven, accessed May 14, 2023, https://www.newhaven.edu/faculty-staff-profiles/henry-lee.php.

2. "May 23, 2019," *Morning Express with Robin Meade*, HLN, May 23, 2019.

3. Ibid.

4. Katie Cox, "Who Is Daniel Nations? The Latest 'Person of Interest' in the Murders of Libby & Abby in Delphi," WRTV Indianapolis, September 29, 2017, https://www.wrtv.com/news/local-news/carroll-county/who-is-daniel-nations -the-latest-person-of-interest-in-the-murders-of-libby-abby-in-delphi.

5. Ibid.

6. Alexis McAdams, "Wife of Person of Interest in Delphi Murders Says Daniel Nations Watched News Coverage," Fox 59, October 11, 2017, https://fox59.com /news/wife-of-person-of-interest-in-delphi-murders-says-daniel-nations-watched -news-coverage/.

7. Ibid.

8. "Police Say There's No Specific Information to 'Include or Exclude' Daniel Nations as Suspect in Delphi Murders," Fox59, October 3, 2017, https://fox59 .com/news/isp-no-info-specifically-includes-excludes-daniel-nations-as-suspect -in-delphi-murders.

9. "Daniel Nations No Longer a Major Concern in Delphi Murders," KKTV, February 15, 2018, https://www.kktv.com/content/news/Nations-no-longer-a-major -concern-in-Delphi-murders-474116613.html.

10. London Gibson, "Tippecanoe County Rape Suspect Fatally Shoots Self During Standoff in Boone County," *IndyStar*, June 28, 2019, https://www.indystar.com /story/news/crime/2019/06/27/boone-county-deputies-standoff-rape-suspect -paul-etter/1586992001/.

11. "Evidence from Man Who Killed Himself in Standoff Shared with Delphi Investigators," *Kokomo Tribune*, courtesy of WTHR-TV, July 22, 2019, https://www

.kokomotribune.com/news/evidence-from-man-who-killed-himself-in-standoff
-shared-with-delphi-investigators/article_077205e6-acd0-11e9-83ca-ff7d3
428b86f.html.

12. Ron Wilkins, "Accused Attempted Murderer Asks for a Change of Venue, Citing Worldwide Media Coverage," *Lafayette Journal & Courier*, July 22, 2021, https:// www.jconline.com/story/news/crime/2021/07/22/james-brian-chadwell-up date-possible-delphi-murder-suspect-venue-change/8025708002.

13. Matt Adams, "Man Sentenced to 90 Years in Sexual Assault, Attempted Murder of Lafayette Girl," Fox59, December 16, 2021, https://fox59.com/news/man -sentenced-to-90-years-in-sexual-assault-attempted-murder-of-lafayette-girl/; "Lafayette Man Pleads Guilty on All Charges in Attempted Murder, Kidnapping of 9-Year-Old-Girl," WTHR, October 21, 2021, https://www.wthr.com/article /news/crime/change-of-plea-hearing-scheduled-for-lafayette-man-in-kidnapping -attempted-murder-case-james-chadwell-indiana/531-2cf92c53-7886-42e3 -8a86-4c7ab9df4100.

Chapter 8: CrimeCon

1. Thomas Fuller and Christine Hauser, "Search for 'Golden State Killer' Leads to Arrest of Ex-Cop," *New York Times*, April 18, 2018, https://www.nytimes.com /2018/04/25/us/golden-state-killer-serial.html.

Chapter 9: Armchair Detectives

1. Sue Montgomery, "Man Who Saw Magnotta as Escort Describes Encounters," *Montreal Gazette*, October 7, 2014, https://montrealgazette.com/news/local-news /lin-juns-friend-describes-search-for-missing-man.

2. Patton Oswalt, "Patton Oswalt Remembers His Wife, Michelle McNamara: 'She Steered Her Life with Joyous, Wicked Curiosity,'" *TIME*, May 3, 2016, https:// time.com/4316653/patton-oswalt-remembers-michelle-mcnamara.

3. Nick Schager, "Inside Michelle McNamara's Obsessive Hunt for the Golden State Killer," *Daily Beast*, June 28, 2020, https://www.thedailybeast.com/hbos -ill-be-gone-in-the-dark-explores-michelle-mcnamaras-obsessive-hunt-for-the -golden-state-killer.

4. Gina Tron, "A 'Big Switch for Me':, Golden State Killer Investigator Paul Holes Reveals Why He Trusted Michelle McNamara." Oxygen Official Site, May 23,

2023, https://www.oxygen.com/true-crime-buzz/how-did-paul-holes-trust-mi chelle-mcnamara-golden-state-killer-hunt-ill-be-gone-in-the-dark.

5. "Delphi Case and More with Kelsi German—Live Call In," Gray Hughes Investigates, interview with Gray Hughes, video, 1:36:51, August 20, 2019, https://www.youtube.com/watch?v=bqGeR0-FboI.

6. Jason Hebert True Crime & Missing Persons, "The Delphi Murders: Anna Williams Interview," October 1, 2020, https://www.youtube.com/watch?v=p9B7B0Nv6cQ.

Chapter 10: Back to the Beginning

1. "Becky Patty, Libby's Grandmother Is Our Guest / True Crime / Websleuths," Websleuths, video, April 3, 2020, https://www.youtube.com/watch?v=Zgp_xg6 VR2Q&t=3508s.

2. "S43E30, Friday, February 11, 2022," *Nightline*, ABC, video, 18:51, February 11, 2022, https://abc.com/shows/nightline/episode-guide/2022-02/11-friday -february-11-2022.

3. Katie Cox, "Delphi Property Owner Pleads Guilty to Charges Unrelated to Teens' Murders," WRTV Indianapolis, April 3, 2017, https://www.wrtv.com/news/crime /delphi-property-owner-pleads-guilty-to-charges-unrelated-to-delphi-teens-murders.

4. Ibid.

5. Ibid.

6. Russ McQuaid, "Investigators to Announce Charges versus Delphi Murders Suspect," Fox59, October 30, 2022, https://fox59.com/indiana-news/investigators -to-announce-charges-versus-delphi-murders-suspect.

7. Demie Johnson, "FBI Search Warrant Raises Questions About Delphi Property Owner's Arrest," WISH TV, May 18, 2022, https://www.wishtv.com/news/i-team -8/fbi-search-warrant-raises-questions-about-delphi-property-owners-arrest/; "Delphi Investigators Once Searched Home of Ron Logan, Owner of Property Where Slain Girls Were Found in 2017," *Inside Edition*, May 19, 2022, https://www.insideedition.com/delphi-investigators-once-searched-home-of-ron-logan -owner-of-property-where-slain-girls-were-found.

8. Demie Johnson, "FBI Agent: Bodies 'Moved and Staged' in Delphi Murders, Suspect Took Clothing," WISH TV, May 17, 2022, https://www.wishtv.com /news/i-team-8/fbi-agent-bodies-moved-and-staged-in-delphi-murders-suspect -took-clothing.

9. Ibid.

10. Ibid.

11. Demie Johnson, "FBI Agent: Bodies 'Moved and Staged' in Delphi Murders, Suspect Took Clothing," WISH TV, May 17, 2022, https://www.wishtv.com /news/i-team-8/fbi-agent-bodies-moved-and-staged-in-delphi-murders-suspect -took-clothing.

12. Ibid.

13. Ibid.

14. Ibid.

15. Ibid.

16. Ibid.

17. Ibid.

18. Jason Hebert True Crime & Missing Persons, "The Delphi Murders: Anna Williams Interview," October 1, 2020, https://www.youtube.com/watch?v=p9B7B 0Nv6cQ.

19. Dave Bursten, "Delphi Police Conference 02.22.17 FULL | RTV6," RTV6, February 27, 2017, https://www.youtube.com/watch?v=P1uSKrtYdDw.

20. Jason Hebert True Crime & Missing Persons, "The Delphi Murders: Anna Williams Interview," October 1, 2020, https://www.youtube.com/watch?v=p9B7B 0Nv6cQ.

Chapter 11: Catfished: Kegan Kline and @anthony_shots

1. Matt Adams and Russ McQuaid, "Court Docs: Child Pornography Suspect in Miami County Had 'Anthony_shots' Account; Link to Delphi Case Unclear," Fox59, December 7, 2021, https://fox59.com/news/court-docs-child-pornography -suspect-in-miami-county-had-anthony_shots-account-link-to-delphi-case-unclear/.

2. Ibid.

3. Ibid.

4. Aila Slisco, "'Yubo' Social Media App Lands in the Middle of a Double Homicide Probe," Newsweek, April 11, 2022, https://www.newsweek.com/yubo-social -media-app-lands-middle-double-homicide-probe-1697064.

5. Lindsay Muntingh, "Catfishing Statistics and FAQs," Screen & Reveal, March 30, 2023, https://screenandreveal.com/catfishing-statistics/.

6. Ibid.

7. "Online Predators—Statistics," PureSight, accessed May 12, 2023, https://www .puresight.com/case_studies/online-predators-statistics.

8. Ibid.

9. "Search Records for Jerry A Kline." Indiana Supreme Court. Accessed June 20, 2023. https://public.courts.in.gov/mycase#/vw/SearchResults/eyJ2Ijp7Ik1vZGU iOiJCeVBhcnR5IiwiQ2FzZU51bSI6bnVsbCwiQ2l0ZU51bSI6bnVsbCwiQ3J vc3NSZWZOdW0iOm51bGwsIkZpcnN0IjoiamVycnkiLCJNaWRkbGUiOiJh IiwiTGFzdCI6IktsaW5lIiwiQnVzaW5lc3MiOm51bGwsIkRvQlN0YXJ0IjpudW xsLCJEb0JFbmQiOiOm51bGwsIk9BTnVtIjpudWxsLCJCYXJOdW0iOm51bG wsIlNvdW5kRXgiOmZhbHNlLCJDb3VydEl0ZW1JRCI6OTIsIkNhdGVnb 3JpZXMiOlsiQ1IiXSwiTGltaXRzIjpudWxsLCJBZHZhbmNlZCI6ZmFs c2UsIkFkdGl2ZUZsYWciOiJBbGwiLCJGaWxlU3RhcnQiOm51bGwsIkZpb GVFbmQiOm51bGwsIkNvdW50eUNvZGUiOm51bGx9fQ==.

10. Rich Nye, "'Anthony_shots' Profile Connected to Another Incident Just Days After Delphi Murders," WTHR, March 28, 2022, https://www.wthr.com/article /news/crime/delphi-girls-murdered/anthonyshots-profile-connected-to-another -incident-days-after-delphi-indiana-murders/531-55323bd6-926d-4605-a6f2 -715a70d5abf7.

11. Jennie Runevitch, "'It Breaks My Heart': Officer Whose Photos Were Stolen by 'Anthony_shots' Profile Wants Justice for Delphi Victims," WTHR, December 20, 2021, https://www.wthr.com/article/news/crime/delphi-girls-murdered/officer -photos-anthony-shots-profile-delphi-murder-investigation/531-0d6b295a -98e8-448e-8348-f8a358075ccb.

12. Ibid.

13. Adams, Matt. "Lawyers for Kegan Kline, Man Linked to Delphi Murders Investigation, Request Change of Plea Hearing in Child Exploitation Case." Fox59, March 20, 2023. https://fox59.com/indiana-news/kegan-kline-delphi-lawyers -request-change-of-plea-hearing-child-exploitation-case.

14. Ibid.

Chapter 12: "Today Is the Day"

1. Rose Minutaglio, "When I Found Out My Father Was the BTK Killer, I Suddenly Saw the Clues Everywhere," *Esquire*, February 2, 2019, https://www.esquire

.com/entertainment/books/a25346777/kerri-rawson-btk-killer-dennis-rader
-daughter-interview/.

2. "BTK Killer's Daughter, Kerri Rawson," CrimeCon, video, 2:50, June 29, 2021, https://www.youtube.com/watch?v=ZjXMORRRqXM.

Chapter 13: Captured, the Press Conference

1. "Delphi Murders Arrest | Full Press Conference | October 31, 2022," WTHR, video, 21:30, October 31, 2022, https://www.youtube.com/watch?v=qBz7y7wZ6As.

Chapter 14: "Bloodlust"

1. Justin Rohrlich, "Delphi Murder Suspect Gets Jail Transfer as Judge Slams Public's 'Blood Lust,'" *Daily Beast*, November 3, 2022, https://www.thedailybeast .com/delphi-indiana-murder-suspect-richard-allen-gets-jail-transfer-as-judge -slams-publics-blood-lust.

2. https://fox59.com/wp-content/uploads/sites/21/2022/11/RichardAllenCourt-Docs.pdf.

3. Matt Christy, "Judge Recuses Self from Delphi Murder Suspect Case," Fox59, November 3, 2022, https://fox59.com/indiana-news/judge-recuses-self-from -delphi-murder-suspect-case/.

4. "Judge Orders Richard Allen to Be in Court for Tuesday's Hearing," WTHR, November 9, 2022, https://www.wthr.com/article/news/crime/delphi-girls-mur dered/throw-myself-at-the-mercy-of-court-richard-allen-requests-public-de fender-in-delphi-murders-case-abby-williams-libby-german-indiana-suspect /531-073da898-f877-463b-8041-a32827dbe3f4.

5. Ron Wilkins, "Court Appoints Two Attorneys to Represent Delphi Murder Suspect," *Lafayette Journal & Courier*, November 14, 2022, https://www.jconline .com/story/news/crime/2022/11/14/richard-allen-attorney-appears-in-delphi -murders-case/69647879007.

6. Rachel Sharp, "Delphi Murders: What We Know About Suspect Richard Allen as Affidavit Reveals He Was on Police Radar in 2017," *Independent*, November 30, 2022, https://www.independent.co.uk/news/world/americas/crime/delphi -murders-update-richard-allen-b2236099.

7. Ibid.

8. Ibid.

9. Paul Holes, and Robin Gaby Fisher, *Unmasked: My Life Solving America's Cold Cases* (New York: Celadon Books, 2022).

10. "Sister of Murdered Teen Debunks Online Rumors and Speculation," HLN, interview by Mike Galanos and Susan Hendricks with Kelsi German, video, 3:25, July 10, 2019, https://www.facebook.com/watch/?v=1257122657798417.

11. Luke Kenton, "Mom of Delphi Murder Victim Makes Plea About Evidence Ahead of Richard Allen Court Hearing & Blasts 'Weird Curiosity,'" *U.S. Sun*, November 22, 2022, https://www.the-sun.com/news/6731633/delphi-update-murder-evidence-unsealed-hearing-richard-allen.

12. Ibid.

13. "Court Documents Released in Delphi Murder Case: Read the Probable Cause Affidavit Here," *IndyStar*, November 29, 2022, https://www.indystar.com/story/news/crime/2022/11/29/delphi-murders-update-probable-cause-affidavit-richard-allen-arrest/69686764007/.

14. "Here's What We Learned from the Redacted Court Documents on Why Richard Allen Was Arrested in the Delphi Murders," WTHR, November 29, 2022, https://www.wthr.com/article/news/crime/delphi-girls-murdered/read-redacted-delphi-murders-case-court-documents-released-richard-allen-libby-german-abby-williams/531-815952ca-6e03-498e-815e-28a2107c7dc0.

Chapter 15: Investigative Insights with Paul Holes

1. "Here's What We Learned from the Redacted Court Documents on Why Richard Allen Was Arrested in the Delphi Murders,." WTHR 13, November 29, 2022, https://www.wthr.com/article/news/crime/delphi-girls-murdered/read-redacted-delphi-murders-case-court-documents-released-richard-allen-libby-german-abby-williams/531-815952ca-6e03-498e-815e-28a2107c7dc0.

Chapter 16: A Closer Look into the Criminal Mind with Dr. Ann Burgess

1. "Death Penalty Facts," IN.gov, accessed May 14, 2023, https://www.in.gov/ipdc/files/Death-Penalty-Facts,-Indiana.pdf.

Chapter 17: The Next Chapter

1. Matt Adams, "Delphi Suspect Richard Allen's Next Hearing Scheduled for June," Fox59, February 7, 2023, https://fox59.com/indiana-news/delphi-suspect-richard -allens-next-hearing-scheduled-for-june.

2. Madison Stacey, "Subpoenas Issued for Facilities with Ties to Delphi Suspect Richard Allen," WTHR, May 3, 2023, https://www.wthr.com/article/news/crime /subpoenas-issued-for-delphi-cvs-westville-correctional-facility-in-richard-allen -case-indiana-libby-german-abby-williams/531-b3b33d78-bfc8-4445-9784 -43cfc71eb613.

3. State of Indiana vs. Richard M. Allen. Cause No. 08C01-2210-MR-000001. Filed April 5, 2023. Carroll Circuit Court. https://drive.google.com/file/d/1gk AowywNKa7Mmf7uI69jSNugqN0e-TLF/preview.

4. Audrey Conklin, "Delphi Murders Suspect Richard Allen's Lawyers Say He Is Enduring 'Prisoner of War' Conditions," Fox News, April 6, 2023, https://www .foxnews.com/us/delphi-murders-suspect-richard-allen-lawyers-say-he-enduring -prisoner-war-conditions.

5. Matt Adams, "Judge Says Delphi Murder Suspect Richard Allen Can Be Moved to New Facility," Fox59, April 14, 2023, https://fox59.com/indiana-news/judge -says-delphi-murder-suspect-richard-allen-can-be-moved-to-new-facility/.

6. Ron Wilkens, "Richard Allen's Defense Attorneys Attribute Admission in Delphi Murders to Mental Health," *Lafayette Journal & Courier*, June 15, 2023, https:// www.jconline.com/story/news/crime/2023/06/15/delphi-murders-update-rich ard-allen-hearing-libby-german-abby-williams/70315237007/.

7. State of Indiana vs. Richard M. Allen. Allen Superior Court. June 28, 2023. https://allensuperiorcourt.us/delphi/